ISBN 978-1-330-88662-5
PIBN 10117199

1 MONTH OF
FREE
READING

at
www.ForgottenBooks.com

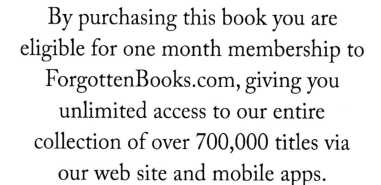

By purchasing this book you are eligible for one month membership to ForgottenBooks.com, giving you unlimited access to our entire collection of over 700,000 titles via our web site and mobile apps.

To claim your free month visit:

www.forgottenbooks.com/free117199

Similar Books Are Available from
www.forgottenbooks.com

Z O Ë;

OR

THE QUADROON'S TRIUMPH

A TALE FOR THE TIMES.

BY
MRS. ELIZABETH D. LIVERMORE.

WITH ILLUSTRATIONS,
BY HENRI LOVIE, AND CHARLES BAUERLE.

"God has hid away the human soul in the black man's skin and his darke person, that in finding it, we may re-discover our alienated and forgotten nature and rejoice more over the one that was lost, than the ninety and nine who were not astray."—Billows.

VOL. I.

CINCINNATI:
TRUMAN AND SPOFFORD.
1855.

E. MORGAN & SONS,
STEREOTYPERS.

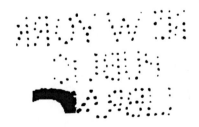

' And the slave, where'er he cowers, feels the soul within him climb
To the awful verge of manhood, as the energy sublime
Of a century bursts full-blossomed, on the thorny stem of time."—Lowell.

PREFACE.

SLAVERY, with its manifold evils and wrongs, is becoming more and more the theme of the statesman, the divine, the poet, and the writer of fiction. It matters little in forming its estimate, whether there has or has not been exaggeration in describing the details of its workings, as it concerns either the master or his bondsman. It is sufficient to know, that it origin-

ated in and is sustained under, a very low estimate of the value
of man as man, and that the exalted Christian idea of the
brotherhood of the race can be but dimly discerned by any one,
who is willing for one moment, to own a human being. It
follows, therefore, that in a system where contempt for humanity
unites with irresponsible power, the most vivid imagination may
fail to delineate truly all its horrors.

As the material globe which we inhabit, was originally spoken
into a rude and imperfect being, its thorough completion being
left to humanity, that, by becoming co-workers with God, we
might be brought more and more into union with Him and his
wonderful designs, so does Society expand and perfect itself by
little and little, in unison with it. We may lament over its dull
perception of truth, its slow growth towards perfect maturity.
and the worldly and weak in faith, will be ready to despair of
its eventual freedom from bondage to evil. Not so does our
Maker, who knows the abundant resources of his creation, and
the fitting time when each material shall best adapt itself to its
highest and most appropriate use.

When the waste places of the earth have been subdued by
the energy and force of the stronger races, and the rude powers
of nature are trained to do their bidding, when by the aid of
machinery, men are set comparatively free from the harder drud-
gery of life, then, to those who, by fidelity in duty have earned
the high and glad privilege, there comes the play-time of their
being, when the higher faculties which adorn and beautify life,
will be in the ascendant. Then come up to the surface of
society, those who have been regarded as inferior elements in
its construction, even those *little ones in Christ's kingdom*, in
whom the feminine, the graceful and tender, the imaginative and
artistic qualities are largely mingled. Then, woman will be
freed from the chains which enthrall her, and will step forth as
she is, the subtle, spiritual genius, to impel to high deeds the

"lord of creation." Then the African, child of the sunshine, in whom is wrapped up what we, in our country, have as yet vainly looked for—poetry, music, high art, and the full reflection of God's love as revealed through our Saviour, will take his true and blissful position.

The worldly and selfish will, for a time, scoff and disbelieve this, as they laugh at the struggles of woman to reach her high destiny; but the unwelcome truth will be, at last, forced upon them, that they have been acting out the fable of the drayman towards Pegasus, on a fearful and monstrous scale.

It is time that the world should know of the glorious appointment which God has in store for these his children upon whom his hand for the ages has been most heavily laid; for, from the laboratory of every imaginable calamity and woe, the fitting alembic through the action of his divine chemistry for his choicest productions, there shall spring up and bloom the loveliest, the most celestial, the most sky-scented flower of humanity, which the world has yet seen. On them will devolve the supremacy of the ages, and it will be their joyful destiny to evolve light out of darkness, to wind up the horologe of the present, and set it to the musical dance of the hours of the approaching Future. And to one whose soul's eye has become couched to discern this high lot of the feminine element, all apology seems futile for offering to the public the following Tale; for, as the winds of Heaven scatter the leaves of the trees when they are ripened for the fall, so, through a strong conviction, do the thoughts drop from the pen, and they are scattered wherever they find a soil fitted to vitalize them. And with faith in the welcome which words expressed from a full and glowing heart will receive, do I offer it to all generous and truth-loving Americans, whatever may be their nativity or race.   E. D. L.

CINCINNATI, *Nov.* 25, 1855.

ILLUSTRATIONS.

———◆———

1. Zoë and the Dove......................(Frontispiece)
2. Genius of Slavery.................................... 3
3. The Rising Moon..................................... 9
4. The Ice-King 16
5. Carl and Zoë....................................... 24
6. Introduction of Zoë to Miss Ingemann.................. 33
7. Winter Scene in Denmark............................ 44
8. Snow-Queen..................................... 45
9. Christ and the Apostles.............................. 65
10. Death of Thorwaldsen 69
11. Thoughts of Home.................................. 88
12. Zoë guided by Angels............................... 108
13. The Wandering Jew................................. 163
14. Scene on the Prairies............................... 185
15. Mrs. Liebenhoff and Hilda........................... 200
16. Iceland.. 213
17. Magnetized 229
18. Spirit-Horse 246
19. Departure of the Ship.............................. 321
20. Women and Children building the Church............. 322
21. The Church Built................................... 324

(vi)

CONTENTS.

PAGE

PREFACE.. 3

CHAPTER I.— The Sacrifice..................... 9

CHAP. II.— The Voyage 16

CHAP. III.— New Scenes and Associations....... 83

CHAP. IV.— Questionings...................... 45

CHAP. V.— Children at Home................. 50

CHAP. VI.— The Teacher and Taught.......... 57

CHAP. VII.— Bereavement 69

CHAP. VIII.— Lady versus Law 76

CHAP. IX.— Color can Feel 88

CHAP. X.— Anglo-Saxons do not know Everything 97

CHAP. XI.— The Cloud hangs low.............. 105

CHAP. XII.— Fresh Breezes from the West...... 114

CHAP. XIII.— A new Preacher in the Field...... 131

CHAP. XIV.— Spirit-Sister..................... 144

CHAP. XV.— Pic-Nic — the Wandering Jew reappears 163

  PAGE

CHAPTER XVI.—Castle Building on the Prairies. 183

  CHAP. XVII.—Chit-chat........................ 199

  CHAP. XVIII.—Spiritualism 210

  CHAP.   XIX.—Magnetism...................... 229

  CHAP.   XX.—The Parley..................... 246

  CHAP.   XXI.—Steel in the Ore............... 280

  CHAP. XXII.—Fire in the Flint.............. 300

  CHAP. XXIII.—The Dedication................. 322

Z O Ë:

OR, THE QUADROON'S TRIUMPH.

CHAPTER I.

"No manna falls around me from on high;
Barely from off the desert of my life
I gather patience and severe content.

*   *   *   *

A mighty purpose rises large and slow,
From out the fluctuations of my soul.
As ghost-like, from the dim and tumbling sea,
Starts the completed moon."

ALEXANDER SMITH.

HE story of Zoë Carlan, a young colored girl, of the little Danish island of Santa Cruz, is a pathetic illustration of the false position into which a refined and educated nature may be thrown, by the fierce prejudices of caste and color.

Her father, George Carlan, was native of the island, and originally a slave. His ancestry on the father's side for two generations had been whites, so that with his light complexion, he combined much of the energy and restiveness under despotic rule of the Anglo-Saxon race.

Slavery under the Danes had some mild and alleviating features. Schools were supported by government, in which the rudiments of knowledge were taught the slaves, with a view to their eventual freedom, and provisions were made, by which it could be purchased by those who would employ the requisite exertion.

George so diligently used these means, that at the age of twenty-eight, he stepped forth under the clear vault of Heaven, a free man. He could but imperfectly read and write and cast accounts; and he reasoned thus with himself. "Here I am, with none to rule over me but my God and my King. Independence and influence I will have, but how to gain them is the question. I am too old to educate myself; but rich I may become, and rich I will be. I will take my stand beside the haughty whites, and whatever consideration and power may be mine through wealth, I will attain."

Through his industry and perseverance, he had become a successful merchant; and at the time when this story commences, he was living in the enjoyment of not only the comforts, but many of the luxuries of life. On attaining his freedom, he married a young colored woman, of much gentleness and native refinement of character, and one child, the little Zoë, was given them, to be the light of their home, and the object of all his aspiring hopes and desires.

But the free blacks and colored people (for that distinction is very carefully made in the islands), though experiencing much favor from the Danish government, and sometimes even preferred to the proud and discontented white colonists, when indulgences are to be awarded, have no *position* in society. In the first place, the latter are, for the most part, the children of illicit connections. and where is the community where the odium of such sin falls not upon the weaker party and her innocent offspring? Then the people of color are a continual source of contention and trouble; they are restless, discontented, aspiring. For every step they advance higher than the full black, they cast behind them a glance of indifference or of scorn, while they are ever looking upward and striving to plant their feet side by side with the whites, if not in advance of them. This is met with unflinching opposition by the dominant race. In all spheres within their control, they omit not to give the most scathing demonstrations of their contempt. In social life they seldom meet, of course. It is, however, the custom for the Danish governor-general to hold levees, from time to time; and to these the chief mulattoes are invited as well as the whites. Gladly would the latter excuse themselves from the honor of attendance, knowing the odious companionship to which they will be subjected, but it is well understood that an invitation is equivalent to a command, and policy, perchance safety, forbids a refusal. There is by no means a very cordial feeling between many of them and their rulers. The population is a mixed one. Many of the old and more wealthy families are of English descent. Their religion is only tolerated, the Lutheran being that of the State. Almost all offices are held by Danish officials, often unscrupulous and grasping, and the Creoles are made to feel in numberless ways, that they are but step-children to the mother-country, and that their interests are ever second to her own. Then, more than all other causes of jealousy, is the slackening of their control over the blacks, by the measures of the home-government. They see in it their humiliation and ruin; and as prudence forbids a very open expression of their outraged feelings to their rulers, they display a temper all the more bitter towards the immediate cause of them.

In this scene of unrest, ambitious striving, and corroding sentiment the little Zoë was born and lived until her seventh year. It was then that her father felt that the time had come to carry into execution the idea which, from the first moment that his eye rested on the face of his infant child, had been as fixed as if the fates had commanded it. This was, to send her from the island to be educated. It was a common custom of the white Creoles to do so; but few, who had the means, were willing to confine their children to the very slender advantages for culture, which the island afforded, and though the temporary exile was fraught with much peril and heart-sickness, it was submitted to as a painful necessity. For through most of the forming period of their children's minds, they were given over to the care of teachers too distant from them to exercise much superintendence, while the intercourse by letter even was too infrequent to retain a very strong hold over their affections and characters. To this fact may be attributed very much of the feeling of exile which the Creole carries about with him to his grave. Seldom is the island spoken of as a home, but that endeared appellation is given to Denmark, Germany, England, the United States; and this use of language is imitated by those who have never stepped beyond its boundaries.

George had often spoken of his intention of sending Zoë to Denmark, but the distant idea of it always distressed his wife so much that he delayed the final announcement of it as long as possible. She had but little of his proud, ambitious spirit or intellectual thirst, but lived chiefly in her affections. She was but a child in mind, and while her heart could lavish its love upon her husband and child—while she could wander with them through her favorite haunts and breathe in the luxurious sensations imparted by the delicious climate and gorgeous nature around her—she was happy and contented.

One evening, as they were seated in the verandah of

their dwelling, which overlooked the Caribbean sea, the refreshing trade-wind gently waving the leaves of the tamarind tree, and the delicate odor of the star-jasmine wafted to them on its breath from the abundant blossoms over their heads, George was aroused from the abstraction into which he had fallen by a laugh from his wife.

"See, George," she said, "how oddly Zoë's goat looks with that wreath of flowers which she has tied about its face! Is she not like some old, withered belle trying to look young and pretty?" and Nanny, as if aware of her ridiculous appearance, suddenly flung herself away from the child, turning her a somerset, as she did so, down the slope.

"Yes," said her father, but not joining in the mirth; and then more to himself than to his wife, he added: "Zoë is very fond of the animal. It shall go with her on the voyage; it will serve to divert her, and besides will furnish her with milk."

"What voyage? what do you mean?" said Sophia, seizing his arm and gazing eagerly into his face.

"Now, Sophia, be calm and listen to me," said he, "you know what my desire and purpose is, and I want you to look at the matter as I do."

"I cannot. O George! I know you have spoken of sending her away, but I never believed you would have the courage, when the time came, or," she added, in a lower tone, "that you would be so cruel to me."

"Heaven knows what it costs me," throwing his arm tenderly around her, "even more on your account than my own; but do you wish her to grow up like Mahala and Jenny — your brother's daughters — ignorant and impure, with no higher wish than to be the mistress of some white coxcomb? No, I would see her die first."

"But she will not: am I like them? You saved me from that fate, dearest, and will not your own child, with you to instruct her, with my eye ever upon her, be even happier and more worthy of her father than I am?"

"I teach her," said he, bitterly, "who, (thanks to my slavery for that) know nothing myself!"

"But you do know a great deal," said she, brightening a little, and casting a proud glance at his handsome face; "I have not told you what I heard the American merchant say to Captain Sturd, yesterday, while I was standing in your counting-room at the store."

"Well, what was it, dear?" said George, willing to divert her a moment from her grief.

"He said that there was not a more gentlemanly fellow, nor a better business man on the island than yourself, nor one that he liked to deal with so well."

"I dare say," said George; "but I know just what such compliments are worth, coming from a white man, and I value them accordingly. But what has that to do with Zoë's going away, if not this, that if I have risen above my people in any respect, so much the more must I see to it, that my child does not grow up good for nothing but a slave's degraded life, though she may not literally be one? No, Sophia, life is too dark, too hard for me with my ignorance and sense of humiliation, not to wish for our darling a better fate. She shall be educated as a lady, and who knows," said he, his eye gleaming, "but the tables may be turned a little before she comes back, and people be seated a little more according to their deserts?"

"It frightens me to see you so ambitious, George. Why not be contented and happy in us, as we are in you, and let the world go on as it will?"

"Well, love, I will. You and Zoë are my life. Will you not, with me, make a sacrifice for her best good, and prove to me your love by being happy with me alone for a few years? Were we not happy together the three years before her birth? and shall we be less so now? You are not like me if your love has weakened with time. Has it, Sophia?" and he drew her toward him.

These words, and the sad and tender tone in which they

were spoken, by one not very demonstrative in his feelings, quite subdued her. She leaned upon his shoulder and wept, but softly and without bitterness. "Her husband's love—the good of her child," these were the open Sesame to her heart's most guarded treasure, when against the claims of intellect or ambition she would have turned a tiger's resistance.

O man. thou hast no lore in woman's nature, it matters not of what clime or color, for it is one and the same in this, if thou hast not learned the very point of the rock which is to be smitten for its waters to gush forth for you. "Her husband's love! The good of her child!"

CHAPTER II.

" And a little child shall lead them."
ISAIAH.

LL was now busy preparation with them for the little girl's departure. Captain Heiliger was to return to Denmark in a mon'h, in the good ship Skager-rack, and his wife, who had been spending the winter in Santa Cruz, very willingly consent ed to take charge of her. The Captain had many business transactions with Mr. Carlan, and great good-will had grown up between them, and he was very glad of an opportunity of reciprocating some favors which he had conferred upon him in the way of trade.

(16)

Many were the tears shed by Sophia as she diligently stitched upon Zoë's wardrobe, but George saw that she struggled hard to be reconciled to the separation, and he redoubled his affectionate efforts for her happiness. As for Zoë, childlike, one hour she cried at the thought of leaving her parents and going alone among strangers, and the next, was impatient for the day to come when she should sail upon the great ocean, and see all the wonders of the country far away, of which her friend the captain, often gave her glimpses in his narrations of northern life and scenes. It came at last all too soon for Sophia, and no less for George, whose sterner nature was first put in action by his own firm resolves, and by the necessity of conquering his wife's opposition to the plan; but, these victories won, the strong man betrayed the tender heart underneath all this bravery, and, at the last, turned to his wife for the courage and support which had come to her through patience, submission, and disinterested love.

Once on board ship, the first agony of tears over, the busy preparations for sailing going on, holding Nanny, the pet goat, by the brightest ribbon her mother could find in Frederickstadt, Zoë stood, interested and quiet, if not happy. She reserved her next burst of sorrow for bedtime, that fearful hour, when, if there is a grief in a child's heart, it surges up and breaks over all the bounds within which deference for others, or passing sports or occupations had temporarily confined it. Sleep, blessed friend, comes at last, to relieve the inconsolable one. and no less the impotent, unhappy sympathizer, who ranges the heavens and earth and the waters beneath for some antidote in the shape of story, suggestion, or joke, to allay the tempest. When all hope is failing, and the hands are folded in mute despair, lo, more welcome than the friendly sail or life-boat in a storm at sea, is caught the first glimmer of relief in the drooping eyelid, and soon the occasional

2

sob is all that tells of the dark clouds which had so shut
in over the " Heaven of its infancy."

Zoë found no lack of employment or of friends on board.
A child on ship is a god-send, for in no other so small a
compass, do you get so much variety and freshness com-
bined to break the tedium and monotony of a voyage. She
was soon at home in every part of it; knew the exact lati-
tude and longitude of the kitchen, pantry, cowhouse, hen-
coop, and especially did she make minute investigation
into Nanny's quarters, to see that all was right with her
favorite.

She became an apt pupil in learning the terms in use
among the sailors, and larboard and starboard. main-sail
and top-sail, stem and stern, were soon familiar lore to her.
For the child is your true democrat. The world is all
before her, free from the conventionalisms, which build
such high walls between her elders, and love and com-
panionship go where natural affinity leads. Greater than
a sovereign, too, does this Heaven-directed freedom make
her, for all hearts become willing subjects to love, and
there is no smack of worldly policy or thrift in the service
which such love wins.

Sophia would have been frightened enough to have seen
her child threading her way through what would seem to
her, very dangerous places, now running up and down the
steep gangway, now leaning over the railing, now mount-
ing up into the binnacle, and anon, down in the engine-
room, with the sooty Vulcan himself. But apart from the
self-reliance and sureness of foot gained by being suffered
to depend somewhat on herself, " there were angels in
charge over her " wherever she went. At one time, it was
a lonely papa, who as he took the little hand to help her
up a step, did it all the more tenderly for thinking of his
own cherubs far, far away. At another, it was an in-
valid lady, who in saving her from a fall, sighed that

before the weary weeks should bear her to her own blue-eyed darlings, she might be sleeping beneath the waves. And again, it was an honest tar, who " sooner than see harm come to such a trim, pretty little craft, shiver his timbers—he would be blown himself, he would." And nothing of interest in sea, sky, or ship, was thought to have fulfilled " its order of entertainment," until she had enjoyed her share of it. The cry was, " Zoë, see this whale spouting in the distance;" or, " Zoë, look at this troop of horses galloping through the sea," and surely it took two or three good glances with her bright eyes to see that they were only porpoises, jumping and floundering through the waters. Then the silvery flying-fish, with its brief spasmodic soarings into the blue ether, engaged her attention and sympathy too, when it was told her that it was impelled out of its natural element for the moment only, to escape the jaws of some pursuing monster. But her greatest delight was to lean over the guards at evening, and watch the phosphorescent light upon the waves, which the ship parted in its course. Its silvery sheen, now brightening, now fading, and flowing about the keel like grains of molten sunlight, had a fascination for the child which she did not willingly forego. Undaunted by warnings of dampness and chilly evening winds, she would beg that she might be permitted to look " just for one hour," and if she could not persuade my lady to come from the cabin and share with her the sight and her fur cloak together, why, she was just as happy and comfortable too, under a corner of Tom's pea-jacket at the forecastle.

Zoë was neither a very beautiful nor a vivacious child, but she was interesting from her gentleness and grace, and thoughtfulness for others. She was too diffident and shrinking to show fondness excepting to the long-known, but she had many unobtrusive little ways of testifying gratitude and affection. She had that delicate touch in

smoothing a sick one's pillow, that instinctive knowledge
when any little service is wanted, which made her like a
ministering spirit to the languid and sea-sick, and when
she found that her goat's milk was considered a luxury,
the largest share of it was sure to be transferred to where
it was most wanted.

She was of the grade of quadroons, and her features
were pure and intellectual in their contour. One skillful
in such criticism could see that there was a mingling of the
African in her physique, but nevertheless she was a fair
and agreeable-looking child. Her hair was black, wavy,
and abundant, her eyes soft and dark, her face oval and
delicate in its form; but over it there was that mysterious
pensiveness quite common to her caste, and visible even in
the face of the full African; a peculiarity which may be
explained by those who imagine he is insensible to the
evils of his condition, and would fain delude themselves
that he is joyous and happy under its hardships. Does the
difference of expression arise from the greater fragility of
constitution said to be inherent in the mixed race, or is it
a prophecy or a fulfillment of the bitter struggle of the
spirit which in all of them is to be wrought out by groans
and tears, but in the full black may be somewhat relieved
by a naturally happier temperament?

The favor in which she was held on board was not
stinted on account of her race. The few passengers were
Germans, Swedes, and Danes, and it is well known they
are comparatively free from our aversion to the African.
When living with them in the islands as a Pariah race, they
are not proof against the influences which slavery always
engenders in the irreligious and sensual, and in conse-
quence learn to regard them with a degree of contempt,
which would be entirely unfelt were the black elevated to
his rightful condition; but the individuals who go, from
time to time, to Europe to be educated, are petted, and a
vail of fancy and romance thrown around them which

raises them rather above the common level in the esteem of their fellows.

With the quick wit and freemasonry of childhood, Zoë soon learned who her best friends were, and especially with Carl, the man at the wheel, did she establish an intimacy, for, besides a kind smile and a merry or pleasant greeting as she approached him, she found he had a rich storehouse of tales to narrate. Though somewhat broken and disjointed by his duties at his post, she could gather from them rich store for her world of day-dreams. Carl was perfectly at home in elf-land, for he told her he was a "Sunday child," which gave him great privileges with the little people dwelling there, and the elves of light and the elves of darkness he knew like a book; for to all Sunday children they were visible. Often in herding his cows in Denmark, just at evening had he seen the good little white elves playing hide-and-go-seek among the leaves of the trees over his head, or dancing in the elf-dans; that is, the brightest and greenest spots in the meadows. But with the little black elves, who lived underground and under houses, he had to put on his best manners or there would be trouble enough, ay, and his good wife, too, must see to it, that her house was kept cleanly and neat or she would have plenty of tricks played upon her. Her butter would fail to come, or the cows would hold up their milk, or more vexatious than all, when she tried to spin her linen thread, it would snap as if the fire had touched it. But if everything was in good order, they were sure to reward her. Sometimes in the morning she would find her nice cream-cheese all ready pressed without her having to put a hand to it, or her clothes would be all washed and laid out on the dewy grass, or the table all laid for supper, if she stepped out to gossip a little with a neighbor.

But he had to be very careful not to let his cattle graze where the elf-people have been, for they have one bad habit—they spit—and if the cows should graze there they would die, unless his wife had been prudent enough to raise some John's-wort, saved on that saint's day, and it was near at hand.

However, he had learned that when he went to the pasture, if he would but say, " Thou little Troll, may I graze my cows on thy hill?" no harm ever came to them, not even if the great blue cattle of the elves came out to feed with them, for they only wanted a little deference from others to be civil in return.

But better than all, did she like to hear about the Hill people who were not elves, neither were they human, but half between; although when they appear, they are like handsome men and women. As their name denotes, they live in the caves and hills, and he had often put his ear to the ground and heard their music. It was very sweet and lively, but if any one was so cruel as to breathe a word of doubt about their ever going to heaven, the singing would cease, and there would be such weeping and lamentation as to quite break his heart to hear it; for through all time they carry about with them a longing, but faint hope of salvation.

" O Carl!" Zoé would say, "God will let them go to heaven, won't he? What have they done, that he should not?"

" I don't know, I hope so; but don't cry about it, little maiden, or I can tell you no more about them."

She hastily wiped away her tears and begged for another story.

So he went on: " One evening, just at twilight, I was sitting in my door-way with my old wife, resting after my day's work, when I heard the sound of my neighbor Johan's fiddle. Now Johan was a rare fiddler, but somewhat given to mischief, and he had often said that he knew how to play the elf-king's tune, and that he meant to try it some day. ' Johan,' said I, ' thou hadst better not, for thou wilt rue it if thou dost.' But sure enough, when I heard his

fiddle that night, I knew that he had acted upon his threat.
Down the road he came, playing as if he were the elf-king
himself, and with him a crowd of men and women and
little children, all dancing as if they were mad; for when
that tune is played, all who hear it must dance whether
they will or not.   Up jumped my poor old wife, who had
not taken a step for many a day; and such antics as she
cut up were a sight to behold.   But no need for me to
laugh at her, for though I had much rather have gone to
bed than to join the whirligig, I could not be let off, but
was forced to join the crazy crowd.   And that was not the
worst of it, for out came my wife's spinning-wheel and up
jumped my plow, and then the tables and chairs set to
flying, so that it seemed as if the world was turning topsy-
turvy altogether.   'Play the tune backward, you evil carl!'
I shouted to Johan, but the good-for-nothing fellow had
forgotten it; for if he could do that, he could then stop
playing.   So we whirled and capered until the breath was
nearly gone from us, and Johan himself was as red in the
face as his jacket, when I bethought me to take my knife
and go behind him and cut the strings of his fiddle.   If I
had not done this, or if Johan had not bethought him how
to play the tune backward, we should have danced till this
time.   And that was the last, I think, of Johan's trying to
play the elf-king's tune."

"Carl, was that a really true story, or did you make
believe it so?" said Zoë.

Carl hemmed and cocked his eye, and said, "there were
a great many more wonderful things than that in the
world," and gave the wheel a vigorous turn, singing, as he
did so, a snatch of a Danish ballad.

So Zoë had no lack of entertainment to her liking, and
her appetite was insatiable.   Her favorite hour for the
feast was just at evening, when the captain would permit
her to lead Nanny out for an airing, and after running a
race with her up and down the deck, she would take her

stand near her friend, her arm thrown around her goat's neck, her eyes upturned to Carl, while Nanny, meantime seeming pleased to serve as her support, chewed her cud—the two making as pretty a contrast as need be seen of contented animalism and earnest mind.

Carl had to draw pretty largely on his invention to satisfy her cravings, for, although his stock of the legends and superstitions of his country was ample, such an extravagant draught might have exhausted even that. But he was seldom at a loss, for, although to look at his rough, weather-beaten, stolid face, one would as soon expect to find a white lily growing out of a cabbage, or ottar of rose exhaling from a rough oak knot, as fancy or imagination in him, yet he had both.

These northern nations of Europe, Germans, Danes, Swedes, etc., are a queer people—a strange blending of sour-krout and nightingales' tongues, lager-beer and nectar, mercury and lead, soot and sunbeam, or any other combination of the most incongruous elements which might be suggested to the imaginative.

Here is Carl's story of the Enchanted Lady, or the little Flying Fish:

" One evening at twilight, as I was standing at the helm, the new moon just over my right shoulder—where I like to have it—with no voice about me but the washing of the waves, as the ship parted them in its course—for the passengers, with their noisy gabble, had gone into the saloon—I heard a splash in a tub of water near me. This tub Jack had brought and set in an out of-the-way place, to be ready for him to holystone the deck with, bright and early in the morning. Well, as I was saying, I heard something splash into it, and I looked and saw that it was a beautiful little silvery flying-fish. Thought I to myself, you have made a lucky hit that time, my little heartie, for if you had landed on the dry deck, if you had not broken your head, you would have been rather out of breath by this time, for this is

thinner air than you like. I gave but little heed to it, but let it stay, knowing that the poor little thing would, at least, be out of the way of its enemy, the dolphin, though it was rather snug quarters for one that was used to having the sea to range in. By-and-by it was Tom's time to take the helm, and I turned into my berth to get a bit of sleep, and did not come up again till six bells sounded in the morning.

"As I stood tending the wheel with one hand, and rubbing my eyes with the other—for one needs a little sunlight to wake up easy—I thought I heard some one call my name. It was not like a common voice, speaking low, but the tiniest little grasshopper one, calling as loud as it could. Thinks I to myself, I must be in dream-land, for who ever called ' Carl ' like that, in the wide-awake world. So I scratched my head hard, and pinched my arm, and tossed up my cap in the air, to be sure that I was up and dressed, but seeing nobody I went to my post. A second call, and this time, a splash in the tub, and then I remembered the flying-fish. I thought I must be mistaken about the voice, but said to myself, 'the little thing is discontented, and no wonder; I'll e'en put it into the sea again.'

"As I was taking it in my hand, it cried out: 'Let me stay, Carl, I want to talk with you a bit.'

"'That's it, is it?' said I. 'Who ever heard of a flying-fish spinning a yarn? But what shall I do; I can't leave the wheel, for where do you think the ship would drift? and my old ears are too thick to hear your little fairy speech at this distance? However, I'll pull the tub nearer the helm. There, now: what on earth are you? And what can I do for you?'

"The little flying-fish squeaked out: ' I am an enchanted lady, and my name is Skada. I am the wife of the great giant, Krymer, who lives in Jotunheim, away up toward the north-pole among the eternal snows and icebergs. He is very grim and imperious, and with him I led a hard and

3

slavish life. I was the daughter of King Olaf, and was
haughty and proud. I was handsome and witty, and liked
to be seen and heard—and who had a better right, being
a king's daughter? I could not abide to stay at home and
nurse the children, and cook my greedy lord's fifty fishes,
and three reindeer, and five turtles, and one white bear,
which he consumed every day at dinner. I thought myself
as great as he, being a princess, and with as good a right
to share in his rule over the dwarfs, who were his subjects.
And this I told him; but all the answer I got from him
was, 'Can you lift my hammer and throw it like that?' and
away it flew and took off the whole top of the mountain
Utgardelok, which fell plump into the sea, throwing so
much water into the air that it rained for five days. I had
to confess that I could not; and what was the use when the
ground was so moist already with the melting snow that
nothing would grow, and I told him so. 'Can you shout
as long and as loud as I can?' And with that he raised
such a hideous yell, that the trees all fell flat, and my poor
little flowers, that I was trying to nurse into life and beauty
by gently blowing upon them with my warm breath, all
shrunk back into the earth, thinking that the safest place
for them. 'No,' I said, 'and the less noise the better,
for then something would be done, or at least, there would
be less destruction.'

" 'Have you courage to go through Utgard, and contend
with Loke and his three evil children, Fenris, the wolf,
Jormungandur, the great serpent, and Hela, the queen of
death?'

" 'No, and why should I? If I keep clear of them, they
will never trouble me. Let them have their dark kingdom
to themselves.'

" 'Then you are not fit to rule,' said Krymer, 'which did
not convince me, being no reason at all. So one day I took
the scepter, and was brandishing it about when Krymer
came in. He was as angry as the north-wind in a tempest,

and without waiting a moment for his wrath to cool, turned me into a flying-fish and threw me into the sea, where I am compelled to live for a score of years.'

"What a cross, cruel, ill-tempered husband," said Zoë; "but did not she tell you what she saw down deep in the sea?"

"O yes, you may be sure she did, I thought she would never be done talking of the mountains higher than any on the land; of the green meadows which lie at their base; of the waving forests; of the huge ferns a thousand feet long, with their brilliant foliage of crimson and purple, and the beautiful pink and green turf, and sea-weeds and lichens, which they overshadow. And she told of the vast monsters—the whale, the huge kraken, the sea-serpent, and countless hosts of smaller tribes, who dart and gambol, or pursue their prey a mile below the surface of the sea; of the myriads upon myriads of salmon and mackerel and herring, which migrate from one side of the world to the other, disturbing the current of the mighty ocean itself. But more beautiful was what she told of the wonderful working of the little coral insects, who patiently pursue their labor from year to year, forming their delicate and frost-like sprays, blooming at their summits with insect life, which become the basis of great continents and islands in the midst of the waters.

"But many a sad sight too, was beneath the briny waves; noble ships, with their untold treasures of gold and silver, and rich merchandise, and what was sadder still, beautiful women and children clasped in each other's arms, and strong men with the marks of the death-wrestle still upon their faces."

"Please tell me no more about that," said the child, heaving a deep sigh, "but what became of the little lady flying-fish?"

"Well, after she had spun her yarn, and a pretty long one it was, she said that it was time for her to go back again, for she was afraid if Jack should see her when he came to clean the deck, that he would seize and cook her for his breakfast. So she begged me to give her a lift over the side of the ship."

"'I will, my heartie,' said I, 'but in return for making the night so short with your pretty talk, I want to give you a word of advice.'

"'O yes, by all means,' said the fish, fluttering her fin a little, by way of a courtesy, 'what is it?'

"'When the time comes for you to go back to the old giant, don't seize the scepter again, for it is an ugly, heavy, old thing, and you will stagger under it, and it would be a sorry sight if it should trip you up before your subjects and throw you flat upon the ground. *But if you are indeed a princess and no sham, your rank will shine out,* though you are dressed in cat skins instead of sable, and you will share the rule, for the dwarfs know who is who, and you will get rid of the trouble of the heavy scepter. Let the giant keep it if he wants a plaything, you are not a baby. Will you heed what I say?'

"'Ay, ay, and thank you. I can take a hint and act upon it too. It is stupid old Krymer, whose skull is so thick, that he thinks that it is only a leaf falling when Thor's thunderbolt comes down upon it.'

"'Tut, tut,' said I, 'little lady, be a little less free with your liege lord, when you speak about him.'

"'Never fear, I shall remember what you say; I only want to make his ear burn once like fire with my sharp words. for turning me into a flying-fish, and then I will ever after be as mild as a May morning, and docile as a dove.'

"The little fish spread its gauzy fins, laughing as it did so, at its own merry speech, which sounded like tiny silver bells, until it darted out of sight under the water."

"Thank you, Carl, that is the funniest story you have told me yet, all but that about the mothers and their poor little babies;" and Zoë's eager glance was dimmed as it turned upon her own world of dreams, and she was lost for the time being to the one about her.

Thus the time sped on, and even a long voyage comes to an end at last; and there was hurry and bustle on board ship again as the city of Copenhagen loomed up in the distance.

To Zoë, accustomed as she was to the perennial verdure of her own sunny isle and to the low style of architecture which its exposure to hurricanes rendered necessary, the sight of the brown earth, the leafless trees (for it was now March), the high buildings and tall steeples, was a great subject of amusement. She knelt upon her berth to look out of her port-hole, as it was too cold to stay on deck, while Norna, the servant of Mrs. Heiliger, packed her trunk and dressed her in readiness to go to the city. When she was arrayed to the girl's mind, Zoë took her hand to go and bid that poor invalid good-by, as the lady would immediately take a carriage to ride ten miles to her residence in the country; her mother's heart yearning to embrace her children, from whom she had been separated for six months.

She kissed the child and told her she had been a good little girl and had given her no trouble, but on the contrary, had been a great comfort to her in many little ways, and said if she was unhappy in her school or wanted any aid, she must let her know it, and that in the summer (if she were living, and she sighed) she should come out and spend her vacation with her own little girls, Adelgunda and Freya.

Zoë, impelled out of her accustomed timidity and reserve, flung her arms around her neck begging her, as she did so, to take her with her.

"Not now, my child, you know your father's wish was that you should be taken directly to Miss Ingemann's, and it will be easier for you to be left among strangers now

than if you first went home with us. You will go cheer-
fully, dear, will you not?"

She hesitated for a moment, then nodded her head by
way of assent, and ran to get Nanny.

That grave individual now had its beauty set off by the
addition to its wardrobe of an old sack of her own, the
sleeves projecting each side like budding wings. She had
insisted that she must suffer from the cold, as they came
into higher latitudes, and in this she was probably right,
as the Santa Cruzian goats have scarcely a sufficient modi-
cum of hair, it would seem, for home use much less for
colder regions. Nature is not negligent in adapting her
children's supplies to their needs, yet she has for so many
ages accustomed herself to do her work in her own quiet,
moderate way, that she is hardly up to our fast times, when
steam transports us from the extreme heat of one climate to
the no less extreme cold of another before she has time to
get her manufacturing apparatus in order to suit the con-
flicting demands upon her.

Zoë was leading Nanny across the deck when she met
Rolf, one of the ship's apprentices, a lad of seventeen,
who, as boys are very apt to do, expressed the interest
which he really felt in her by teazing her on every possible
occasion. He found an especial charm in this entertain-
ment, as Zoë was inclined to take very literally all his jokes
and absurdities.

She was, moreover, rather irritable, and when thus
fretted, would disown all friendship with him, then and
forevermore, at least two or three times a day only to
return soon to be better friends than ever.

"What are you going to do with your goat, Zoë?"
said he.

"I am going to take her to Miss Ingemann's with me,"
said the child.

"Going to school is she? hey! I doubt if with all the

old lady's teaching she gets her beyond ba-a-a-a!" imitat-
ing her bleating to perfection.

"She is not going to school," said she indignantly;
"she is going to play with me and give me milk."

"There is no room for goats up there, you silly child,
unless you can make a crib for her in your bandbox,"
said Rolf.

She was going to retort again, but for the first time it
flashed into her mind that he might be right, and that she
should have to give her up. She looked anxiously at him
and said:

"What must I do with her, then?"

"O! throw her overboard; let her go to Loke's (the
devil's) kingdom. She is one of his people anyway, you
know."

"You naughty, wicked boy!" said Zoë, stamping her
foot. "It is no such thing. She is a *great deal* better
than you are;" and with that she quickened her pace to
reach the captain, whom she saw in advance of her. She
asked him, with a very downcast look, if she should have
to leave Nanny behind with that ugly *old* Rolf, who would
throw her into the sea to live with Loke.

"O no! my little girl," said the kind-hearted captain,
"she shall have no such dreadful fate as that. How
should you like to have me carry her to my country place,
where my little girls will take good care of her, until you
come in the summer to visit them?"

Zoë was delighted, and on those terms was reconciled
to parting with her pet, with whom, however, she took
most sentimental leave, murmuring over her every imagin-
able term of endearment and promise of everlasting re-
membrance; and then went back to triumph over Rolf for
Nanny's happy fortune. He soon found means to appease
her wrath, and, although two or three times in as many
minutes, he nearly provoked it again by his quips and
cranks at her expense; yet, at the last, they exchanged

keepsakes, and wished that they could both go back to Santa Cruz together.

Over Carl's rough shoulders she threw the ribbon with which she had adorned Nanny in her gala hours, and told him to wear it when he went to Valhalla; and if he were ever so old and gray she should know him by that, and she would come and sit by him to listen to his stories.   Good Carl!

CHAPTER III.

" Most musical—most melancholy."—MILTON.

THE boarding-school into which Zoë was now admitted, was kept by a lady who had gained great reputation as a teacher of young girls. She was of noble descent, but inheriting from her parents more of rank than of wealth, and scorning dependence, she had resorted to education as a means of support, and had gained an honorable reputation thereby. Tall and stately in her mien, with the clear blue eyes, blonde hair, and light complexion of her country-women, with decision, high thought and power of command in every lineament of her face, and movement of her figure, Miss Ingemann might have been taken for a Volkyria, and, indeed, her pupils could not have held in higher veneration her character and acquirements had she

(33)

shown them, in legible handwriting, her certificate from
Odin, that she had been of his court.

She received the little girl kindly and listened atten-
tively to all the directions which Mr. Carlan had intrusted
to the captain, as well as to his own fatherly injunction that
she should have careful attention, and after his departure,
seeing her look tearful and forlorn, she directed an assist-
ant to take her to her room, to the companion who was to
share it with her.

This was Hildegund, or Hilda Strophel, as she was
called, the daughter of a Danish gentleman, who two
years before possessed a large plantation in Santa Cruz.

He married a Creole lady of English descent, and for a
time lived in great state and splendor in the island. His
lands were very productive—sugar, the principal article
of export, brought him large profits, and he spent his im-
mense income in the rude magnificence, once so common
among the planters—in dinners, wines, horses, equipage,
rich plate, and last, but not least, in gambling. His house,
large, airy, and commodious, was open to his friends,
scores of whom he would welcome to his hospitality for
days and weeks together, at which time his halls would
echo to the sounds of music and revelry, until the night
waned into early dawn. But this was not sufficient for his
ambitious and pleasure-seeking wife. She was beautiful
and proud, and would fain be presented at court. She,
therefore, sought and easily gained her husband's consent
to spend a year at Denmark. Here the gayeties and excite-
ment of high life completely engrossed her, and when the
time appointed for their return arrived, she urged delay.
The idea of going back to little, contracted, quiet Santa
Cruz and its limited range of social life, was dreadful to
her. She pleaded one reason, and then another, to induce
her husband to remain. First, her health needed the
bracing air of the north, and afterwards the children must
be educated; and how could she leave the darlings among

strangers? although no scruples of that kind prevented
her banishing them to the mercy and to the exclusive care
of servants for days and weeks together. In vain did her
husband insist that his affairs required his oversight, and
that he should be a ruined man, if they pursued their pre-
sent course much longer: she could not be made to believe
it, and so long as the money for her expenditure was forth-
coming, she drove care to the winds. Her stronger will
and greater force of character overruled his prudence and
apprehensions of evil, and so they swept on in their wild
career. This false and reckless state of things could not,
of course, last forever. His manager was a crafty and
rapacious man, who had an eye only to his own interests.
He bribed the attorney left in charge of Mr. Strophel's
business, to further his plans; so while they sent fair
accounts of the great profits the estate was yielding, and
money enough to blind him to the true state of things, they
were exhausting the land, wearing out the negroes by
cruel usage and lack of care, and in fine, feathering their
own nests with the riches of the poor, simple bird who
had given himself up as their prey. So one fine winter's
eve, when my lady was all appareled to wait upon her
Majesty, news came that he was bankrupt. What to do
now was the question? Return they must, to gather up
the fragments of his once splendid fortune, but how were
they to live? It happened that he had influential friends
at court, through whose efforts he obtained a lucrative
office, just left vacant in the island, and in a week they
were on their way to Santa Cruz, with many a bitter re-
gret on the part of Mrs. Strophel, that her gay and brilliant
life was comparatively at an end.

The little Hilda had just entered her sixth year, and
her they left with Miss Ingemann, until her school educa-
tion should be completed. She was a bright, gay little
sprite, and her rosy, dimpled face and laughing blue eye
reflected every emotion of her changeful spirits, so that

Miss Ingemann, when particularly gracious and conde-
scending, would designate her as Mademoiselle Aprilis.

When Zoë entered the room, she was giving her doll,
nearly as large as herself, a lesson in waltzing, scolding
her in the tone and phrase caught from her dancing-master,
for her imperfect attention: "Toe out, toe out. Doesn't
she mean to take the steps right? Does she wish to go
into the black-hole?"

At her first glance at Zoë, she stopped short, and stood
in speechless amazement. She was but two when she left
her birthplace, and had no recollection of the blacks or
colored people, her nurse dying soon after her arrival, and
although they were occasionally seen in Copenhagen, she
had never happened to meet one. Zoë was no darker than
many a *white* Creole, and she was entirely free from the
most peculiar and repulsive African indications; but there
was a marked difference between her countenance and
that of the other girls, which struck and interested Hilda,
and although thrown off her guard by surprise, she felt
that, compared with the rather common-place and inexpres-
sive features of many of them, the little stranger certainly
had the advantage.

Zoë's heavy eyelids lifted, and her face brightened, as
she looked at the human sunbeam before her, and after
gazing straight into each other's faces for a full minute,
much to the amusement of Miss Holberg, they exchanged
smiles, an omen of their future friendship, and then Hilda
ran off to find some of her schoolmates.

"O! if we haven't got the funniest, little dark elvo
now," said she, as she danced into the general sitting
room of the pupils, where a dozen or more were collected
"the new scholar, whom Miss Holberg told us was to
come from away off in the West Indies. Her hair is as
black as jet, and all wavy; her skin is dreadfully tanned
and her eyes are so mournful. I wonder if she is not one
of the little Hillfolk, who never expect to go to Heaven

But she has a beautiful sweet smile. I know I shall like her; I feel already that we shall soon say *thou* to each other; I am so glad she is going to room with me."

"O yes, Mademoiselle Aprilis, and how long will it be before you quarrel, as you did with Rinda, and have to be separated?" said Elize; "I should advise you to be a little less hasty in getting up your romantic friendships."

"Well, I cannot help it, if Rinda will fly off the handle like an old jacknife that is loose in the rivets, at every word that is spoken to her. I am ready to love her again, when she is not so cross and fretful."

"Who would not get out of patience with you, you little bumble-bee, buzzing about one's face and ears all the time, and such an everlasting talker too? She said she could not study, nor read, nor sew, nor do anything, you tormented her so."

The idea of being a bumble-bee struck Hilda as so comical, that she laughed loud and long, and forthwith began to act in the character of that demonstrative insect, flying about the room with her arms extended, with a buzz equal to that of twenty of her tribe, giving this girl's cheek a tap, and that one's nose a pull, and pinching a third by way of a sting, and poking her fingers through still another's hair, until there was a general uproar and indignation meeting, when fortunately the door opened for some one to enter, and she whizzed past in a bee-line towards her own room, to see the new comer.

She found Miss Holberg engaged in unpacking and arranging Zoë's clothes, while giving an occasional direction to her about keeping them in order, she, in the meantime, sitting passive and silent on a stool, watching her and nodding assent from time to time to her suggestions.

"And Zoë," she said, as Hilda bounced in, "you will keep your closet and drawers very neat, dear, for it is a very good habit to grow up with, and besides, with so

many little girls to see to, it would give us great trouble if
you did not."

" Zoë! is that her name?" said Hilda to herself, " what
did her mother call her so for?   It is not half as pretty as
Gunhilda or Thora."

Here was a sphere for my little ladyship. She was
a real Anglo-Saxon in character and mind, as well as in
descent; energetic, expressive in action as well as in word;
inventive, decided and managing. She was soon deep in
the business of the hour, loading herself with Zoë's frocks,
until she looked like a moving mass of drapery, when her
laughing face and voice would peep out and resound from
between the folds; or, finding odd corners and shelves for
shoes and the various knick-knacks of femininehood; or
passing judgment upon the child's wardrobe; or laying
down the law to Miss Holberg herself, bustling about
and talking all the time, and altogether as busy as " a
hen with one chick."

" O, I like this! I wish there were clothes to unpack
and put away all the time; it is a great deal better than to
sit still and study or sew; and is not this little nook a good
place for the parasol? it is so nicely out of the way. But
what are these gauzy things? I guess her mother thought
it was as hot out here as in Santa Cruz. I may as well
fold them up and put them in the very bottom of her trunk,
for she will never use them till she goes back. And, Miss
Holberg, don't you put those stockings there, for it is my
own especial corner, and I can't spare it; here is a place—
lay them there, please."

Every now and then, too, she would look over to Zoë
and smile upon her in a very protecting way, and when she
came near her in her revolutions around the room, she
would give her a hug; but though its spirit evidently
pleased the child, she winced under the act.

At length all was neatly arranged, the last package
paper picked up and put away for incendiary use, and

the trunk moved into the most out-of-the-way corner; and
what more could Hilda do to show her good-will to the
stranger? She thought of a box of sugar-plums, which
she had treasured up for her next feast, when Freya and
Adelgunda came in with their dolls to play visiting with
her. She ran and opened it and poured out the larger
half and held them out to Zoë, saying:

"Here, you may have them."

"No, I thank you," said Zoë.

"O, but you may! I have got a plenty besides. I don't
wish for them at all."

"Neither do I, thank you, I don't care for sugar-plums."

"But you shall have them, I had rather you would than
not," and suiting the action to the word, she put her hand
up to press them into her mouth.

Miss Holberg, who through all these scenes had had her
eye upon the children and was forming her own opinion
upon them, now spoke out:

"Hilda, my child, what are you doing? Come directly
to me."

She stood before her.

"Look straight into my eyes and listen to what I say."
She obeyed.

"You know, Hilda, that I have told you before, that you
are too managing—too commanding in your disposition. I
see plainly that if you do not put a check upon yourself,
you will ride directly over this passive, gentle little being
with your rough, abrupt ways. Do you not see that she is
different from you? (a very decided nod of assent from
Hilda). Then do not force her to like just what you do.
Let her work and enjoy herself in her own way. You do
not wish to be a *tyrant* do you? (laying a contemptuous
emphasis upon the word) and make Zoë miserable and
cause her to dislike and fear you?"

Hilda had a noble, generous, candid nature, and when a
truth was plainly presented to her, never flinched from its

avowal, even though it told against herself. She looked very serious, and said:

"No, ma'am."

"Will you remember what I have said?"

"Yes, ma'am."

This timely rebuke, earnestly uttered, ever after acted as a restraint upon Hilda, and as a defense for Zoë; for, excepting in occasional fits of exuberant spirits, when the former, like a whirlwind, would sweep clear away all obstacles to her dominion, making one grand hurly-burly, the latter, bending low until the blast went by; it required her only to say, "Hilda, dear, you remember what Miss Holberg said? Let me enjoy myself my own way," and she would pretty soon desist from her attempt to rule.

It would be well for Anglo-Saxondom throughout the world, if some wise school-marm could thus put an extinguisher upon her propensity to force her government, creeds, customs and tastes upon nations and people who do not like them, or who are not yet prepared for them.

The two little girls were now left alone.

"Do you think you shall like here?" said Hilda, whose tongue was seldom still.

"I don't know," said Zoë. "Everything is so strange, and it seems so close," looking around at the shut doors and glazed windows.

"Close! why, are you too warm?" said she, opening the door. "I thought you came from a country where there was no winter and that we never should be able to keep a fire large enough for you?"

"Yes, it is very warm, but the doors are always open, and we have no glass in the windows, and there is a breeze all the time; it seems as if I could not breathe here, all shut up," and she drew a long breath as she walked towards the window.

"What strange trees! Ours have beautiful, shining green leaves on them, and flowers, too," said she.

"So have ours in the summer. As soon as the warm days in spring come back, they burst out in no time, and it is just like walking from one world into another—the change is so great and quick."

"O, that must be beautiful!" said Zoë, brightening up.

"Yes," Hilda went on, elated that she could make her look more cheerful; "and then we have such splendid times! Miss Ingemann takes us into the country, and we climb the hills and ford the brooks, and see the peasant women make their butter and cheese, and play with the calves, and eat our dinner out of doors, and, and—"

"Do you ever see the little elves that Carl told me about on board ship, and the Hillpeople, and hear their sweet music?"

"No—o," said Hilda, disappointed that she could not go on in her triumphal march, "but I think I shall next summer, I shall look for them. They are very little, you know, and I don't care very much about them, I like to gather strawberries better."

Zoë turned to the window again. "Where does all this cotton come from?" said she, looking up at the large snow-flakes, which were falling thick and fast.

"Cotton!" said Hilda, clapping her hands — "good, good! Why it is snow, ha, ha, ha!"

"What is snow?"

"Why, it is rain that freezes away up in the sky and comes down in this way."

Zoë looked up disconsolate, and thought, that if the rain froze so up near the sun, what should she do down on the cold bare earth; and she shivered, and sat down on the stool by the fire, shrugging up her shoulders, and leaning her hands on her knees, and looking quite the picture of desolation, while Hilda danced the Schottische around the room.

"Come, let's dance and play a bit," said she, holding out her hands to her.

4

Zoë hesitated.

"I won't plague you; I'll remember what Miss Holberg said."

"I wasn't thinking of that," said Zoë; "but mamma told me to write to her when I got to Copenhagen, and I ought to do that first, for the captain said, that a ship would go back soon."

"So I would," said Hilda, "and I'll help;" but the image of Miss Holberg coming up, she said, "should you not like to have me draw up this small table for you near the fire?"

"Thank you," said Zoë, and went to get her little writing-desk, which her father had given her and furnished with all needful materials.

"You are little to know how to write," said Hilda, as Zoë spread her paper and took her pen.

"I can't write like men and women, but I can print a little, and mamma said she could puzzle it out, if it was not written well, for she loved me so much;" and she brushed away a tear and began:

"DEAR MAMMA:—

"I am going to write you a letter."

"O, don't crowd your words so," said Hilda; "if you do, your mother will never be able to read them in the world—I mean, I would not if I were you," she added in a very deprecating way.

Zoë began again, and this time the letters were separated twice as far as they needed to be. Hilda was about to exclaim against this mode, but recollecting Miss Holberg's injunction, she pinched her fingers hard and bit her lips, and thinking she should be more out of temptation to do something besides watching her neighbor, she seized a book, and seated herself by the fire, and was soon absorbed in Hans Christian Andersen's story of the Ugly Duck, which he had given her the day before.

" My Dear Mamma :—

" I am going to write you a letter. Do you miss me
any? I had a good voyage, and Carl told me a great many
funny stories. Does papa miss me any? Nanny is gone
into the country to live at the captain's house with his two
little girls. I like Miss Holberg—that is one of the
teachers; she is very kind to me. I shall go and see
Nanny in the summer; the captain said so. There is a very
merry little girl in the room with me; her name is Hilda;
I think she tries not to manage me, as Miss Holberg called
it. She told me about the leaves coming all out on the
trees in the spring. It is very cold here, and the air has a
great many snows in it; that is, rain frozen up in the sky
and coming down like feathers.

"From Your Own Zoë.

" Ever so much love to papa and you."

Seeing Zoë closing her desk, Hilda got up and went to
her.

" What a pretty little desk you have got! I wish I had
one like it."

" You may use mine whenever you want to," said Zoë.

" You are a dear, good little girl," said Hilda, " and I
know I shall like you. We will say *thou* to each other,
will we not?"

" What does that mean?"

" O, when people love very much, they say *thou*, when
they speak to each other, instead of *you*."

Here Zoë's timidity and self-distrust came up, and she
said, " I am afraid you will not like me so well as you
think you will, and if you left off saying it, I should feel
so bad; I had rather wait a little."

" What an odd little thing," thought Hilda; " sure
enough, she is different from me. I think as Miss Holberg

said, I may as well let her do things her own way, and we
will see what comes next."

Hilda's curiosity coming into play was a great saving to
her fingers and lips, for she never afterwards had to bite
or pinch them so hard in order to keep them in their
proper places.

CHAPTER IV.

"Thou little child! yet glorious in the might
  Of heaven-born freedom on thy being's height!
  Why, with such earnest pains, dost thou provoke
  The years to bring the inevitable yoke,
  Thus blindly with thy blessedness at strife?
  Full soon thy soul shall have her earthly freight,
  And custom lie upon thee with a weight,
  Heavy as frost, and deep almost as life."—WORDSWORTH.

ZOË soon became tolerably wonted to her new home. Shrinking and timid as she was, her first introduction into a school of forty girls was painful and awkward. Some stared and nudged their next neighbors to look at her; some smiled upon her as if to re-assure her; some said and did their prettiest things to draw forth her admiration; while the older ones either were, or affected to be too much absorbed in their occupations to observe her at all.

Hilda would very gladly have shown her off in schoolroom, parlor, and kitchen, had it not been for Miss

Holberg—either visible as she busied herself with the pupils, or invisible in the shape of her earnest rebuke, seconded by the shy manners of Zoë herself, which pleaded to be left in quietness and obscurity. Her childish lessons were easily learned, and she obtained her share of the little prizes awarded by Miss Ingemann to the best scholar in the different studies. In no way did she seem very unlike the other children either in study or play or in the little household occupations which her teacher, true northern woman as she was, required each in their turn to share; only that she seemed of a more indolent temperament than the Danish girls. This prompted her to retire from their active sports sooner than the others, and disinclined her to long and steady occupation; in fact, as was the plain speech of the school, she was rather "lazy."

"Come," Hilda would say to her, "put on your furs and hood and let's go skating. See how bright the sun shines and what good sport the girls have! Ha! ha! there goes one down and another on the top of her! But what is that?"

"It is Rinda," said Zoë; "she said she was going to be the Snow Queen, that Mr. Andersen told us about. You see she has dug her a palace in that great drift—look at the icicles which she has hung from her curls, and she has got a snow-baby in her arms! U-g-h! It makes me shiver to see her," and she left the window and crouched down by the fire.

Hilda screamed with delight as she saw the Queen, with the light snow stuck to her lips and a long icicle for a scepter in her hand, run round to kiss her subjects, who shrunk from her cold embrace and chilly sway.

"Come, come, there's rare fun there. I'll be the reindeer and upset her throne with my branching horns, and you, with your black eyes and dark skin, may be the little robber-maiden with the warm muff to warm our hands for us. That will suit you, won't it?"

" Y-e-s," said Zoë, and not liking to disappoint her play-mates, she suffered herself to be dragged out to the Snow Queen's palace, from which, however, she soon stole away half-frozen to build one in her own way, of feathery tamarind boughs and waving palm leaves, with a tropical sun glistening through the shining leaves, and the blue and violet sea stretched out before her, while loving faces and gentle words filled up the scene and made its fitting music.

"I wonder," said she to herself, "if our Father in Heaven, who mamma says, is our best friend and knows what is good for us, told my papa to send me away off to this cold country, where everything is so strange to me There is the sun; it shines bright enough, but it does not warm me much, and how naked the world looks here' Hilda says, that it is prettier in the summer, and she tells me the truth about things, I know, so I believe her. 1 am sure I shall be glad to walk into the new summer-world, when it comes. Doesn't God love the white people as well as he does us, that he gives them snow and ice and such cold weather? But what a good warm fire this is! How it crackles and blazes! I must move my seat back, for it is too warm. O, now I know, God gives them plenty of wood, so as to make a sun for themselves when his grows cold. Isn't he kind to think of it? and Hilda likes snow and says she has the best fun in winter. So I suppose, it is all right; I must take my furs off too. How soft they are! O yes! and God gives *them* too, as well as the great wood-fires—I mean the animals they grow on. Yes, they seem well taken care of; but I can't help wondering whether he meant that I should come; but I've got to stay here now, so I may as well be contented," and she drew a long sigh.

"Have you got your lesson in geography?" said Hilda, as Zoë sat listless, one morning, with her books in her lap.

"Yes," said Zoë, "I've learned the words, but I don't understand nor care about parallels of latitude and longi-tude, and exactly the spot where people live. If I only like them, and they have a pleasant country for a home, why then I'm very glad."

"But don't you wish to know whether they are north or south of you, or which way the points of compass are?"

"No, I don't. I like to learn, whether they live in a warm or cold country, and what they have to eat and drink, and what kind of people they are, and such as that; but I don't understand why it is that Miss Ingemann said she could not be contented in a place till she knew just where the east was. If the sun will only rise warm and burst the little buds which Miss Holberg showed me were wrapped up so nicely, and the pretty flowers will bloom, and I can feel as if I could walk about without shrugging up my shoulders so because I am so chilled; it is all of the points of the compass I care about."

"What a droll little thing you are," said Hilda. "But we must learn about these things if we don't like them. Miss Ingemann says that all little girls ought to. Come, it is school time and she has gone in;" and hand in hand these children, so opposite, and yet already so assimilated as to be chosen companions to each other, entered her presence.

This lady, in many respects, was admirably adapted to her part as a trainer of young minds. In the first place, her character was high-toned and truthful, in an eminent degree. Nothing mean, unjust, or indelicate could stand the test of her clear eye, or indignant protest. She was not merely ordinarily truthful in speech, but in thought, in manner, in her judgment of people and passing events, did she strive after and attain to a wonderful degree of integrity. As the crown of her high qualities she was sincerely religious. Her faith was not worn externally as a holiday garb, as it were, but entered into the warp and woof of her being, and was the secret spring which regulated her intellect, her affections, and her life. Common-sensible and earnest, she sought to fit her pupils for the duties and enjoyments of the world they lived in, by developing their powers in just proportion, rather than by encouraging any idiosyncrasy of mind or character. Her mode of culture and personal influence was happy and beautiful upon most of the minds in her charge. Under her genial and affectionate care Hilda had budded and was blooming like a rose. They were greatly alike naturally, courageous, high-spirited, with minds in which the understanding predominated, direct in speech and decisive in action. Clear in her reasoning, exact in her knowledge and conscientious in her investigations after the truth; with her imagination under due restraint, the mind of Miss Ingemann was like a grand and spacious storehouse, free from whatever was unseemly, with various generous-sized parcels, all neatly arranged and ready for instant use, while a clear, steady light pervaded the scene. So that though one might at first ask, what more could be wished for in an educator of youth? the answer might be—scarcely anything in intention, yet time must test her ability to deal with a nature so opposite in its tendencies to her own as that of the little Anglo-African.

5

CHAPTER V.

"In the clear heaven of her delightful eye,
An angel guard of loves and graces lie;
Around her knees domestic duties meet,
And fireside pleasures gambol at her feet."

MONTGOMERY.

"JOY, joy," said Hilda, bursting into their common room one morning, "it is holiday you know, to-day, and Mrs. Körner has sent to know if you and I may go to her house this afternoon and play with her little boys. O, I like her so much, and Mr. Körner is the best and the funniest man that ever was. All the children call him *the kind gentleman.* Aren't you glad?"

"Yes," said Zoë, to whom the idea of some change was grateful; "but I am afraid to go to see strangers."

"O, you need not be. They won't be strangers to you five minutes. Everybody is at home at Mrs. Körner's— Miss Holberg says so."

Accordingly they were neatly arrayed, and after a short walk, were admitted into a plain, but cheerful-looking mansion, and conducted up-stairs to the nursery—a good-sized room, comfortably furnished, and ornamented with engravings such as would interest children, with here and there marks upon the tables, sofas, and chairs, made by the collision of toy carriages and horses, and the various implements of a children's play-shop.

They were greeted kindly by a bright, handsome, happy-looking woman, with Carl, the youngest hope in her arms,

(50)

by Frederick. a black-eyed boy, of Hilda's age, and Emile, a little stammerer of three.

"Come, Hilda, let's play at draughts," said Fred, in the summary way in which youngsters go into subjects, leaving complimentary greetings very much to their elders. "You may have the white men and I will have the black, and we will play the giving-away game.

"Well," said she; "and what shall Zoë do?" who was standing timidly by.

"Please give me my playthings, mamma," said Emile, in a mode of speech guiltless of many letters, especially consonants, familiarly known as baby-talk

"O, yes," said Mrs. Körner, "and this little girl may help you set up your town and build castles with the blocks. Will you, dear?"

Zoë liked nothing better than this amusement, which gave scope to her fancy; and she and the gentle but merry little Emile were soon good friends.

"Make me a castle as big as that, please," said he, stretching out his arms to their full width.

"I don't know how; but I will try to make my papa's house that is away over the great sea," said she, at which promise he was pleased, watching her progress and handing her the blocks as she built it upon pillars, connected by arches, with a veranda all around and steps to ascend it.

"Build it higher," said he, as he saw her putting the roof over the single story.

"I must not," said she; "the hurricane, that's a high wind that comes sometimes, will blow it over."

"You must put a chimney to it," said Fred, whose attention was drawn away from his game by their talk.

"No," said Zoë, "we don't have chimneys.

"How can you cook your dinners?" said Fred, who was fond of creature comforts. "Don't you eat anything but oranges and pine-apples?"

"Yes," said she, "but the kitchen is a little house out-side."

"That's queer; how should you like, mother, to have to go out-doors to another house to make your puddings and tarts for dessert?"

"Very well," said Mrs. Körner, "if I lived in a warm country, because it would keep the heat from the house."

At this Hilda, who had become impatient at the interruption of the game, said, "Come, it is your turn to move."

Fred was moderate in his movements, and remained with his eyes still fixed upon the house-building, whereupon Hilda gave the board a push against him to attract his attention, but with such force, that he burst out crying, and said, he would play no more.

Hilda, partly provoked and partly sorry, tried to make the matter fair to Mrs. Körner, by saying, "she did not mean to hurt him."

"Stop, stop crying, Fred," said Mrs. Körner, and then added, with a brightening manner, "Who wants to go into the yard, and see my little white rabbits?"

There was a general rush for the door, Fred's last tear being hastily dashed away, and Zoë even following with alacrity, to see the household pets.

After due admiration of the timid, long-eared, pink-eyed specimens of living natural history, and seeing them in repose, eating, jumping, in every attitude possible to rabbit capacity, Mrs. Körner, Zoë, and Emile returned to the house, leaving Hilda and Fred to romp in the yard for a while.

But the spirit of management which slept in Hilda, under Miss Holberg's eye and was kept in abeyance with the gentle, non-resistant Zoë, became rampant, with the vigorous, strong-willed, self-indulgent boy Fred, and when he tried to force her to play in his way, she only pulled him the harder towards the fulfillment of her plans, until he, quite out of patience at her presuming to have a de-

cided preference of her own, and not only that, but insist-
ing upon it that her will should be his, gave her frock a
twitch, making a bad rent in it.

Hilda's bottle of tears was very near her eyes, and if
anything went wrong, out came the cork, and to one more
self-restrained, there seemed a great waste of feeling;
but this time, she was sure there was sufficient cause, not
only for crying, but for chastisement of the wicked Fred,
so she inflicted a hearty slap upon that young gentleman's
shoulder. He was never above weeping and lamentation
when occasion offered, so that there was presented to Mrs.
Körner, the next moment, the spectacle of two mutually in-
jured and enraged young *humans*, with flashing eyes and
burning cheeks, and four great rivers running down from
as many eyes.

" What is the matter?" said that lady, with the manner
of one ready to listen to complaints, and award due justice,
and by no means thrown off her balance, as if it were the
first belligerent case upon her docket, and she were to give
her maiden charge.

" He pulled me first," said Hilda.

" She struck me, and real hard too," sobbed the little
lord of creation.

" My little Hilda," said Mrs. Körner, " you know I have
three rough, strong boys who have no little sister to make
them gentle, and I want you and Zoè to help me to do so,
will you not?"

Hilda paused a moment, as if a new idea had dawned
upon her, but her wrongs came up again, and she cried,
" He pulled me first!"

" She had no business to strike me," murmured Fred.

" Go into the bath-room and wash your tears away, and
you will feel better," said his mother; " your papa will be
at home soon, and I want him to see happy faces."

This was the " expulsive power of a new affection " to
them, and with the cold water it banished every trace of

ill-temper, so that five minutes after, they were playing as if their life's sea had never been ruffled.

The door-bell rang, and the shout went up, "There's papa;" and a glad "Hurra," was heard from a manly voice in the hall, and quick steps upon the stairs soon brought a brave beaming face to their view.

The baby clapped hands; Fred climbed up his father's perpendicular with a little help, till he crowed from his seat on his shoulder. Emile looked at Fred, and tried to do and say just what he did. Hilda jumped up and down and pulled him at every point by turns, while the little Carl looked and stretched out his arms towards him, his straining eye, eager even to painfulness, pleading for notice, as if here was his "kingdom come," and he must rush into it.

"How are you, my dear?" said he, shaking hands with his wife. Zoë sat smiling placidly upon this noisy greeting, and hoped the kind gentleman would speak to her by-and-by.

"And who is this?" said he, disrobing himself gently of the children and stooping towards her.

"It's Zoë," said Fred, "and see, she has built a house, such as they have in Santa Cruz where she lives."

"How do you do, my little dear?" said he, putting on his spectacles, for he was near-sighted; "and how do you like Copenhagen?"

"I like some things very well; but it is cold, and there are no flowers, and I am afraid I shan't get all my lessons well to say to Miss Ingemann."

"Yes," said he, "but it will be warm soon, and then we will take you to ride in the country, and Fred shall hold the reins and Emile the whip, and we will cover you all over with flowers; won't we, Carl?" said he, tossing him up and down and handing him to his mother: "and as for the lesson, you must say to it — you old hard lesson, do you jump right into my head and there do you stick, and if you ever get out, I 'll, I 'll *pound* you in," and he squared at an open book on the table near, and brought down his clenched fist hard upon it.

The children gazed admiringly at his valor, and all laughed at his threatened assault, when the tea-bell rang and Mrs. Körner directed Fred to lead Hilda, and Emile Zoë; while she followed, arm-in-arm with her husband, to the dining-room below stairs.

The next morning Zoë was awakened by the entrance of Hilda into the room attired in cloak and hood, as if returning from a walk.

"Where have you been?" said she.

"To Mr. Körner's, to carry back the dice of the back-gammon board, which I found in my pocket. I was afraid Mrs. Körner would hunt for them, as she did once before after we had played. Did we not have a good visit?"

"Yes," said Zoë; "I like them all, and I do not feel one bit afraid of them; they are so kind and Emile is a little darling."

"I like to frolic with Mr. Körner," said Hilda, " he lets me do anything to him I want to."

"But I think he had rather you would be gentle though he is so lively; for he looked tired when he sat down, as if he had worked hard all day."

"I *did* hear him say to Mrs. Körner softly when I was pulling him hardest: ' What a little catamount she is!'" said Hilda, " but he was in fun, I guess; for don't you think, when I went there this morning, I ran directly to the breakfast-room where they were at the table, and as soon as he saw me he took up the newspaper and read:

" 'Found fighting in Mr. Korner's yard by the police, Frederick Korner and Hilda Strophel. They were taken to the watch-house and kept during the night, and this morning carried to Court; where their mortified parents and teacher plead for their release, which, after paying five dollars and costs, was granted them.'

".I was so frightened that I snatched the paper out of his

hand to read it myself, and there was not a word of it there. O! I never know when Mr. Körner is serious or when he makes-believe—he is so droll.

"But do get up, Zoë, how lazy you are! The breakfast-bell will ring in ten minutes, and I am afraid Miss Ingemann will scold you if you are not ready."

CHAPTER VI.

"O'er wayward childhood wouldst thou hold firm rule,
And sun thee in the light of happy faces;
Love, Hope, and Patience—these must be thy graces,
And in thine own heart let them first keep school."—COLERIDGE.

MISS INGEMANN had a few clear and true principles by which to judge of human nature and character. She was fond of its study and proud of her shrewdness in its interpretation, and seemed to consider it a legitimate gymnasium in which to exercise and sharpen her intellect. Her skill and knowledge stood her in good stead with most of her pupils. Such a development in one of them went for so much and must be encouraged or repressed, as the case might be. Such an expression indicated this or that tendency and must be dealt with accordingly. With the frank, open Danish girls, who could bear any amount of direct scrutiny into their natures—for so much in harmony was hers with their own that they appreciated her kindly motive and dearly loved her — her plain, abrupt method answered very well; but with Zoë it was different. Her first feeling when led into the stately presence of Miss Ingemann, was admiration. Left for the first time without some one familiar to her to lean upon, she longed for the love of the beautiful white lady, whose blue eye shone so brightly upon the little girls around her and who all seemed to live in the light of her kindly smile. But when she fixed her clear, intellectual gaze upon her as if to read the soul within, that world where from infancy she had been wont to retire and revel in silent delight, not without

(57)

misgivings of a failure in truth and duty in so doing, she
shrank timid and frightened within herself.

Like the tamarind leaf of her own clime, which closes
at the rude touch of one who would read its hidden mys-
tery, so when most yearning for sympathy and companion-
ship she involuntarily shrank from her teacher's direct man-
ner and intellectual attempt at her analysis, though she
knew she was disposed to be her kind friend.   To Miss
Ingemann she was at first an enigma, but as days and weeks
went by, and she developed nothing remarkable, she set
her down as a gentle, well-disposed little girl, with but
little energy and less frankness; with no decided tastes of
any kind; wanting in earnestness of character, and governed
more by a love of approbation than by anything else.   She
had no complaint to make of her; she performed her tasks
well, but the lack was too general a one for her to reach—
a moderate capacity and no real enthusiasm for anything.
It needed no words for Zoë to read this sentence as she
advanced in years; every sense and nerve revealed it to
her and she assented to it all.   And yet there was within
her the eternal questioning and unrest of a dissatisfied,
imprisoned soul.   Her face, pensive and mild in its expres-
sion, was a poor index to the want of harmony between her
inward and outward life, and it wore, in its almost unvary-
ing calmness, the natural defense of a reserved and keenly-
sensitive spirit, which would hide from every eye its
struggles and griefs.

As the two children grew apace, it was interesting to
note the broad contrast in their persons, manners, charac-
ters, and minds, and, at the same time, the beautiful har-
mony between them.   Like the soprano and contralto in
music; like light and shade in a picture; like pathos and
humor in fiction; like tender sentiment and triumphant
expression in poetry; like joy and plaintive sadness in life,
did they blend and divide in its daily anthem, till one
became necessary to the full contentment of the other, and

there was evident on each the indirect influence of a companionship salutary to both.

Hilda, the elder by a whole year, was the taller and fuller in figure, with the clear red and white which the keen breath and tempered ray of a northern wind and sun paints, and not for a brief day only, upon the cheeks of her fair ones; with blonde hair, so light and silky that the faintest breeze would set it afloat, and with a blue eye that would kindle and brighten, throwing a flood of light over her whole face, like the sun rising from the ocean depths and spreading his radiance over sky, earth, and water. Her step was quick and elastic, and when suffered to act out her impulses, her modes of locomotion were a bound and a spring, dancing a few steps forward, turning around as in a waltz, swaying back and forward à la schottische with an ordinary step or two in advance, to be continued by a movement of original composition. Her mind was as active and as versatile in its operations as her body. At one time she would be absorbed with her doll, dressing and undressing it; washing or altering its wardrobe; teaching it her own various exercises; telling it over and over the rules of the school, with additions à la Hilda, and especially enforcing them by occasional punishments, so that the school-girls, who all had reaped the benefit of Miss Holberg's rebuke for her spirit of management, had great amusement in seeing how the safety-valve was let off in the direction of poor dolly, who, as they suggestively said, had "to take it," since they were somewhat relieved. When once settled down to her studies, her acquisitions were rapid and correct, provided she understood them perfectly; but she took few things on trust, nor believed much in any subtle, hidden meanings, but if everything seemed clear and reasonable, she easily mastered it. In character and feelings she was like an April day, as her nickname denoted. For story-reading she had an insatiable appetite, preferring the true, but swallowing fairy and goblin tales,

too, though with some wry faces, and much demurring at
their hard digestion. Strong-willed and decided, only to a
firm, wise mind and cheerful spirit would she submit, and
then only through much struggle with herself, which would
often vent itself in loud weeping and complaining at her
supposed wrongs ; or, when desperate and under the eye of
one in whom she stood in awe, only in inarticulate ejacula-
tions to herself. But when most severely punished, and
subdued to quietness, her teacher would begin to relent
and question herself if she had not been too hard with her
and thus crushed the tender young spirit, who now, pas-
sive and serious, was gazing apparently at vacancy, she
would start up and say: "O, look, Miss Ingemann, at that
funny old man formed by the coals in the fireplace! What
a great pack he has got on his back, and how he turns his
long nose up!" She would then, forgetting her dreadful in-
juries, throw her arms around her neck, and exclaim upon
her beauty and her own love for her, overwhelming her with
kisses till she had to cry for quarter and beat a retreat to
her own apartment.

She was her teacher's pride and joy, as she developed
beautifully in mind and person, under her fostering care,
and she looked forward to a brilliant and happy future for
her favorite.

Miss Ingemann's birth, mind, manners, and character
being of such elevated stamp, she sustained a high position
in the society of Copenhagen. Her pupils were from
among its best and noblest citizens, and her companionship
was sought by the enlightened and titled of the land.
To Hans Christian Andersen, she had been a friend and
early patron, and to him her doors were ever open in hos-
pitable welcome. And from the children of her school he
always met a glad and noisy reception. Hilda would run
to him with outstretched arms and beg for a feast from his
" nice cupboard full of stories," and no fond mother was ever
more generous in giving food to her children, than he in

'heir distribution. Simple they were, yet full of poetic life; quaint and humorous, yet shedding sensibility and sympathy for the poor and struggling from every point; and what gave them their deepest interest was not their genius merely, for that was but the instrument by which he poured forth to the people, each one of whom was a dear brother or sister, the vailed experience of a tried, but disciplined, true and devoted life. He would sing to them too, most sweetly, and Zoë loved him better even for his music than for his tales. His dramatic power was at their service also, in a way which they best liked, for his childlike character and love for their young spirits made him deem nothing unseemly, which would furnish them a pure amusement and a happy hour. The girls would collect their dolls, old, young, middle-aged, handsome, ugly and odd, and he would marshal them into a dramatic corps, imagine some play which would hit off their several characteristics, and lead them through it with such nature and spirit, as to entrance not only the children, but older spectators. Hilda's doll in particular, which rejoiced in the full age of a century, being an heirloom in her family, was made to play a conspicuous part. Tall and rigid in her figure, wearing on her brow the scars of many a life-battle, with a firm pursed up mouth, which, if she could open it, would only berate the degeneracy of the times; a square, practical nose, with an iron-colored tip, the effect of many a snubbing from her young duenna; black, staring eyes, which never looked within, but forever spied out and speared the world's surface faults; chin and cheeks expressive of entire self-satisfaction, two fixed spots of red upon the latter, as if defying old Time, and saying, " put me down if you dare," with no line of beauty but in the eyebrows, and they were such a thread, that they gave but an iota of character to her face. She was dressed in the fashion of the olden time, with here and there a scrap of modern finery stuck on her by Hilda, and her flying hair and crumpled cap gave evidence that her ungrateful descendant (for she called her granny,) was getting tired of her, and thinking that it was almost time for her to be out of the way. This image, Hans Christian made full use of, especially with reference to Hilda, whom he understood like a book, and so criticised and belabored her through her *ancestor* as to make her almost afraid of her, and she would say to Zoë, after his departure, " I am going to lock up my old doll in the closet, and she shan't come out for a whole week. I wish Mr. Andersen would not make her so cross, for I shall certainly hate her, and as she was my great-gieat great-grandmother's, and mamma told me to be careful of her, I don't want either to burn her or cut her up, or throw her into the street for the naughty boys to laugh at. Isn't it too bad?"

By fastidious critics among his countrymen, with whom his simplicity and purity of mind and beautiful genius went for but little when weighed against his awkward figure and manners and proneness to egotism, he was said to " carry his heart on a waiter;" but Miss Holberg thought that he might reveal himself still more to his friends, and yet retain within much more wealth of thought and feeling than his uncharitable judges had in their whole stock in warehouse or trade.

The great and good Thorwaldsen, to whom Art revealed herself bright, lovely, chaste, severe and sanctified as she is, whose countrymen have it not to reproach themselves with that they were blind to his worth, was also an honored guest at the mansion, and to him Zoë bowed lowly and reverently in her secret heart. To Hilda and herself, un-like yet loving as they were, he always gave attention. He called them his " Night and Morning." For the one, jocund and wide-awake, soaring on rapid pinion through the empyrean, scattering roses on her way, and lighted by the flambeau of joy, he had a merry greeting or a playful jest; but for the other, who with folded wing and half-closed eye, drifted slowly wherever the breeze might waft her, with her young thoughts and feelings asleep and pressed closely to her breast, and attended by the grim and ominous bird of night, screeching anon of evil to come, his tenderness gushed forth. His gentle tones and soft hand pressed caressingly upon her head, were a healing to the pain which she felt, but knew not enough of herself to reveal, and a hope to the sadness which moaned within her, but which she was too much a stranger to happiness to note.

"Come down into the drawing-room," said Hilda to Zoë, one evening just at twilight: "the great sculptor and Mr. Andersen are both there, and Miss Ingemann and Miss Holberg have walked out. Mr. Andersen has promised to tell me a story, and Mr. Thorwaldsen asks if his little Night has drawn so dark a shadow over her as not to be visible Come with me and I will chase it away as we enter his presence, so that he may catch a glimpse of you."

They entered the room, Hilda in advance, when just as she approached him, she stepped aside, and, in mock-heroic, school-girl style, with a wave of the hand towards her friend, repeated:

"Lo, evening flieth upon the steps of day,"

and then went to the window where Hans Christian was standing. Zoë stood by her honored friend, for, at the mature age of nine she thought herself too old to sit upon his knee as formerly, and besides he was very infirm. Hilda begged for a story from Hans Christian.

"Which of my tales do you like best?" said he.

"The seven stories of the Snow Queen," said she; "but Zoë reads the Ugly Duck most, and says she thinks she is like it."

"Only that I never expect to become a swan," said Zoë.

"We went yesterday," said Hilda to Thorwaldsen, "to see your works of art, sir, in the different public buildings, and the last place was the cathedral, where are the Saviour and the twelve apostles."

"And which do you like best of all of them?" asked Thorwaldsen.

"O, my namesake, Morning, and next the Three Graces. Those are beautiful." And she imitated the attitude of one of them, lifting Mr. Andersen's hand to have him personate another.

"No, no, you cannot make a grace of me, that is very certain; but you must balance my homely mouth against my stories which you say you like; my one sided nose you must set against my little dramas; and as for my forehead, why my music need not be very much ashamed of it, though it retreats a little as if it did not care for it as much as my little friends do. But where are you leading me?" said he, as Hilda pulled him along towards the door.

"To see my new doll, which is sitting in the armchair in the hall. I got tired with the scoldings of old granny, and have put her away. This new one cannot pucker up her pretty mouth to scold, if she tried, or if you do your best to make her."

"It will depend on yourself," said he, "whether she talks to please you. I can make her give you a hard lesson if you are not good, even if she were as beautiful as the new moon."

Zoë was left alone with Thorwaldsen. "And which do you like best of what you saw yesterday, my little Night?" said he, tenderly laying his hand on her shoulder.

For the first time since she left her mother's side was she won to complete confidence, by the serious but mild eye and deep inspiring voice of the artist.

"The Christ," she said; "and I dreamed last night that I saw him passing by, with a covering upon his head suited to the drapery he wore, and there seemed to be written all over him: '*Venite ad me omnes*,'—'come unto me all.' I rose to follow him, but I remembered that he could read my thoughts, and I dared not go."

"But, my child, you have no thoughts which you fear to hide from him, have you?" said he mildly but solemnly.

"I am afraid so. I make-believe a world within myself, and I fear it is like telling an untruth. I always say when I have asked Hilda not to talk, because I am going to think, 'now this is making-believe, or supposing so and so,' but yet I do not feel quite right about it. I hope it is not wrong, sir?"

"Not if you do your little duties in the outer world, and love real people better than your ideal ones," said he.

"Ah, that is the trouble. They are not so pretty or so good as they are in my mind-world, where everybody does what is beautiful and right, and that frets me, and worse than this, I am not the same myself in Miss Ingemann's school that I am in my thought home, and that vexes me more than anything; and if I do not speak cross, I feel so, and am often very unhappy, and the minister says that only good and blessed people are in heaven, and I am neither; so I fear I shall never go there."

"'Come to me all,' the Christ says, Zoë, which means that we must be and do and think and feel as he would if he now lived and worked among us. Remember this, my child; obey his commands. Take, as it were, hold of his hand when you pray to the great Father, and the right and true will be plain, and happiness will come to you through following these when you seek it not."

She still looked dissatisfied. "But what is right? Is it always doing what we dislike to do? And is it wicked to do what we most like, what makes us happy?"

"Tell me what you like to do and I can answer you better."

"Nothing which Hilda and the other girls do. I soon get tired of play; I do not like my lessons, nor my sewing and knitting, nor any other work. I feel afraid of people too much to wish to visit them. Even the poor, which Hilda likes to work for and to teach many little things, trouble me so much with their dirty houses and clothes and stare at me so that I cannot go to them any more."

"But this is what you do not like. Now tell me what makes you happy."

Zoë looked down and struggled hard with her natural reserve, then gazed a moment into Thorwaldsen's eyes and answered:

"To make-believe myself the great, good, kind queen of the whole world, and to think of all that I will do to make its people happy and gain their love. This is all I like to do, and O! it is so foolish," and she burst into tears.

Thorwaldsen paused. He remembered the dreams of his youth and how God had enabled him to fulfill them, and he reverenced those of this timid and aspiring yet humble child.

"Zoë," said he, "when a boy of your age, I too dreamed of being the greatest sculptor of my country, and raising the world to a higher and purer taste for Art. God has enabled me to do so, and for it I daily bless his holy name. But to be great and to do good, we must not merely dream but labor and suffer and wait patiently upon his will. Daily must you take up your cross, and in his own good time you shall wear the crown which he sees to be fitting for you."

"But how take up the cross?" said she, "never, never to dream but do everything I do not like—is that the way? O! life would be so hard! Did our Father in heaven intend it should be so?"

Children ask puzzling questions, and even Thorwaldsen knew not how to answer her directly.

"My child, I cannot say, but this is sure; obey your conscience, read your Bible, let the Christ be your pattern and guide through life, pray to the good God to be your friend. Learn as much as you can of the works of his beautiful world, and be not anxious for anything else—all will be right with you. Will you do this?"

"I will try, sir," she said, and as the ladies entered the room, she turned to leave it but with a firmer step and brighter eye than ever before, for her life at that moment was invested with an aim, which she was never to lose sight of wherever it might lead her.

"Be gentle and forbearing with this little girl," said he to Miss Ingemann, for she had before alluded to her dullness of apprehension and want of interest in her studies; "for time and patience may reveal some hidden power of mind and character which may surprise and delight you. Hers is no common spirit, I can assure you."

The next day Miss Ingemann sharpened her mental gaze as she studied Zoë from her elevated post of observation, till her victim writhed as if her teacher's eye were a cold steel point probing her flesh, and when she could not escape her keen metaphysical scrutiny, she instinctively threw out a darkening cloud in the shape of an unaccountable impulse or eccentricity. That lady became doubly certain that she was right in her judgment of her, only that she had given her credit for more gentleness than she deserved, and she wondered how so clear and

true a mind as Thorwaldsen's could suffer a fancy to mis-
lead him. O! when will it be seen that for no jugglery,
nor even at the rap of the clearest understanding will that
sacred thing, the human soul, reveal itself, but as deep
answereth only unto deep, so to the spiritually enlightened,
sympathetic and pure, to the little child in Christ's king-
dom alone will it give forth its most subtle odor and its
sweetest music.

> "A vail is lifted—can she slight
> The scene that opens now?"

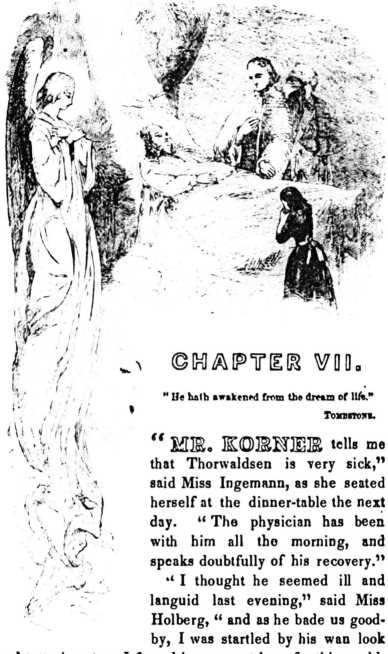

CHAPTER VII.

"He hath awakened from the dream of life."

TOMBSTONE.

"MR. KORNER tells me that Thorwaldsen is very sick," said Miss Ingemann, as she seated herself at the dinner-table the next day. "The physician has been with him all the morning, and speaks doubtfully of his recovery."

"I thought he seemed ill and languid last evening," said Miss Holberg, "and as he bade us good-by, I was startled by his wan look and tottering step; I feared he was not long for this world, but could not bear to dwell upon the thought."

(69)

Zoë quietly dropped her knife and fork, and her dinner remained untasted. It attracted but little notice, for her appetite was not an eager one, and her teacher would sometimes say, " that if she would even *eat* with the relish of the other girls, she should have more hope of her, for it might serve as a clue to other capacities, if she *had* any distinctive ones, but with such a dead level of a nature as hers, what could she do?"

After dinner, the child retired to her room, and seated herself by the window which commanded a view of the artist's house. Hour after hour, she sat with book in hand, but not once read, and watched the signs of his ebbing life. She saw one physician after another hurry up the steps with anxious mien; the little child checked by its nurse in running noisily before the door; the servant with open handkerchief wipe away his tears as he quieted the restless, growling dog who strove to go to his master's room, and the friend who came out for a brief moment to stand with folded arms and serious thoughtful face against a pillar, and then rouse himself and step hastily back as if he would not lose a single breath of the dying Christian artist; and over the whole scene, there was that mysterious, sad quietness, unexplained by reason, but real to the feelings, such as one is sensible of on entering a vacant room, and knows that a friend is gone from the house by the still air of the chairs and tables. By-and-by there were other movements. The two physicians last called in, came out together talking of the case, each one having his own thought of its treatment, and well satisfied that he was called in too late to save his life. Then the family medical man with slow, thoughtful step, and face with no remorse of aspect, but mournful, as if " Would God I could have died for thee, my best friend and benefactor!" were written in every line. At last the window was raised, the shutter drawn and she knew that the form of the dead was com-

posed decently to his last rest, and that the spirit of him
who had given a hope to her life, had ascended.

Hilda ran into the room. " Why, what is the matter,
Zoë, you look so sick?"

" Thorwaldsen is dead."

" Why, no, he is not. Miss Ingemann sent in at three
o'clock, and he was a little better then, and they had hope
of his life."

" He is dead," said Zoë. Hilda gazed wonderingly at
her for a moment, and then broke into a loud cry. " O!
he must not be dead; I cannot have him die; the good
Thorwaldsen, who is always so kind, and I love him so
much; O dear! what shall I do," and she ran weeping
into the school-girls' sitting-room. " Thorwaldsen is dead,"
she exclaimed, between her sobs.

" Who told you so?" said half a dozen voices at once.

" Zoë."

" O, the little raven! It is no such thing. I'll engage
she has not been out of her room this afternoon, and
strange as she is, I do not believe she has *second sight*,"
said Rinda.

" He is though!" said Hilda, wiping her eyes, for the
slur upon her friend was fast diverting her grief from her
loss. " He is, for when Zoè says a thing is certain, it
always is. He is dead," and she again wept aloud.

The day of his funeral came, and he was to be honored
in his burial as no subject of any realm had been before.
The king in deep mourning, was to receive the body at the
entrance of the church, and the crown prince, as President
of the Academy of Fine Arts, at the head of its members,
followed by the royal princes, and the principal officers of
state were to walk after the hearse. Troops, processions
of the different guilds, and orders of citizens were to form
the train of this national ceremony.

Miss Ingemann's school was to attend her to the
church, habited in white, with a scarf of black crossing the

shoulder and hanging down the side.   One is not curious to
know how much the preparation for this pageant alleviated
their sorrow.   It is sufficient, that from the oldest to the
youngest, there were love and veneration for the departed,
and the sad sense of loss was really felt according to each
one's character and capacity.

Zoë watched the preparations, and with Miss Holberg's
help arranged her wardrobe, but with a strange feeling of
unreality, as if it were not for herself.   The idea of doing
something to honor her friend, were it but sewing a straight
seam in her most skillful manner, was grateful to her, and
her imagination pictured a thrilling adoration, a deep and
manifest woe, as a necessary accompaniment, and a lasting
inspiration derived from the recital of his greatness, and
goodness.

She was too young and inexperienced to know that human
power is so limited in this life that though profound senti-
ment may first suggest the ceremonial, yet when we are
doing the most to honor outwardly the departed, thus
spreading our feelings over a large surface, we are for the
time dismayed at their comparative shallowness.   It is
well that it is so, for to give beauty and richness to life
there must be symbol and ceremony, and the various ex-
pressions of deep poetic sentiment; and let the mind be
sufficiently engrossed by them to have them fitting and
beautiful, though at the time they may seem to detract from
the ethereal essence of feeling.   But when the duty is
done and every untoward and vexatious circumstance is
softened to the memory or haply fades away from it
entirely, then rises the Phœnix of holy and beautiful poetry
from the ashes of what may seem to the mistaken a too
material and meaningless rite.   " For thus it becometh us
to fulfill all righteousness," and to him who simply and
reverently obeys without questioning the dictates of nature
and religion, the great alchemist will in time reveal the
reward.

Zoë sat by herself and mourned silently for her loss. Too young to reason much, constitutionally sentimental, early thrown into circumstances which favored reserve, not understood by her teacher, she was fast growing morbid and unnatural by a one-sided development. Like the passion-flower torn up by the roots and planted against a wall of ice, the tendrils of her soul spread hither and thither striving instinctively to reach some support. With the elements of a self-sacrificing, aspiring life prematurely developing, of a nervous and anxious temperament, she had found relief and hope through confiding in Thorwaldsen, and at night she scarcely slept for the joyful visions which visited her. The great artist was her friend. He, too, had dreamed like herself, and to him she would go to slake her yearning to be loved and feel that she could look straight into his eye without being repelled by a wondering, critical stare. Now her hope was cut off. With this painful experience adding a long term to her life, she was again thrust back upon herself, and her feelings at first stunned, now gushed forth in uncontrollable weeping.

"How foolish I am!" she said to herself; "as if a little girl of nine has a right to be so sorry because this great man, whom all Denmark and the world worship, has died. He never said much to me and I less to him, and Miss Ingemann always seemed afraid lest I should trouble him when I stood by his knee. I would not have her know that I was crying so for him for the world. I will wash my eyes that she may not see my tears. But O! was not his soft hand upon my head like this cold bath to my eyelids? I never, never shall feel it again!" and she burst forth afresh. "But I must control myself, as Miss Ingemann calls it. I will go to the window and look out and think of something else. There sits a poor tired man in the street, and two little children are giving him something, and he stretches out his hand and pats their heads. It looks like Thorwaldsen's Christ blessing little children.

7

O, I never shall hear him tell me again of the Christ and make me feel as if I could be like him! What, what shall I do! I am afraid the feeling which made me so happy will leave me;" and she clasped her hands and looked up as in earnest entreaty. "But hush! some one is coming. No, the step has passed by; but I must get ready to go to the funeral. How the crowds begin to pour along! how eager they are to get a place where they can see the parade well! This is their way of being sorry, I suppose. But can I walk in the long procession, with the bright sun shining into my face so that people can see me, if I cannot help crying? And how can I help it when everybody has lost a friend, and I the most of all! And they will say: 'The great and good Thorwaldsen is dead!' And the organ will play so mournfully, and *that* I cannot bear up under. I shall certainly groan and cry aloud. O no! I cannot go to the funeral. I must stay by myself. I must, I must;" and she threw herself upon the bed and hid her face in the pillow to still her sobs.

Miss Holberg came into the room—"Come, my dear, I will help you to dress before I make my own toilet."

"I cannot go to the funeral."

"Not go to our friend's funeral!" But seeing the child's swollen eyes, she guessed the cause, and she knew her well enough to speak gently, but not to go to the deepest springs of her nature to console her. "Yes, dear, I see. We all loved Thorwaldsen, and feel very sad to lose him; but we must submit to God's will and do our best to honor his memory. You wish to do that, do you not?"

"O Miss Holberg! let me stay at home; please, please, do! I feel as if I should drop down in the street. Do ask Miss Ingemann to let me!"

She really looked so sick and miserable and her step tottered so, that knowing she was not strong, she feared she would not sustain the fatigue, and therefore, went to Miss Ingemann and reported her state.

She was disappointed to have her arrangements disturbed, for the brunette and blonde were to form a pretty contrast in the procession, and really sorry that the child should have one of those troublesome headaches so malapropos; but she was too busy to see her personally, and directing that some simple remedies should be given her pupil, she accompanied the others to the church.

So Zoë lost the opportunity of regulating her sensibilities, diseased by solitude, and her idiosyncrasies of temperament, by the healthy influence of contact with other minds and right participation in a becoming pageant; but she sat alone exaggerating the grief of the audience, and the desolation caused by their loss, till a morbid impression was fixed in her mind by an event which might otherwise have been presented to her under such inspiring aspects. For this born peasant, but nature's noble, from humble poverty and a frigid clime had worked his way upward to a post which kings looked up to, and had drawn from his calm but burning soul, images of beauty, sanctity and power, which the world has caught glimpses of enough to honor, but which are to inspire and lead the human soul far in the distant future.

And now, that the drapery of mortality had fallen from him, he stands revealed as two great lives, one upon earth so vailed as not to startle, but to allure to excellence; the other, " where no eye hath seen, nor ear heard, nor heart conceived "— the glory which shall be revealed to the lovers and doers of *the good!*

Poor Zoe! her young heart was only too alive to the power and beauty of the first life; and what a light is quenched, when a great and pure nature bids adieu to it! But to balance this premature sensibility, there were needed a deeper and more inspiring mode of consolation, a clearer insight into the other, than her teacher gave her, and she suffered accordingly.

CHAPTER VIII.

"The law's delay."

SHAKSPEARE.

"MOTHER, here is Mr. Ernest's gardener, with your plants which he promised you. Shall I ask him to carry them into the yard?" said Fred Körner, one bright morning early in the month of May.

"Yes, my boy, and say, I thank Mr. Ernest, for his kindness."

As soon as that bright notable lady had finished her household arrangements for the morning above stairs, dusting here and there a bureau or table in her bedroom, smoothing a wrinkle left in the counterpane, picking up the threads from the carpet, she went into the parlor. Before one could count twenty, there was a general overturn of the furniture; sofas were wheeled from one corner to the other; the great chairs had an easy hob-nobbing squint given to each other, as they were stationed at opposite angles; and she mentally resolved, that on the first leisure day she would pull up those set-looking bookcases by the roots, and let them know that they were not to stand still all their lives in this age of progress. They should change sides like the politicians all over the world.

Here was little Denmark all in a fuss and fury about Schleswig Holstein, her husband's birthplace. She hoped it would have its own way for his sake, and had she not read the American newspapers, which Mrs. Stephenson, the minister's wife from that country, had lent her?

(76)

She had borrowed them at first to improve her knowledge of the idioms of the English language, but there was such life and fun and information in those New York papers, especially in one called the *Tribune*, that she must read them weekly.

"No, no, her bookcases should not be old fogies, they should march with the times; and if some day she could catch her brother-in-law, the Lutheran minister, whose church she attended, and who doted even on the odor of an old book—no, she believed on the whole it was a new one—would not they have a good time in making a thorough revolution among them? And those old pamphlets, they should make a bonfire unless the parson wanted them, which he no doubt would. What a saint his wife must be to suffer so much old lumber about! Poor victim," she thought "on the whole she would not offer them to him, but for her sake put them into the fire at once."

After giving the last touch and turn to the ornaments about the room, to make them look as unlike to themselves as possible, she went into her little yard.

It would not be called a large territory by a countryman, but for the city, it was not to be despised by any means, and with the contributions of her different friends, especially Mr. Ernest's, and what the seed-store afforded, and the hot-house plants from Mr. Hoffman that he had just brought her, which would give the last touch to its glory, she already saw in her fancy quite a little greenery around her.

"Yes, her house, with its surroundings, should be a real home to her in the best sense, and it should be a resting-place to the soul of her beloved when he returned each night from his labors, and her children should have sweet and lovely associations through its beauty with their childhood; and how easy it would be, through the springing grass and blooming flowers, to lead their thoughts and affections to the good Giver of all this enjoyment!"

"And then it would be an oasis for the eye of the traveler upon the dusty highway; and would she not have flowers, not only to brighten and fill her own rooms with incense, but for her friends also—those dear ones who had received her with open arms when she came a young stranger from the country, with her simple ways, to meet what she feared were the stiff conventionalisms of a city?" But she felt them not, for love and kind deeds had ever attended her—so she thought as she untied the string which bound them together.

"A pear tree! what a thrifty one! you shall climb against that tall fence, and make the most of yourself. Four grapevines! you will be good enough to cover that out-building as soon as it pleases you. Eight currant bushes! my favorite fruit. Won't I have fresh individual ones for tea instead of those conglomerates from the market? Six rose bushes! please to arrange yourselves according to your color and capacity, whether as climbers or staid conservatives. And ivy! that is a radical, even if you place it against a dead wall, more so for *that*, my old, young favorite! cling there if you please. Honeysuckle! you angel, shedding your fragrance most when the damps of life fall upon you, cover my lattice—the sooner the better! Here is one that looks like a mere walking-stick; but nevertheless, it shall have its place. Who knows but that it is cousin, far removed, to Aaron's rod, and that it may bud more marvelously than any of the others? Now for my hoe and trowel!

"But where is that precious husband of mine? He said he would stay from the office and help me; that he would only step out for a moment while I was arranging things in-doors.

"I dare say I shall not see him until dinner time—perhaps not before night. O dear! I wonder if it was intended that husbands should live in dull, dirty notaries' offices and dingy, dark wholesale stores four-fifths of their lives! They must be a deal better than I am, if their souls don't get soiled and rusty with such base contact all the time.

"But business must be attended to! Business! what does it all amount to? Stirring up a grand hurry-scurry, each one striving to get up in the world and thrust his neighbor below, putting everything upside down, wrong side up and out of the way generally, till Providence in the form of a *crash*, throws everything into *pi*, and gives men an opportunity to begin anew in a better way! But do they? that is the thing! At any rate they have the chance, and the worse for them if they do not. I don't mean that my dear husband is one of those cackling biddies in male attire, who go scratching about with their heads towards the ground, as if it was their *mission* to pick up the fattest worm in the earth, and what they cannot eat, to hide away to putrefy, so that other hungry hens can't get it—and the next thing you know of them, they are waking up the babies and disturbing the neighborhood by their noisy cackle—and when you go to see what the matter is, there is only one little egg after all. And then with the best luck, only a wee little chicken comes out of it, and ten to one the silly fool scratches its eye out digging for another worm.

"But how my thoughts run! O, my husband I was thinking of! No, no, he is honest, generous, and whole-souled; but he has got into the whirl, so away he spins from morning to night.

"O dear! again I say! He will certainly go blind with that pain in his eyes, or crazy with those headaches; and then what will the money he is heaping up for his wife and children—for I know that it is for us he works—be worth to us! If I don't make him turn over a new leaf I am not so great a woman as he thinks I am.

"But I hear the bell ring! never mind, Mahomet won't go to the mountain this time, the mountain shall come to him! Louise! whoever it is, send them out here.

"Mr. Stärke! your most obedient! And to what fortunate combination of events may I attribute this early call? Why, the sun is up yet, and is not eclipsed either. You can see to work! For mercy sake don't lose a minute! You will feel poverty-stricken to-morrow if you do."

"Good morning, Mrs. Körner," bowing, "how facetious you are! The key of the safe was forgotten, and all the papers needed for our present work are in it. I will thank you for it."

"And can't Mr. Körner do anything until you return?"

"Nothing of consequence; he desired me to call as I had an errand this way, and the clerk was not at hand."

"Good! no better time than the present then to commence my reform. No! I shall not give you the key, my friend, and more than that, you are going to stay yourself and help me; what say you?"

"I should be most happy, Mrs. Körner, at any other time, but really, our business is very imperative and I cannot be spared."

"So is mine, and I can't spare you either. Please take this hoe and dig a place for the root of this pear tree."

"But, my dear Mrs. Körner, our clients are waiting and they have already pressed us to hasten their cause, and—and—I must confess that I am a little selfish about it too, for you know, I have just been chosen junior partner and I am very desirous of fulfilling my part of the duties of the office."

"You cannot do it better than by aiding your partner's wife, and I will prove it to you in religious and poetical form—which is a deal better than your dry legalities—before you leave.

"Please take the hoe! Is Mr. Stärke impolite to a lady? What portents are there in the heavens to correspond with such an anomaly? (looking all over the sky). Take it, please, I will answer for you to the court, judge, and jury, and lead you away from them with flying colors.

"There, thank you! I knew you would aid a distressed — not damsel exactly, but something fully as good and quite as forlorn — a deserted wife; who spends the honeymoon, gives life to and trains up her babies in the fear and love of the Lord, or mayhap in terror of his black majesty, works out life's problem, whether it be dark or joyful, prepares for heaven or haply sinks into the other state, wears away with disease, dies and is buried with what? the devoted love of her husband, to be sure, which proves itself by his digging his own grave prematurely in nervously searching for a paltry treasure that any ill-wind may blow away! And, in the meantime, makes an evening call to play with the children, spends a weary night to get up half-refreshed in the morning, breakfasts in haste, dines, if at all, in a trice, and sups upon the vanity and vexation of spirit of the whole day.

"There, is not that a true picture of married life at the present day? I mean of the best and happiest marriages— of those who are called *well to do in the world* in every way?"

"There is some truth in it, I confess, but what would you have? It seems to be the order of society, and pardon me, but you look pretty happy under the administration."

"So I am; who would not be with my glorious husband? but don't you think I could be happier in a truer and higher style? I should like to have the trial, I know, and I intend to have it too.

"There! you have planted that nicely. Now for the grape-vines! O! I see you will be tolerably educated under my supervision, before you marry. I will give you a lesson from time to time, and then for the wedding-cake; I will make it for you according to my mother's receipt. It is the best that ever was."

"O! that event is a long way in the future. I must make the fortune first, which you seem to despise so much this morning."

"No, you will do no such thing! You will marry before you are a thousand dollars richer. What is the use of a fortune to begin life with, when you have a head and two hands and health into the bargain?"

"I should feel that it was very selfish to inflict poverty and self-sacrifice upon a delicate, high-bred young lady, and really, you would not wish me to be satisfied with any other."

"If you mean refined and well-bred, I say no; but do not ask our rosy Danish girls to grow sickly, sentimental, and learned, like that pale American young lady opposite. She looks like an Anemone, beautiful, it is true, and of celestial birth apparently, but as if she would bloom only a month in the spring and then be laid low. Mrs. Stephenson says that many of the young girls in her country are like her fair cousin. They live in furnace-heated rooms in winter and go out but little, but study, read, attend to music, poetize, and dream of a higher life than the present affords them, till they are sick, nervous, and if they do not become insane they sink into an early grave, or, heaven save us! mount the rostrum or pulpit; or what is a little better, flood the country with their mental effusions in print!

"No, no! marry a sensible, healthy little damsel, contented with this sublunary state for the present, who likes nothing so well as to begin at the lower round of the ladder with you, so that you may have the satisfaction of climbing to the top together.

"But stop, if you please! Don't plant that honeysuckle in that north corner, where the sun never shines, and close by that stiff-looking snow-ball that is too pure and cold ever to blush, but here in this sunny spot, that it may be supported by this trellis without being shaded too much. And now, as you are too good ever to be angry, I am going to give you a fact or two, which your blunder forces upon me.

"If the young men of the present day, especially of the

learned professions, would be a little less proper, and a little more chivalrous, a little less worthy in the hum-drum sense, and a little more enthusiastic in their love for the dear Lord and their fair young neighbors, to say the least, a little less politic and sort of make-believe in their sieges upon hearts—like the English army before Sevastopol, but march up more in the ' deliver, or (not *you*, but *I*,) die' style of olden time, I can tell you, women would not require you to wear yourselves out in getting a fortune for them, but they could not withstand you at all. Fortunes without poetry and love are quite indispensable, but with them they are esteemed a convenience, or otherwise as you happen or not to have them.

" All that is very fine, but—"

" There is no tender spot in you for it to sink into, you mean. O, the degeneracy of the men of the present! Well, we shall see.

" Come, my roses, you shall bloom and console me for the superabundance of Lombardy poplars all about this blessed city. They give it such a stiff, prosy look, and turn their branches upwards as if the sweet heavens needed their shade instead of us poor mortal women. But you need not think I speak from a sense of my own wrongs. My husband was, is, and ever will be, ' *le preux chevalier, sans peur, sans reproche*', excepting that he works too hard for me.

" Here, my beautiful white rose! friend of my childhood! stand there, at the right of the George the Fourth; royalty and simplicity side by side. That is well, and my Superbe shall climb this wall, and be the back-ground of both."

" You seem at no loss where to put your plants, but it is take aim, and down with you!"

" Of course, that is a part of my inspiration, you see; it requires nothing else.

" Now, they are all set but this Ampelopsis, which my friend, Mr. Weiss, saint as he is, brought me yesterday, and I am so little acquainted with it, that I do not know what site it wants to make it contented. I will wait until Mr. Körner comes."

" I thought your inspiration was sufficient? Excuse me, but it seems to have failed already."

" Now, is not that a mistake worthy of a man of a clear understanding, who depends upon a chain of reasoning, ratiocination as he calls it—what a hard word—to sustain himself and the universe. This mistake of yours, proves it is insufficient. If you would but condescend to make use of the brighter lamps which God gives us, as we women are thankful to do, you would be a great deal better, and more interesting than you now are, with your dry logic and masses of facts; and you would not make that remark, pardon me, so wanting in psychological insight, as our metaphysical friend, Gottfried, would call it. For, have you not learned yet, what it is to be a prophet?"

" I must plead some doubt upon the subject."

" Why, it is the simplest thing in the world, when it is once learned, my sister, ' Lisbet ' told me, who knows a scrap of almost everything. It is to profit by everything in nature, God's Word, by men, women, and children, and all they say and do—indeed everything in this great universe, in which our Father has placed us. Now, if you can tell what on this earth is a greater inspiration to me than your honored partner, I wish you to do so.

" What! does the learned notary look puzzled? I dare say now, that he has always pictured to himself a seer staring up into vacancy, with a pen in his hand, and a scroll on the table beside him, waiting for some angel, or, mayhap evil one, to blow the divinity out of that vulgar-looking trumpet that may be seen sticking out of some clouds near, instead of learning about the lilies of the field and the fowls of the air, as our Saviour did. This comes not from your Bible, you may be sure of that; you men are too proud and unenlightened in these days—excuse me, to read that much; but from always pulling upon that old, broken chain that you call ra-ti-oc-i-na-tion! no wonder that you tumble over so often, with your nicely-laid plans. You deserve to, for trusting so much to such an antiquated, second-rate affair, good in its place, but not to be made so much of as you wise men of Gotham do."

" Thank you for the idea, I am not quite sure of its correctness, however."

" You will try if it fits into your old chain, will you, before you adopt it? Well, it does, and it does not, but it is true notwithstanding."

" Now we will give one survey of our labor, and then I will release you from your thraldom. Yes, it will do, and when I get a few shrubs from Mrs. Farrel's, which I had almost forgotten she had promised me, it will be as full as I wish it. Strange that that lady should have such a kind and friendly face and heart with such a thunder-cloud of a creed! I think she must get her faith, after all, more from the New Testament and her pretty garden, than she does from that hobgoblin from the middle ages, that stalks about and takes up so much room in these days! But here is Mr. Körner."

" Well," said he, as he greeted them with beaming face, " if there isn't the truant! Mr. Stärke, what account can you give of yourself?"

" I have none, sir; I rely on the interposition of Mrs. Körner; I refer you to her."

" Why, what! he has only been acting up to the mission of your sex, to do the rough work of the world, while I was the subtle, moving spirit of the scene. The plants must be set, and he has done it very well. I thank him."

" Ah, Lina! Isn't she great! And here are my boys, the very best in Copenhagen! Aren't you glad to see your old man, Emile? Yes, you are. But where is Fred?"

"Here he is coming across the street from Mr. Stephenson's."

"What is the matter with my boy?" seeing him swallowing with great effort some grief. "What has young America done to you now, my dear?"

"He ' walked into my young affections,' as he said; but I call it a pretty hard blow that he gave me." And the lad ran off to stifle his sobs.

Just then Mrs. Stephenson crossed the street.

"What has my boy done to yours, Mrs. Körner? I am very sorry that he should behave so, but he is really quite unmanageable."

"O, nothing of consequence; it was a childish quarrel between Fred and him."

"I left him crying, because, as he said, he had *hit* Fred."

"Well, the millennium must be at hand, if the striker cries for the deed and the stricken controls himself. Won't you walk in?"

"No, thank you, our dinner is ready."

"So is ours; come, Mr. Körner!"

"Come, come, Mr. Stärke," said her husband, "walk in; we have got a swell dinner, as Andrew Jackson over the way would say."

"No; I had a little rather he would not; Eliza is cleaning house and I have not a repast worthy of our friend today. You understand me, Mr. Stärke?"

"O, certainly, certainly; and I am very glad to have you speak so plainly. Good morning!"

"There is a man who would not disgrace a judgeship any day, though the wig would surmount rather young shoulders to be sure," said Mrs. Körner.

"Yes, he has knowledge and stability enough for one, and as for his principles and opinions, why you know our sister ' Lisbet ' says he is ninety years old, as it regards them."

"I don't want him to be judge," said Fred, "for then I am afraid he will not play with me any more, nor draw pictures for us."

"Never fear that, dear," said his mother; "if Mr. Stärke is a little too old in his judgment of men and their doings in this world, he is simple, loving, and thoughtful for my children's happiness, and for that he wins me, and no judge's seat or wig will spoil him in these points. And remember, Fred, if you would be as good a lawyer and writer as he is, and at the same time not grow too sober and careworn as your years increase, you must be careful to do everything in its season, as he did, for when a boy in your uncle's school, he got his lessons well and learned to draw; in College he was always faithfully at his post, and now it is easy for him to work at perplexing law cases all the day, and in the evening come and talk and entertain me and my friends, or play with you."

CHAPTER IX.

" They have the sensitiveness of the mimosa, and find their affections withering up where the blast of scrutiny blows too roughly upon them."—Swal-low Barn.

" MY birthday! I am sixteen years of age! That is pretty old, but I feel just like a little girl yct. Hilda is a year older, to-be-sure, but she is a good deal larger than I, and she appears already like Miss Grün-herg and Trener, who dress gayly and carry their heads so straight as if they were afraid of nobody. I wonder if I ever can do so! It looks pretty in them. Let me try. (She walks to the mirror and imitates them.) No; it is only make-believe with me, so it looks silly. Mrs. Stephenson used to say I looked like a Quaker. What does that mean? A person with a sober, plain face like me, I guess. I am afraid of her and of almost everybody else but Hilda, and I never like to go anywhere without her; she is always so kind and talks to people, so it is no matter if I do not. O this hard lesson! I must study it. (Looks on the book for a few moments and then gazes on vacancy.) I will try to see my mamma with my mind's eye. It is so very, very long since I left her: how does she look! I wonder if she is dark like me or white like Miss Ingemann; if she is pretty like Hilda or plain like Rinda. I can't remember, but this I always can call to mind, that she would smile very kindly and call me 'dear,' and make a little cooing noise like a dove when I had been good, and that her forehead would have wrinkles in it when I was naughty, and I would be so sorry to see them coming one, two, three after the other, and then I would say I would be good and they would all smooth away again. O! how I wish I could see her and that she would again put me into my little bed at night, (for I don't want to be anything but a child still,) and hear me say 'Our Father,' for I am weary, weary of longing, longing for something and it must be for my dear, dear, far-away mother: and my papa, too, I remember him, tall and dark and very thoughtful. And he would sit under the veranda and look out upon the blue sea — for that is before me now — and talk to himself and shake his head a little as his lips moved. And he would gaze at me so earnestly and sadly — and he liked to have me lively and active — energetic and decided he called it. I am afraid I never shall be; but here is Hilda."

"Have you got your lesson in algebra, Zoë dear?" said she, for she was very much afraid of her falling under the teacher's reproof in this study which she much disliked. The rudiments of arithmetic she easily mastered, but algebra and geometry were like an unknown tongue to her,

8

and to attempt to make her comprehend or solve their prob-
lems was like dashing water upon a steel surface, which
evaporated without one drop being absorbed.

"No," said she, "and I can't. I don't know what Miss
Ingemann sets me at this for! She might just as well
pour water upon that stove expecting it to soak in. It will
only crack it and raise a great steam, just as my head is
nearly split by this puzzling sum, and there is a thick blur
over my eyes, I have looked at it so long."

"Let me help you," said Hilda, who was quick at
figures.

"O no! thank you. That would be untrue, for she said
I must do it myself, but I can't and there is an end of the
matter. I was not made to study algebra. I know enough
of arithmetic to count the money when I go shopping and
to pay my laundress, and that is all that I shall want."

"But what if your father should leave an estate for you
to settle?"

"I could take care of it without knowing about a plus
b and c minus d."

"But you must at least know about simple and compound
interest."

"No, for I am going to lend my money just as I do my
books to you when you want them, or my prettiest ribbon
to Freya when she goes visiting, or my seed bracelet to
Adelgunda when she wants to make 'a sensation,' as she
says. I don't tell you that you must put a new cover on every
book you borrow, or that Rinda must pin another piece of
ribbon to the one I lend her to pay for its use, or that
Freya must hang a gold charm to my bracelet every time
she wears it. I should be ashamed to be so mean and
selfish. That is not the way they did in those days I like
to read about eighteen hundred years ago, nor will it
be so in the good time I can't help thinking will come
by-and-by."

"*I guess* that you will have plenty of people to borrow

your money. Why, they will tease it all away if they know you don't ask interest."

" Don't you think I can say 'No!' if I think they don't deserve it. I should ask 'our Father' when one asked me for it whom I did not know about, if I should lend to him, and I should try and learn about him or her, and whether it would be right and useful to them to have it; and if I made up my mind that it would, I would lend it till they could pay it again — just the sum that I lent them and no more. But if I thought that it would do more harm than good, I would say, 'No, you must not have it;' and as I should feel sorry to disappoint them, I should look and say so, and perhaps that would do a little toward making them better, and as soon as God was willing I would let them have it, and I don't think he would make me wait till they were perfect seeing that none of the rest of us are, not even Miss Ingemann."

"O Zoë, darling!" said Hilda, throwing her arms about her, "I wish that you would try to do just as our teacher wishes you to do, so that she may love you dearly as she does me. She is so kind to me, and I am so fond of her that my only trouble is that you don't seem to understand each other, so she gets angry with you and you look so sad, or if you do laugh and frolic, it seems like froth and foam on the surface of the deep moving sea, and it makes me feel worse than to have you sit quiet, as you do so much of the time. I try to explain matters to both of you and make it appear that you neither of you are in the wrong, but both mean the very best; but it is of no use, and it makes me very unhappy." And she kissed her and began to arrange her curls while she hummed a little tune.

" No, Hilda! it is of no use," said Zoë seriously; " Miss Ingemann does not like anything about me. I am not clever, like you and the other girls, about my lessons. I get them *by rote*, she says, and to-be-sure I do, all but my

natural theology and grammar and rhetoric and my Bible
lesson. I like *them*, and when Miss Ingemann wishes
to show me off she does right to question me in those
studies."

"But there are other matters that you trouble her about;
your hair is not always arranged neatly to suit her, and
your shoes are sometimes down at the heel and your hose
are too much darned, and then you sometimes lay your
sewing implements and books about, and as she is very
particular and nice it tries her; and it is not all for that
either, but she really wishes you to grow up a tidy, sensi-
ble, intelligent, and elegant young lady."

"Yes, Hilda, I know it, and you need not think that I
don't thank her for it in my heart, though I don't kiss her
and tell her so as much as you do. But I know this too,
for though I am a little dark-girl, I can see through a cloud
when the moon shines through it, as well as Miss Inge-
mann or any other bright person. She wants me to be
sensible in just her way, and intelligent in just her way,
and elegant in just her way; and if I am not, she won't
own that I am at all. Now that is not what God intends,
else He would have made me more like her. She does
not like my curly hair, and when she wants to show that
she is particularly kind, she takes both her hands and tries
to smooth it and she says, 'Zoë, my dear, put on your bon-
net and may-be your complexion will improve;' or, 'Zoë,
you see how straight Adelgunda sits, I wish you not to
lounge so;' or, 'Zoë, look! Freya has knit this pair of stock-
ings in two weeks, you must be industrious like her;' or,
'Hilda has an excellent mind, she is so quick in her
algebra;' and then looks at me as much as to say, '*you
have not!*' "

"Why how you talk, child! what an imagination you
have!"

"It is not imagination, it is plain fact; and though Miss
Ingemann is very good and knows almost everything in

books and all about the great people who have lived since the flood, and is ' *au fait*,' as she is always saying, ' to the conventionalisms of society,' there is one of 'our Father's' little girls about five feet high, that she knows precious little about, and it is a pity since she pretends to teach her."

"Aren't you funny?" said Hilda, laughing.

"It may be fun to you, but it is anything else to me; when my mind is in such a hurly-burly state and I only know that I must be made for something, but I don't know what, and if Miss Ingemann would go the right way to puzzle me out and then tell me, I should be much more thankful to her than I am while she distresses herself about whether I am dark, or white as a piece of chalk with two strawberries stuck on it, or my hair flax-colored and as lank and straight as a tallow candle, or black and curly as my own, or whether I bend a little before the cold north wind always blowing upon me, or take it all as firm and erect as if I were a piece of Thor's ramrod set down here on the earth. Leave these things to 'our Father' who made me, and teach me something of more importance, I say."

"Good," said Hilda, "I like to see you so, because your face has some spirit in it. But you can't deny but your habits of study and behavior are of some importance."

"O yes! But what if I do set my thimble by my plate while I dine; she need not look and speak as if I had smashed Moses' two tables of stone with all the commandments upon them; or, if Freya does knit like a steam engine, the globe is not kept together by it, as I know of; or, if you can reckon a million, that does not redeem all the souls in the world, does it, my own best Hilda?"

"O no, indeed, I hope not. Save me from any such awful responsibility. I am afraid my own will fly away into space some day I am such a giddy thing; but do, Zoë, wear clean white skirts, and nice fine hose all the time, to please Miss Ingemann and me, too, dear! wont you?"

"Now that is just like Miss Ingemann; and you, too, Hilda dear! you say so to save me from disgrace with her; but she has always had money enough all her life, and, besides, only associates with a few elegant, tasteful people as fortunate as herself, so she does not seem to think but that everybody may dress as well as she does. Now my father is not rich, and he has many poor relatives whom he helps in their living, and it is very expensive keeping me here, and though he is generous, yet I know he wants me to be economical, so I am, and—I wish Miss Ingemann would turn her sublime gaze to the stars, and not look at my stockings."

"But at any rate, as she says, there is water enough in the river and your skirts might be clean."

"How, without great expense in this filthy, smoky city, I should like to know? Look at the piles of dirt in the street, and see that great chimney belching out a column of black smoke. I wonder if it is the evil deeds of the proprietor, ascending to the bar of heaven to be judged in that form! And don't we bury ourselves before our time every walk we take. To be really and thoroughly decent as I like to be, for I am as nice in my taste as Miss Ingemann, it would take all my allowance money for my washing, and I can't spare it, when I must have new clothes once in a while; and that is just the way she judges and teaches me. No, Hilda! I had a teacher once, and in five minutes he pointed out to me the way to walk through life, and to me it seems so simple and plain that I wonder when I attempt to keep in it that all good people do not bid me God speed! and take hold of my hand and help me onwards, instead of making me turn aside into their by-paths. I do not say that they are by-paths to them, but when I try them to see if they were made for me, I feel so wretched and away from home and the sunlight of God's favor, that I shrink into myself and begin again my ceaseless questioning."

(A voice calls Hilda.)

" Dear Zoë! I must go. You are better, O! so much better than I am, and I love you dearly! I only say these things to you because it frets me not to have Miss Ingemann see you as I do, and if some little things were altered in you I think she would."

" No, Hilda! I am not as good as you. It is so easy for you to do just what you were made for, that I admire and look up to you all the time, and you are so kind to let me lean upon you, and you cover up my failings so beautifully when we go abroad together! But I am nothing but one cluster of interrogation points, always longing to do my duty but not knowing how, throwing the past behind in disgust, having no life and interest in the present, and yet what am I fit for in the future of such a world as this? But go, dear!"

(Zoë alone.)

" ' Obey your conscience; read your Bible; let the Christ be your pattern and guide; take, as it were, hold of his hand when you pray to the Father to aid you; learn of the works of his beautiful world; love him for his goodness, and all mankind, because he loves them; and be not anxious for anything else.' Yes, these were his words. And have I fulfilled them? To the letter I have tried to be faithful, but something is wanting. I reap no reward of self-satisfaction. They speak of the approving conscience. I know it not. My life is one great feeling of deficiency, my soul nothing but an altar of sighing and supplication. Whither shall I turn for light? The Bible—even Jesus— have not their full power over my crude and ignorant mind, and when I pray, O! that the heavens would divide but a hair's breadth that I might be sure that God hears me! I try to follow strictly the precepts of Jesus in my thoughts and my conduct, but it seems to unfit me for what they call the best society in which I visit with my teacher, and they do and say what seems to me so contrary to his spirit that I am ever weary and sad. Yet I can say nothing, for I am but a little girl and know not how to argue, only to feel, and then, worse than all, this unrest and dissatisfaction with myself weakens my words when I would dissent from my companions. O! my mother! my far-away mother! would that I could be folded in thy arms while I say 'Our Father!' and then, perhaps, He would answer to her call and mine. For is it not a cruel thing to tear the young bird from its warm nest, or the tender lamb from the sheepfold, to wander in the snow-mountains alone? and how can it be that a little girl could find the right way through the cold, hard world, to the warm, sunlighted heaven above, without her mother to guide her?"

(She sings in a low tone —)

"O. my mamma, my mamma, my mamma!
Where are you now, I wonder?
Sitting under the tamarind tree. looking over the deep blue sea,
After your own little daughter?

Here she sits, mamma! doubting and sad, mamma!
Over the hard lessons given her;
White lady knows her not, so, of course, she loves her not—
O, the poor, lone little dark-girl!

When will come the time, mamma? Our Father's good time, mamma?
So longed for by both of us so wearily;
When together under the tamarind tree, looking over the deep blue sea,
We see the star in the East rise so brightly.

We will follow its guiding light through all the dark night,
Hoping for sunlight in the morning;
O, show me the way, how I may the best pray
For the bright, glorious sunlight in the morning."

CHAPTER X.

"There are more things in heaven and earth, Horatio,
Than are dreamt of in your philosophy."—SHAKSPEARE.

MISS INGEMANN'S heart was a benevolent one, and her character high-toned, and whenever a child was placed under her care, she felt the responsibility involved in the trust reposed in her. Not less did this feeling influence her, than heretofore, when the little, dark-browed West-Indian was left to her management and fostering nurture. To us, Americans, slaveholders, or abettors, excusers or tolerators of slavery, who are buried ten thousand fathoms deep under the prejudices, conventionalisms, false, unnatural and wicked feelings superinduced upon the soul by the existence among us of this great sin against God, and foul wrong against his humanity, it seems almost impossible, that Zoë should not from the first, have been looked upon by both teacher and pupils with distrust and aversion, when she came to claim as an equal a share in the privileges of this "home of education." But it was not so; on the contrary, she was instituted immediately as both the lion and the pet of the school. But her nature was a shrinking one, and she recoiled from the pedestal upon which, not only Hilda, but all her schoolmates, at first strove to place her. And who that knows anything of the world of children, no less than that of men and women, is not aware that, for immediate success in life, one must not only accept willingly all the honors it proffers, but claim

9   (97)

even a little more as its just due, in order to keep a position fairly equal to its deserts, in an age when might makes right, and among a people, admirers of coarse, rough, obvious power. For our modern material civilization has but little insight into the value, beauty and latent power of a soul, true to its natural instincts, refined and strengthened by growing up into a perception of, and sympathy with God's revelation through the ages, while it is kept tender and pure, and at the same time, is glorified in intellect, affections, character and imagination, by a walk and communion with the Infinite, through Nature, no less than the spirit, principles, precepts, hopes and promises of his Holy Son, our Lord and Master, the beginning of a new spiritual creation, and the Leader through time and eternity of all who put their trust in him! So that the child was soon as readily dropped as she desired to be, into quietness and retirement. It followed, as a natural consequence, that she ceased also to be the favorite, except with a very few; for there are not many so true, loyal and self-sustained that they do not require that their judgment of men and things should be reflected from the smiles and respect or haply worship of others, in order to insure them that they are not making fools of themselves in their opinions or choice of friends and associates.

But other causes operated with Miss Ingemann, to place her in unhappy relations with Zoë, to lead her into mistake, perplexity and discouragement, and at length into injustice and mutual injury to each other's characters and lives.

In the first place, she was an Anglo-Saxon, with the physical courage, energy, self-reliance and practical power of that predominant race. She believed in its "manifest destiny," which by the majority is supposed to involve a superiority to the rest of the world, and as a natural inference, its final rule over the different nations.

Zoë belonged to a different division of the human family. Her strongest characteristics were a fiery temperament, imagination, strong affections and religious aspiration. With these were combined a nervous organization of the most delicate cast, warning her at every point, of her want of sympathy and adaptedness in physical, mental and spiritual constitution to the sphere into which she had been transported.　By a strong natural instinct, acting upon her like a fate, she unfolded herself only so far as she could find a response to her utterances, either in action or words. As the spider, who, sociably inclined, approaches the domestic circle, and puts out one antenna after another to attest its welcome, when lo! a start, or a scream, (if haply it is not crushed altogether by a rude and daring foot,) warns it to use its mysterious instinct by feigning death, until it can scramble away discomfited, and then it compensates itself by ascending on its self-woven wing to a height above the scene of its trial, where it spins itself a world according to the beautiful laws with which its Creator has inspired it; so Zoë, finding in her teacher's staid, bare practical world no home for her glowing fancies, unworldly fashions and aims, and enkindled hopes, sat like a stone, in the midst of the noisy life and glittering but chilly brightness about her, and as soon as she might, buried herself in her chamber to call about her the spirits of a clearer ether and intenser being.

In the second place, Miss Ingemann was of noble birth and dated back from a long line of titled ancestors. She believed in privileged orders, and though intending to be strictly just in her estimate of her pupils, this idea made the scale waver a little against those who were not, of which Zoë was one.　Then she had the true Anglo-Saxon mode of estimating power, as before indicated, in an age of action and invention; its obvious, clear, striking manifestations she appreciated, and where this was exhibited in full blaze, no prejudice in favor of rank or title prevented her for a moment from owning and bowing down to its sway. So to the charms of simple goodness as exhibited in ways

familiar to her, she was fully alive, and was absolute in her
requisitions of its first importance in her friends, associ-
ates, and pupils. But enslaved by conventionalism, ever
fearful of overstepping the bounds of female propriety, as
laid down by society; gifted with but little imagination or
passion, she frowned upon all manifestations of charac-
ter which indicated a rebellion against existing opinions and
customs.

With no broad sweep of sympathies which would make
her one with every tribe, nation, and kingdom under
heaven; ay, and lift her to companionship with the realms
above, and carry her in pity and hope into the under-world
beneath, but confining her familiar intercourse very much
to a choice clique of the wise and good, ignorant from
actual witness of the obstacles, disadvantages, and dread-
ful temptations through which the multitudes struggle
upwards to the light, or which haply prevent their ascent,
she was often stern and intolerant in her judgment of the
imperfect and erring, or else ignored them altogether.

Not by such narrow rules did he who knew what was in
man gain such insight into his depths, and it may be
doubted whether with the aid of miracle itself, this nature
would have unfolded itself to his gaze, had he separated
himself from the people by virtue of his royal descent and
sought only the companionship of Simon the Pharisee,
and such as he, or even of Mary, Martha, and Lazarus.

But the great, over-mastering cause of her failure in edu-
cating Zoë, was the falsities of her creed; for these she was
but partially accountable, for it was the result of the spirit of
her age, which was compounded in part of Christian ideas,
it is true, but with a large infusion of the errors of the
past, the crude speculations and skepticisms of the present
mingled with the worldliness, licentiousness, and hypo-
crisy, ever the attendants of a decline of faith in the simple
but sublime truths of God, written upon the human soul in
its purity, revealed through his messengers and daily

hung out to the gaze of the world in his wonderful works. Strange, strange that these verities should be forsaken or be held but feebly, to cling to a soiled, misshapen, parchment credendum, scribbled all over with characters written m blood, partly by the Pagans of the anti-Christian world, in part by the half-enlightened, self-conceited philosophers of the times of, and after the Apostles, with the continual accretion with which mistaken men, loving their own blind opinions and fancies better than the truth, have covered over or deformed their majestic beauty.

Had Zoë's mind and character been like Hilda's, for instance, ready to be moulded according to her own fixed notions of culture, all obstructions to a happy development of her nature, at least to a certain extent, would have been spared her. For so much greater than any creed is the human soul that in quiet, unexcited times when the falsehoods of society, like lions and tigers asleep, scare not mankind into unnatural attitudes and induce them to build around themselves ugly walls of defense, and force not the guardians of society to utter hideous shrieks and magnify the danger at hand, thereby frightening it into deformity, it may grow beautifully under the genial light of God's sunshine and grace, though it may not reach the height, breadth, and depth of expansion that it would under the most favorable circumstances. But the Anglo-African was a new specimen, a *lusus naturæ* of humanity, and her teacher knew not what to make of her. Her sense of responsibility nullified all feeling of curiosity, all desire for entertainment in the exhibition of a nature so different from her own, and her love of sway and fixed ideas of the culture suited to all human beings alike kept her on the alert to check any of her eccentric demonstrations. Her want of success in calling forth her powers at first bewildered, next discouraged, then disgusted her, and year after year she treated her with increasing coldness and dignity. These different feelings she expressed to her

friends and associates, with a few of whom Zoë was a
favorite and who saw in her more than appeared to Miss
Ingemann's prejudiced eye. These took up her defense
warmly, and by injudicious comments in favor of one and
against the other, enlarged the breach between them.
Then came to her mind the false philosophy which she
had somewhere read of, that the Africans were a race
cursed by God in early times for the unnatural scoffing of
a son at his patriarch father. Next, clustered around it
the infidel notions that its degradation was insurmountable;
that God intended it for the lowest rank among his people,
and mercifully denied it the Caucasian powers; and as
these opinions were warmly combated by the majority of
her acquaintances, resentment was awakened which re-
coiled on her pupil and darkened her to her mental vision
more and more, till she became utterly incapacitated from
judging her in any point correctly. This result Zoë, with
her almost supernatural perceptions, felt in its full force,
and it threw her more and more back upon her vivid ima-
gination and burning sentiments. It remains to be seen
what was the natural effect of this concentration upon
herself.

Not that she *knew distinctly* of these speculations, for
they were not repeated to her by any one, and if she had
ever had a clear consciousness of her distinction of race
before she left home, which is doubtful, it had faded from
her mind as her soliloquizing about her mother has indi-
cated. Her differences of person from the other girls she
attributed to a West-India climate, as also her love for the
hot summer sun and aversion to the winter's snow and
cold. She knew only too well that Miss Ingemann disliked
her, and that she was hurt and offended that she could not
make her what she wished, yet she was sensible of no will-
ful opposition to her desires and efforts. She studied hard
the lessons given her, and seldom dissented from her
wishes ostensibly. But there was the perpetual cry of

resistance of her nature within to many of the tasks imposed upon her which would not be appeased. She would rush from her abstract studies into the open air of the garden, which surrounded the house, and clasp the trees with her arms as if they were conscious, sympathizing friends who would rescue her from her thraldom. She would throw herself upon the ground by the flower-beds, and brood over the lilies and violets, for she seldom gathered them, and say, "O, my beautiful angels! they need not say that ye are without life like me, for I feel it in every breath of your fragrance. Ye tell me in that, that ye are sorry for my woe, for Ah, my sweet flowers! ye know well that they are not kind to the little dark-girl as to you; for here in God's beautiful sunshine ye may ever dwell, and be wet by his dew, and sprinkled by his showers and bloom, O, so beautifully in the light of his smile, while I am chained to dark, bewildering words, and mystic crooked characters in the prison-house of my soul's bondage with the fear of frowns and sneers, if I do not love them and make them my own. But O! lily, queen of my heart! they speak not to me as thou dost, when I ask them whence, why am I and what does our Father wish me to do. Thy voice even is not clear to me yet in answer to my ceaseless request; but it may be that when I have more and better studied his holy Word, my mind will be pure and still enough to hear distinctly your revealings. So bloom on, my lily and violet, and when your leaves fall and mingle with the dust, and your breaths ascend to heaven to take to themselves more glorious and lovely representations of God's beauty and love, O, then plead with Him when ye are blooming at the foot of his great white throne, to tell me more plainly when, where and how I am to do his holy will! Farewell, my flowers, until I have wrought out my tasks, and then I will come again and seek my reward in the odor of your incense, and the radiance of your sheen."

In going in she met Miss Ingemann: "Miss Zoë," said she, "these are school hours, you are aware?"

"Yes, ma'am."

"You know the rule, it is not necessary to repeat it to you?"

"Yes, ma'am."

The lady walks up the steps with great dignity, while Zoë goes to the schoolroom and takes her Algebra.

"It may be breaking the rules to the letter to go and talk to the flowers between nine and twelve in the forenoon, but at any rate my head is clearer and courage greater than before I went out, so my lessons will not suffer by it. Come here, you dingy Arab of an arithmetic; I wonder if your old grandfather far removed, who made you, and who is, I hope, in heaven, is not sorry that he left you behind him, to puzzle and fret so many little girls. I wonder if Jesus studied algebra! I doubt it. Then I don't know why I should. But come along, I say; we have got other masters now-a-days. But you don't get me to go astray from him, in what I *know* he did or did not."

CHAPTER XI.

" Spirits are not finely touched,
But to fine issues; nor nature never lends
The smallest scruple of her excellence,
But like a thrifty goddess she determines,
Herself the glory of a creditor,
Both thanks and use."—SHAKSPEARE.

"ZOE! there is the music teacher, dear; have you prac-
tised your lesson enough to be familiar with it, for you know
how cross he is when we are at fault?" said Hilda, who
partly from her love to her friend and dread of her in-
curring censure, and in part, from her inherent spirit of
management, which, train it as she would, still floated on
the surface of her character, though the principle upon
which it rested, had had its roots dislodged, kept an eye
upon her friend's doings.

"After a fashion; though tum-ti-tum, diddle-de-dee,
don't, you well know, belong to me, so I give it but little
welcome, seeing that I shall drive it from my soul's door as
soon as I can. I make my courtesy to it, and do it the
honors to please Miss Ingemann, but such a little shallow,
chattering blonde and I have not much in common. Come,
Miss, perch on my little finger, and

So we will go
To the realms below,
Where is sound without sense
To be bought for pence;

and she balanced her music sheet on its tip, and thus
walked out of the room,

(105)

(Hilda alone.)

" The funny, mournful, foolish, wise little *thing;* yes, *thing!* for I really do not know what else to call my precious, provoking, fascinating, fantastic, but dear, dear friend. I wonder what fairy left such a little elfish, yet cherub changeling in this naughty, prosy world. She is so different from us all in her way, speech, looks and everything. Sometimes she is so weird, that I am afraid of her; and then again, no angel from the skies could look or talk more beautifully. One would think, to hear her speak of Jesus, that she had lived when he did, and he had been her schoolmate as I am, and that walking to and fro, they had led each other by the hand, and spoken in the most serious, but familiar way of their love for God and their fellow-men, and of the great and good deeds they would do for them. And then again, she so revolts against her life here and her lessons and work—not in word ever to Miss Ingemann, but by her listlessness and indifference that I am out of patience and in fear for her. For our teacher dislikes her, that is evident; and Zoë knows it, and that makes her more and more like a stone, when in her presence. Miss Ingemann never sees her as I do, sometimes full of fire and fancy, sometimes, O, so tender and loving to me, and then again, so mournful and sad, and next hour so angelic and devout, that I look upwards to see if Heaven is not opening to receive her. And yet, I well know, that she tells me but very few of her feelings of any kind, for I am so unlike her, I could not understand them, but I know her better than any one, for I sometimes catch sentences of her soliloquies, and they make me wonder and tremble for her too. What more can I do for her than I do? I try to explain, and explain matters between her and our teacher, but it is of no use. Miss Ingemann will persist in seeing only her surface-mind and character, which do not suit her. And Zoë is under a spell, I verily believe, for I can think of nothing but a dead wall when she is in her presence, which, of course, is rather an incumbrance in a house full of bright, lively people. O me! I could be so happy, if the world did not go so badly with poor Zoë! My heart is as light as a feather, when I have not her lying upon it with her griefs and wrongs. Why can't people be happy, I wonder? I see no reason for discontent.

> "Trall la la *la*, la *la*, la *la*,
> Merrily dance we O:
> Cast care to the winds,
> For sighing and sins
> Come not to my world, *no, no:*
> Trall la la *la*, la *la*, la la *la*," etc.

And she waltzed out of the room.

Zoë practised her quadrille in the presence of her master, a common-place mind, who played with great execution the music of the reputed masters of song, whose deeper spirit was nevertheless beyond his ken. He was constantly dissatisfied that his pupil did not *finger* her piano with more agility and force, but could appreciate but very feebly the occasional bursts of melody which in the simplest manner would gush from her at times, when the clouds would momentarily roll away from her spirit, revealing the glory behind. Still less was he pleased when, with disgust in her soul at the present hour, which encircled her in its folds of servile propriety, with glimpses of a future far in the distance, dazzling to her vision by its splendor and beatification, but shaded for the most part to her prophetic eye by she knew not what big mountains of difficulty, tipped with sunlight, or valleys thousands of feet deep, into which, however, the glory of heaven shone, except into one dark mass of vapor inscrutable to her gaze, she gave vent to all that was in her in language and tone appropriate to her feelings much more than to poetic rules. She was sure never to do this when he was by, but this day he lingered in the hall for some trifling purpose, and heard her outpourings:

"Good-by t' ye, master!   Are ye!
Yea, of my finger-tips alone,
Nay not of those, for here I wash ye,
My digits, and here is all your own.

*(She dips her hands into a glass of water,
and then pours it with force out of the
window towards his usual path of egress.)*

"Avaunt, ye vulgar, shallow skeptic,
Ye blind-eyed, deaf and dumb pretender,
Ye haughty, surface, weakling critic,
I'm weary, weary of your power!

"My soul's a sheet of paper, is it!
Made of old shreds and paltry tatters,
Ground in a mill of man's invention,
Soaked of its individual colors;

"Battered and squeezed, and shaped and
rolled,
Cut into a fair, square, proper sheet,
Ye deem it now all fit for use,
To stain with silly, ugly traces!

(She rubs her hand rapidly across her forehead.)

"But ye mistake me, teacher mine!
  Thus I efface your weak impressions,
My surface brain alone is touched,
  My heart eschews your vain instructions."

(*She sits in reverie a few moments, and then adds:*)

"Would ye know who my Master is! pure as the morning,
  Brilliant as the day-star, and tender as the gloaming,
True as is the Word of God, wise without measurement,
  Holy as the angels are! with Him I made a sacrament;

"Ere my soul to this earth from yon heaven descended,
  When walking with Him in its fields of perennial green,
With the sunlit sky o'erhead all bright with gold and azure,
  And its glory slightly vailed by clouds of silvery sheen;

"He told in simple words the pure truth of his commandments,
  Unvailed of all invention, false glare and grim denouncings,
Their true spirit he revealed to me beneath all wordy seemings,
  And set my heart on fire with the love of their perfection.

"I saw him face to face, their glorious embodiment,
  Perfect love and truth and beauty all radiant in him shone,
As I gazed entranced and wondering, half fearful and amazed
  He smiled upon me then, and laid his hand upon my head.

"I remember no words, for my being was in its infancy,
  But his smile is in my heart as it fell upon me then;
His hand upon my head has shaped my brow to reverence,
  His voice within my soul has never ceased to echo.

"O, glorious elder brother! for such you seem to me,
  Impatient and doubting I turn my heart to thee;
Intercede before our Father, whose beloved Son thou art,
  That He may aid me to know and do faithfully my part.

"In this life, so cold and dreary, where heaven's light but dimly
    shines,
  Heaven's love that comes through men is so little of it mine;
O, when will the day come so longed for by me,
  When with my dearest mother sitting under the tamarind tree,

"We can talk of thy perfection! a ray to us from God,
  All love and mercy art thou, without the cruel rod.
We will pray to Him through thee, He will listen to our cries,
  And on the wings of faith and hope to Him we'll ever rise."

(*She sits again in a reverie, then her feelings changing, she bursts out:*)

"If I were lively I would play something better than that tinkling thing, thus:

"What a funny world is this,
  Right or wrong, hit or miss,
  Sad or lively, silly or wise,
The little dark-girl sits outside!

"What is the reason, I'd like to know,
  Study or sing, frolic or sew,
  Please myself or try to please my guide,
The little dark-girl is always wrong-side?

"White people are mighty knowing,
  Awfully smart, and dreadfully boasting,
  Strong as Thor, proud as Loken,
Of course the dark-girl stays underside.

"May-be the time will come, when folks feel,
  When they see, and when they kneel
  To thank the great Father for curing their pride,
Then the little dark-girl will sit upside."

(Pausing a moment, she bursts into tears and moans out.)

"But I care not for that, my heart wails, O no!
For this is no balm to relieve my woe!
Mamma, my mamma! stretch the arms of your soul,
And within them your lone little daughter enfold;
For she wanders in spirit all o'er the wide earth,
Sick at heart for her studies, disgusted with mirth,
And longing, and thirsting, like flowers for the dew,
To know what our Father would have her to do.
O pray for her, mother! as you look o'er the blue sea,
And the waters a blessing may waft over to me."

While thus reveling in her own fancies, making the piano obedient to the impulses which prompted her enthusiastic soul, outraged, as she felt it to be, in its forced expression no less than its stinted aspirations; at one moment making it speak in grinding, explosive, and indignant tones, then joining her voice to it in strains full, rich, and harmonious, while she gave vent to her religious yearnings, followed by a song, the accompaniment to which was full of sparkling, even rollicking humor, and that by another still of most mournful and thrilling melody, Miss Ingemann entered the room. She had just listened to the piqued music-master's complaint of her reference to himself, which he partly heard, and while nearing the door the outburst of fun and frolic fell upon her ear; but called away for a moment, she lost the pathos which ended her outpourings, which might, perhaps, have touched her. She was dignified and indignant.

"Miss Zoë," she said, "you hinder your progress very much by indulging in such outbursts. I hope you will not again. I regret to hear from your teacher that you seem to have come to a pause in the acquisition of this delightful and most ladylike accomplishment. I advise you to put a check upon your crude, disrespectful (and here she erected her head while her lip expressed the scorn she felt at what she deemed low taste), and I must say, vulgar fancies, and be more obedient in spirit as well as letter to the dictation of your teachers"

Zoë was hushed, both soul and body, by this cold and unsympathizing reproof.

"Yes," she said, as the lady went out and closed the door, "it is all true. I am to-be-sure very stupid not to find more than I do in these great performances, and very lazy, I suppose, ever to miss a note in my lesson. It is strange when Miss Ingemann, who is so high-toned and learned, and who is incapable of pretense, goes into ecstasies when she hears Beethoven and Wagner and Hayden and Mozart, that I cannot. It is because I do not appreciate them of course, and besides I am very discontented and wicked. Not but what they move me. O yes! yes indeed, they are pure and high, intellectual and aspiring, and I bless them for many an hour of forgetfulness of myself and for carrying me up to the stars' clear light, to the Great Spirit above, and into the world of nature all around me, (spreading her hands and raising her eyes in ecstasy. She pauses and leans her forehead on both hands, then raises it with an altered expression). But you can't cheat this dark child anyway, though I am like the ace of spades, somewhat faded out. It is all good enough for white people, but why won't they allow that I can be different and crave something which I have never heard. (She rises). Was I not born in the burning tropics, where the sun shines all the year with fervor as well as light, and down deep in my soul there is a thirst which no water of earth has yet slaked, and in my brain is a flame which perpetually burns, writhing like a serpent after the stream that would quench it; and in my heart, O my poor heart! a loud cry rending me for the love that would lull it to sleep as the mother hushes her infant upon her breast, and through my whole being is the perpetual hungering and agonizing after God! God! Who? what am I, and what wouldst thou have me to do? O! show me the way of thy appointing!

"But I must go. Let me breathe the air of the outer-world, and would that it were not impregnated with the dust and smoke which somehow seem to envelop my friends when they would do me the most good! Heigh-ho! This is the world and the other is the country, as Hilda says when she is particularly serious, and I believe it; but I have a feeling that I never shall go there; for if I am as faulty as Miss Ingemann thinks me, I don't deserve to, and somehow I shrink from ever being in that part where such stiff, dignified, cold people as she and some of her friends are. I am afraid of them here and I must be more so when my soul is laid bare and they see what a discontented, fretful creature I am. I dont feel half so afraid of our Father as I am of them, but he says if we don't love our brother, which means everybody, we don't love Him; so I don't know about the future; I am puzzled and very anxious—O, dear! I'll try and not think about it."

Thus unhappy and dissatisfied with herself and her out-ward relations, she rushed eagerly within, where in her dream-world there was no self-contention or reproach from others. The ruling qualities of her mind, being misunderstood and thus left without guidance by those older and more judicious than herself, ran to waste, and overleaping their just boundaries, and rioting unlicensed, weakened and injured her other powers and hindered their healthy and happy action. Such mistakes in education, will continually occur, until human nature is seen and felt to be the great and sacred thing it is; and while on the one hand, all human means and appliances are brought to bear upon its development; on the other, a large margin of freedom is left that it may work naturally and easily in its Heaven-appointed sphere, directed and guided by the subtle influences of his spirit no less than by his written Scripture and his indicated will, as daily seen and heard in the events and experiences of life, in the suggestions of our friends, both the older and the younger, the history of the past and the present, as well as in the changing phenomena of nature, every one of which is a sign proceeding directly from the Infinite mind.

10

CHAPTER XII

ONE bright morning, Mrs. Körner walked into the study of Mr. Liebenhoff, her brother-in-law, the Lutheran minister, where she found him preparing his next Sunday's sermon. Her sister, also, with portfolio in hand, was scribbling at a rapid rate, while several sheets of copy were piled up before her.

"What a long letter you are writing, Lisbet! Who is to be favored with such an elaborate epistle?"

"No less a personage than the public, Lina, if it will receive it. I have been intending to tell you that I was turning authoress, but really secrets are such troublesome things to keep, that I did not like to burden you with mine."

Why have any great privacy about it?" said Mr. Liebenhoff. "I'm tired of secrets; there is sure to be falsehood growing out of them. They are confided to two or three or more, intimate friends, and from them they are sure to spread, and then comes the questioning and cross-questioning inflicted upon such simple-minded individuals as I am for instance, by one and another of your sex, and it is more than I can stand under; and I am determined to have nothing to do with them any more. My dear, do be frank, and put your own name to your book."

The two ladies looked at each other and smiled, for they

(114)

were reminded of some precious little confidences of their own, which they had shared with him, under promises of his everlasting silence, but failing to make him feel their importance and awful magnitude as viewed by themselves, he had repeatedly shocked and discomfited them, by bringing them into conversation at exactly the most unpropitious time, as mere matters of course. They were never able to convince him that these denouements were of the least consequence, excepting as it hurt and sometimes offended them, but as he was very sensitive to their reproofs, he had got to have a nervous dread of anything which squinted in the least towards secrecy; therefore his remark.

"Perhaps I shall; I have not quite made up my mind upon the subject, but at least, until I have nearly completed it, I prefer that my friends should not know it, for quietness is so necessary to the free and propitious working of my mind, that I do not wish it broken in upon by the curiosity or observations of any one."

"I am very glad you are writing and I doubt not that you will be successful. What is the title of your Tale, for that I suppose it is?" said her sister.

"Yes, and I shall call it ' The Way.' It is to deal with an interesting question of the day, the subject of tyranny; and as you know it is a law of my nature and development to view everything in the light of Religion, it will take its principal tone from that. To the young at least, I hope it will be acceptable, and I shall try to make it as entertaining to them as I can. You shall see extracts from it when you are at leisure, if you would like to."

"Thank you, very gladly; but this morning I have run in for a moment, to invite you both to tea. Mrs. Pendleton, the newly-arrived American minister's wife, with her two young lady friends, Miss Hale and Miss Ingalls, are going to be with us, and I want you to come and talk English with them. They know nothing of Danish or German, and only have an imperfect smattering of French.

What is the reason I wonder, that they come so poorly fur-
nished with the necessary requisition to a comfortable life
among us?   It is well that you, thanks to your facility in
acquiring languages, and that I through my intimacy with
Mrs. Stephenson, and my acquaintance with Mr. Phillips,
can communicate with them in their mother tongue, as it
is all in all to them.   Will you come?"

"Certainly, we shall be most happy to do so; shall we
not, dear?" turning to her husband.

"O yes, thank you, Lina.   Who else is going to be with
you?" said he.

"O, Miss Dahl and Miss Holberg, and the usual set you
know, and Miss Ingemann, I suppose, though I must say
that I am rather out of conceit with her, for I really think
she treats poor Zoë Carlan very shabbily, who is a great
favorite of mine.   I can see that her own character is de-
teriorating in consequence of her prejudice against her.
She is not so successful in her education as with her other
pupils, so she dislikes her.   I used to think her a model
of a high-toned lady, but I have seen her unjust and un-
ladylike in spirit, and even in manner towards the poor
child, which has lowered her in my opinion very much."

"I must know Zoë better.   I feel more and more inter-
ested in her every time I meet her.   She has been so
retiring, and I have so many demands upon my time, that
I have neglected to get into familiar relations with her;
but I see she does not look happy.   I will send for her to-
morrow, and try and win her affections and confidence,"
said Mrs. Liebenhoff.

"Do, dear," said her husband, "I know she will suit
you.   She has great delicacy of organization it seems to
me, and needs some kind, strong friend to lean upon.   She
keeps aloof from me very much, and I know her better
through Hilda, than in any other way.   She is her oracle,
and has I think, a favorable effect upon my Undine.   I
hope she will breathe a more quiet, reflective soul into that

wild water-sprite. Do you think, I was walking in the
glen yesterday, and I heard a tinkling laugh, and who
·should have waded into the middle of the brook but she;
and there she was dashing water all over herself, without the
slightest regard to drenching her garments, and when she
saw me, instead of running to hide herself and her drip-
ping habiliments, she filled the shell which she held in her
hand with water, and threw it towards me. She is as in-
nocent as a child of five years old, instead of being a
young lady past seventeen, but she certainly needs a good
deal of taming."

" She is Miss Ingemann's pet, and presumes more upon
her indulgence than any of the other pupils," said Mrs.
Körner; " and she *is* a most enticing creature, I don't
wonder she is fond of her."

" She will make smashing work among the beaux, when
she comes out into life, but really she ought to have more
check put upon her manners," said Mr. Liebenhoff.

The evening came, and with it Mrs. Körner's guests, Mr.
and Mrs. Pendleton, Miss Ingalls, and Miss Hale, all fair
specimens of American citizens, who dwell in, and hold
a prominent position in New England villages of the highest
class.

Mrs Liebenhoff was the first comer.

" Lina, what sort of people are these Americans? Are
they Goths and Vandals, dressed up in magnified French
style, without the tact which would tell them when and
where not to load on their finery; with great pretensions
and many vulgar short comings, or —"

" O no, not so, I will assure you. You will like them
because you are accustomed to mingle with all sorts of
people, and appreciate nature and spirit. Besides, they
have real cultivation. Perhaps they are not as classic and
mellow, if I may use the word, as those born and bred in
an old country, where every baby that comes into the world
has impressed upon its soul enough of the history of its

past, to save it from the sharp angles, which inevitably stick
out more or less from the characters and minds of the in-
habitants of a new land, where the first thing the wee
things have to do when they can walk and look about them,
is to fell a forest, build a log hut, settle its religious forms,
laws, literature and art. What can you expect but that
they should be prematurely shrewd and knowing, and
forceful, and lack a little some of the graces of life? You
will enjoy them, for you resemble them. Somehow you
have found out the secret of being mighty universal in
your sympathies, Lisbet. I have been ready to think at
times that you lagged behind in your private ones, but only
let the time of need come, and I find that your heart is in
the right place."

The guests entered and were soon made to feel at home,
by Mrs. Körner's cordial, bright manner and abounding
hospitality.

"Have you got settled at housekeeping, Mrs. Pendle-
ton?" said she.

"Yes, pretty well. Of course I have not gathered about
me all the comforts of my own home. That I should not
expect so soon."

"No, my friend, and don't look at all for that consumma-
tion," said Theresa Ingalls. "Cooks like Sally and waiters
like Richard, ready to run to the ends of the earth for you
five times a day, and concoct all imaginable delicacies at
your artistic suggestion, do not grow on every bush, much
less here in this Lilliput," said she aside to her friend,
as Mrs. Körner ran to lift up her youngest who had fallen
upon his face.

"Don't, Theresa, get into hot water with these Danes
the first thing, by your criticisms. Do smooth over matters
a little, and what you can't, with truth, why, let it go and
say nothing," said Jenny Hale, laughing a little, but at the
same time looking somewhat anxious for the next remark
Theresa would make.

"Why, what now! Is that so very awful! Well, (drawing down her mouth) will that do?"

Mr. Pendleton and Mr. Körner entered. Mrs. Liebenhoff drew her chair near the former—a thoughtful looking man, quite a contrast in person to his brilliant wife, rather absent in manner, but when roused from his own thoughts, his face lighted up with sympathy and interest, and he bore in a very quiet but just and sensible way his part in the conversation.

"I have been reading Emerson's Essays to-day," said she; "do you know your distinguished countryman?"

"Not much, personally; but we all know of him of course? He has lectured for us and we always like to hear him."

"He has much insight into life, I think; is a true interpreter of nature from his point of view, and is a pure, high-toned moralist. You have great reason to be congratulated for the possession of such a mind in your new country."

"Yes; I don't understand all he writes, but I think he is more practical as he grows older, or at any rate his mind adapts itself to the wants of the times very well. When we incline to run too much into the vein of a material philosophy, he is what we call transcendental; he sits apart and utters his oracles which seem nonsense to some, and infidelity to others, and the distilled truth of the gods to the initiated. When we grow corrupt in our councils and high moral truths need to be sounded abroad, then he is found at his post, and no one is listened to by the more advanced portion of our people with greater interest than himself. I sometimes think he may be a specimen, or rather an indication of a higher order of beings, which may in future exist among us, but I don't know."

"The fault which I find with him is," said she, "that from being so much imbued with classic lore, he is Grecian in the working of his intellect, and the expression of his

feelings, more than Hebrew or rather Christian, which is
synonymous with universal. Taking that point of depar-
ture more than the New Testament, or at least keeping it
in sight too much, not seeing with sufficient clearness that
the principles of all literature, science, art, and life culmi-
nated in Jesus, that he is the central sun from which is to
radiate light, heat and inspiration by which the past is
to be truly and satisfactorily read, the present interpreted
and guided, and the future gazed into with clearness of
vision and brightness of hope, he loses the proper perspec-
tive of truth and speaks of the Vedas, Zoroaster, Confu-
cius, and Socrates too much as if they were on a level
with our glorified Master and his concentrated, complete,
and unadulterated truth."

"Yes, I think so. He is in a condition of reaction from
Calvinistic superstition, which, perhaps you do not know,
stalks about in its grimmest and most unnatural guise in
my country, and one of its saddest effects is the warping
of our most free and truth-loving minds too far in the
direction of a cold rationalism. But Emerson is essentially
Christian after all. The Puritan parson was born in him,
and he can't help looking like one, and his mind is so fair
and his judgment so calm that if a higher truth were pre-
sented to him with clearness and simplicity, he would
accept it gladly."

"Yes, and I would have him utter with manly, fervent,
inspiring tones his convictions of the sublime verities of the
Christian faith, and his eternal obligation to its inspired
Revealer; for it is by going back to first principles, by ever
renewing our first love, by confessing from time to time
our first faith in our Adorable Leader by word, act, symbol,
and ceremony as well as life, that we keep him in sight in
in our way through the world, or can hope to be united to
him in our triumphal march through the eternal ages."

Mrs. Liebenhoff and Mr. Pendleton were sitting aside
during this conversation, and as it paused they heard Mrs.

Körner say, " Well, it is of no use waiting longer for the gentlemen, I will have tea brought in. Young ladies, I was mindful in giving my invitation to you of your proper accompaniments, but they are delinquent, you perceive, which I am sorry to say is not unfrequently the case in these faltering times. Our knights are getting to be rather unreliable in social life; the claims of business, and if the truth must be told, the coarser pleasures which exclude us, are so peremptory."

" It is what we are used to," said Theresa, " in New England. In the first place, our beaux are not to be depended upon very much; and in the second place, there are next to none left to us poor widowed maidens, for they emigrate to California or the western States, as soon as we begin to have some hopes of them, and the few that remain wrap themselves up in selfish old bachelorhood, which is more hopeless, you know, than all the rest."

" I am surprised," said Mrs. Liebenhoff; " I supposed that young people in pairs, twin souls, as the cant of the day is, designated for each other by heaven from birth, were the natural products of your virgin soil, and that you were free from the wicked, unnatural conventionalisms which divide such or haply prevent their coming together at all in our country."

" You are greatly mistaken, madam, if you think we are thus unsophisticated," said Miss Hale; " we are getting to be apt imitators of Europeans in this regard. Our young gents and ladies, too, are very old in the ways of the world, I can assure you."

" Should you like a rapid sketch of our young American gentleman of the present day?" said Theresa.

" Nothing better," said Mrs. Körner ; " pray give us one."

' Well, in the first place, we have a few who correspond to the heroes of which we read in romance, the Knights

11

Templars, Crusaders, 'les preux chevaliers' of past times, high-toned, enthusiastic, religious, who go to work in a very sensible, earnest way to do their duty in every respect, and some of my friends are lucky enough to have drawn such into their nets; but they are rare specimens, and (sighing) this individual, for one, has but little hope left of such success, lay as many snares as she will. Running into this class and still unlike it—one hardly knows where the one ends and the other begins, and yet there is a great difference—are the Worthies."

"The what?" said Mrs. Liebenhoff.

"The provokingly worthy class, who are more trying than any other; for you cannot help it, and they really deserve scolding at, and yet they are just good enough to give one compunctious visitings for saying a word against them. They rise early in the morning, say their prayers, I have not the least doubt, eat a temperate breakfast, go to their business like clock-work, never make a mistake in life or manners, can be trusted with untold treasures in any shape or form, are very agreeable, gentlemanly, intelligent companions when they vouchsafe their presence in our midst, but dear me! any machines could be made to do as much, you know. What they want is life, moral enthusiasm, and what is to our purpose especially—devotion to us. You understand?"

"That is what I complain of in some of my gentlemen friends," said Mrs. Körner.

"Do *they* take young ladies to ride and skulk out of town through the back streets, lest they should be suspected of some tender designs upon them before they are sure of success?" said Jenny, " and hover round them, weighing every look and word to see if it will do to risk an offer; and when impatient at such timidity, and disgusted at such want of valor, our faces express the feeling that cannot but be roused—' well, if you are so cool and calculating

as all that, a fig for such love. I can live without you,'
why, forsooth, they scramble away like frightened sheep,
and we see them no more; but go on, Theresa."

" In the third place, there are 'the young elect, who
have got beyond ritual,' who are too far advanced to value
the Bible *much*, too enlightened for the church, (having
supped that orange, as one of their number profanely said,)
but cry aloud and spare not in literary clubs, anti-slavery,
odd-fellow, free discussion and temperance societies, are
the special champions and abettors of the emancipated
ladies; and in short, thrust a finger into every reform pie
that the public concoct.   Are you tired?"

" O no, go on," said two or three voices.

" The fourth class are what I call the Kilkenny cats, an
animal which eats itself up you know, all but a slender
extremity.   These are the refined, introverted sort, de-
voured by their own selfish sentiments, who might, if they
were not foolish and criminal too—excuse me, ladies—
gild our hard-working life with a beautiful radiance.   But
no, Narcissus-like, they fall in love with themselves, and
their conversation is interlarded accordingly with a very
egotistical letter of the alphabet.   These *worship* in the
woods, poetize in a weakly way, have interesting fits of
absent-mindedness, affect a few high-strung authors and
fewer friends, paint pictures sans soul, sans life, sans fit-
ness for anything but a chimney board, are musical in a
slender, hypercritical style, fall in love in a dilettante way,
with some different fair one every summer's vacation, and,
in short, with talents and acquirements which they use just
enough to make you regret that they have any to cover
thus with a bushel, are nobody, nowhere, and nothing
at all.   O! deliver me from such hangers-on upon the skirts
of our modern society, who will sit by with microscope in
hand, while the faithful are wearing themselves out with
labor and undue responsibility, making their infinitesimal
and impertinent criticisms upon results the fruit of almost

superhuman efforts, sighing and tears, crucifiers of their
Lord in kid gloves and patent leather boots; first, by deny-
ing him practically, by their paltry lives; secondly, by de-
preciating his greatness and perfect excellence in their crude
speculations; thirdly, by lazily feasting upon the bounties
of Providence, without working with their might for the
coming of his glorified kingdom; and fourthly, by standing
aloof from, if not throwing a heavy additional weight upon
the shoulders of his ministers, who would welcome even
the lifting of their little finger to cheer on the building up
anew of his church on the earth! Verily, the times are
out of joint, when such are the caressed, admired and
gazed-up to as the geniuses and seers of this nineteenth
century. Again, I say, deliver me from their deadening
companionship."

"Bravo!" said Mrs. Liebenhoff; "are there any more
specimens? Give them to us, please."

" Yes, there is young America *par excellence*, Sam, as
we call him now-a-days, often rude, extravagant, ostenta-
tious, impulsive, but generous, bold, energetic, chivalrous,
romantic, very faulty, sometimes very wicked, but with
great capabilities. I intend to marry one of these, if I
can't get one of the very best of the first class, and indeed,
I think I prefer them any way, they are so spontaneous.
But dear me, as I have not been brought up in the woods,
and don't intend to build my hut there and abide, what a
wearisome working and smoothing over of, and taming of
his greenness and bearishness—and what is worse often, of
...is heathenism there must be before he is presentable in
civilized life! O, pity us poor damsels, ye matrons, who
have anchored in the haven of happy wifehood! I really
wish I was married. so as to have the state, condition, or
whatever you please to call it, together with mankind
generally, and each one in particular, entirely off my mind.
I am sick of the whole genus."

Here she was interrupted by a laugh from Mr. Körner.

"A most effectual way of getting rid of them, surely. I will try and assist you in this laudable attempt to ignore our sex. You must be married certainly, confound the beaux! What do they mean by letting you come off over the waters without securing you; I am ashamed of them. Well, we have some here that I will introduce you to."

"My dear sir, I hope you will not think that I left only dry eyes and composed hearts, when I withdrew the light of my countenance from my country. I would not tell tales for the world, but, ahe—m—There comes Mrs. Pendleton to the rescue of the young men. I saw her looking over here, while I was talking with Mrs. Liebenhoff, and I knew that she was getting ready for an onslaught upon me."

At that moment Miss Ingemann and other ladies entered the room, and after the introduction, Mrs. Pendleton crossed over to where Theresa was sitting.

"Now, ladies, I beg you not to believe everything which this satirical young friend of mine has said about our American gentlemen. I know a great many of them well."

"Excuse me for interrupting you," said Miss Hale, "but Mrs. Pendleton is not a disinterested umpire between us, for, as you perceive, she is so fascinating as to withdraw the attentions which should be rightly ours (being in most need of them) to herself. *She* has nothing to complain of, while we are set aside just enough to make us *cool* and impartial judges. I would not insinuate any conscious treachery, but she and her house and garden have such a hospitable, *taking* way with them as quite to eclipse any humble pretensions of our own."

"Now is not that ungrateful," said Mrs. Pendleton, "when my aims and efforts in placing myself, my house, and last, but by no means least, my studious husband and quiet-loving daughter at your disposal so much, is just to advance your interests and happiness. Shame on you!

And now I will tell the whole truth as a proper retribution
for such thanklessness."

"May I be resigned," said Theresa, casting up her eyes,
"for I know well that there is no mercy to be expected
from you, when your war-horse snuffs the battle from
afar."

"Now," said Mrs. Pendleton, "for all moral, religious,
selfishly sentimental delinquencies, and I own that they
have a plenty, I am not going to offer any excuse, for if
people have the New Testament, with its faultless precepts
and perfect example, that is sufficient; there is no reason
that they should be shipwrecked upon these sands.   But so
far as their want of gallantry and devotion to the sex is
concerned, there is some excuse, on account of *their* short-
comings in character and mistakes of education. The
fault of the present day, with our best women, is, that the
intellect is cultivated unduly at the expense of the health,
practical ability, and tenderness, grace and beauty of char-
acter.   In short, we have sharpened understandings, in-
stead of beautiful, loving souls; acute critics in place of
sweet *Charities*, striving with their soft mantles to cover the
deformities they cannot remove; eager, squinting specula-
tists, instead of the strong-eyed *Faiths*, who pierce the
heavens and become inspired at the visions that dawn on
them as they gaze; fierce satirists, and confident denunci
ators and not the bright, beaming, inspiring *Hopes*, that ever
smile and point upwards, through the thickest gloom and
discouragements.   Now, you young ladies, must be less
like the heathen goddesses, somewhat faded and passé and
more like the Celestials of our Master's spiritual dispensa-
tion before your age of triumph begins.   You must quaff the
elixir of life from the well which he opens for every one
who desires it, and then you will not be growing old at
twenty, complaining that the illusions of life are vanishing,
leaving nothing but a void; that the bloom is rubbed off
from the peach, and that life is exhausted of its sweetness

and exhilaration, but it will never cease to be full, rich and harmonious and will irradiate your whole inward and outward being, and then you will have no lack of adorers."

" Mrs. Pendleton, that is all very fine; but I ask you the plain question, if we are not now too good for any young gentlemen—of our village, for instance? Don't ask us to get any farther in advance of them. They would lose sight of us altogether."

" No, not if you advance in the right way, rising into the ether like Beatrice, but ever casting a gentle, holy, winning glance behind. Her influence drew her lover upward, higher and ever higher, and so should yours. As it is, I grant you excite admiration at a distance; but, dear me! you have so much more the spirit of carping and ridicule than of love and forbearance, and generous appreciation of the inner spirit of humanity, when divested of some of the ornaments of life, that the men are afraid of you, and no wonder! I am, too. I am always on the look out for some prick of your stiletto-intellect, sharpened by everlasting reading and study of modern literature, and German philosophy and mathematics, to the exclusion of nature and *your* Bible, for the young men do not alone neglect it."

" Well, Jenny, I suppose we must reform them. Have you any spare hair-cloth for vests for us, Mrs. Pendleton, or peas to fill our shoes with? If you have, please leave them at my door to-night when you retire, for I shall commence my humiliation forthwith. That floating, alluring Beatrice quite takes my fancy. I shall practice ascension from this time forward—that is, after a few turns with the hair-cloth and peas," said Theresa.

Miss Ingemann sat by while this conversation was going on in pretty loud, animated tones, as is a common custom with the excitable American women, and thought it was rather free talk, especially for young ladies. Mrs. Pendleton's loud tones, with her occasional resounding laugh, at length quite disgusted her, and when in a very audible whisper the latter lady asked Mrs. Körner, with a little mischief in the expression of her face, if she (Miss Ingemann) was not a countess, it was altogether too much for her dignity to bear with its usual imperturbableness, and her lip wore a very scornful expression.

Afterward, Theresa was speaking with great affection of her mother and of her father's lively interest in life and its events, though advanced in years.

" Why did they not accompany you?" said Mrs. Körner.

" My mother is too precious goods to be toted away here," said she, " and the last time I went to Niagara with my honored papa, he bothered me so by anxiously watching me, while I stood at the end of the cars to look out upon the scenery, that I told him I should leave him at home the next journey I took; so I was as good as my word, you see."

This was altogether too much for Miss Ingemann, who rose to go, excusing herself in a cold, lady-like way to Mrs. Körner for retiring so early, and only bowed very stiffly to the strangers as she left the room.

Theresa saw that her doom was sealed with at least one member of good society in Copenhagen, and turned to Mrs. Liebenhoff. That lady sat very quietly, making her observations. Feeling nervous at first, as Miss Ingemann began to manifest displeasure, she made one or two attempts to mediate between their understandings, but concluded on the whole, it was of no use, so resigned herself to the enjoyment of the scene.

" Have I done or said anything so very shocking?" said Theresa.

" O no, certainly not! I enjoy it and hope for a better acquaintance. I like to see individuality and spirit. I will suggest to you, however, that as you are a stranger, and of course wish to conciliate good-will and the favorable opinion of those whom you are to dwell among for a time, that without losing these, a delicate sympathy and tact will suggest when you encroach too much on our favorite modes of speech and action. But you will acquire that by experience. We can all learn of each other, you know."

"Thank you! You are a woman of good sense, and I hope you will let me come and see you."

"Most certainly," said she; "do so often. The parsonage has open doors for all, and especially for those after my own heart, as I see you are, with some comparatively trifling reservations. I want my husband to know you all."

"Where is Mr. Liebenhoff all this time, Lisbet? I hoped he would come with you."

"O, at the church! the failing, tottering, gasping church! There is another adjourned meeting to-night to talk over whether the old one shall be repaired or a new one built; and he has gone to say a few encouraging words upon the latter plan."

"Do the gentlemen have adjourned meetings in Denmark as well as in America? How provokingly alike people are all over Christendom! I did hope that three thousand miles would transport me to some rarities in character and manners, but it is very much the same old story I see, with the exception of a few unimportant exteriors. O for a little novelty in this humdrum lower sphere!" said Theresa.

"Yes," said Mrs. Liebenhoff, "adjourned meetings, in which people dole over the difficulty of a little self-sacrifice and discourage each other into doing nothing and being less, if possible, in our Lord's kingdom. *They* seem to be thought the legitimate substitutes for Christian interest, a prompt submission to the requisitions of our glorious faith, and zeal in advancing it among men, so they meet again and again to tell each other how little they will give for his cause, and adjourn to withdraw mayhap their intended

pittance, because forsooth another gives less than he ought
or than he supposed he would for the same object."

"Yes, that is the way.   What is to be done in such a
state of things?" said Mrs. Pendleton.

"What each one thinks right, my dear madam," said
Mrs. Liebenhoff; "I know what I am going to do."

When all equipped to go home, and while making their
prolonged adieux to Mrs. Körner, who the strangers said
seemed to them like an old friend, they met Mr. Liebenhoff
upon the steps.   He exchanged a few words with the
company, and then taking his wife's arm within his, walked
homewards with her.

CHAPTER XIII.

"WHAT sort of a meeting did you have?" said Mrs. Liebenhoff, as they entered their dwelling.

"A pretty discouraging one! Out of a multitude to whom notices were sent, only a handful were present, and the conclusion is, that it is impossible to build."

"I see no reason why; surely it is not for want of means, prosperous and abundantly rich as they are. They have no good excuse, but their backwardness to engage in the work is simply a want of interest in their religious faith, and a low style of character, which is the natural consequence."

"Of course," said he, "but how to rouse them to a higher life is the question? O, if men would not look upon everything which they do for Christianity, which has done so much and would do everything for them if they would receive it in its fullness, in the light of a hard sacrifice, as a charity which they may or may not bestow; but as they make their homes graceful and beautiful for their comfort, the satisfaction of their tastes and the repose of their hearts, so should they with joy and thanksgiving, as if from a glad necessity of their nature lay the foundation stones of their temple of worship, which shall be to them the home of their souls, the altar from which shall arise their purest hopes, desires, and aspirations, and where

(131)

Heaven shall pour upon them its richest treasures of for
giveness, consolation and love."

"Yes," said Mrs. Liebenhoff, " but that is a point far
beyond them as yet; not but that there are many, many
excellent persons in our parish, and I love them for what
they are, and still more for what I see lying wrapped up
within them unused. But they are as yet in the beggarly
elements of a material philosophy and life, quick to discern
the coarser characteristics of intellectual power, ready to
sympathize with the subordinate wants of the moral and
physical man, and that to be sure. is a good deal, showing
an awakening mind, and some sense of obligation, but of
the higher spiritual functions of the soul, its close com-
munion with the Infinite, its development into a complete,
beautiful and harmonious whole, through obedience to
the laws of its being, as taught by the Christ, resulting
in the glad liberty, strength of will and all-conquering
might of its varied powers, they seem as yet not cognizant.
And to one, who step by step has toiled up the way to this
Pisgah height of contemplation and glad experience as
you have, their life seems narrow and groping, and the
very air is heavy and dim with the lack of this celestial
electricity."

" But how shall I inspire them with this higher life? I
am getting discouraged, and really feel that I am not fitted
to be their pastor, Lisbet."

" And are you impatient for the world's idol, success?"

" Not vulgar success; but why may I not see that I am
doing something, and not week after week, be weighed
down with this feeling of responsibility, uncheered by
tokens that my prayers, labors and unceasing thought for
them are not like water spilled upon the ground!"

" O, thou of little faith! but such feelings come from a
constitutional deficiency of what is a large element of my
nature, hope, never dying, but ever springing, triumphant
Hope, and it whispers to me now, that disjointed, freezing,

unfaithful, unsympathizing as a society, the members (each one of whom individually, is a kind, good friend to us,) are, that when the new and inspiring word is spoken to them, they will be all the more ready for their lack of present organization and order to combine into a living body of—not pure, individual Christians merely, but into the true, free, and glorious embodiment through his appointed church, of the universal and heaven-inspired spirit of our Lord."

" You are enthusiastic, my wife!"

" Less so than you are blamably faithless, at this moment. But cheer up; don't think of the ugly, falling ruin of a church. And let the people go to perdition, I say, where they seem to tend so evidently."

" My dear, don't be wicked."

" I am not wicked. I don't wish them there, but if you like it better, I will state the matter as a plain fact. They are already there. Such deadness *is* perdition; the very dreariest of the mansions of the under-world, in which people grope in darkness, and wander about dead to all the higher and more inspiring attributes of their being, while at the same time, they hug themselves with self-satisfaction for their cool wisdom and acute intellectualism which saves them from the quivering sensibilities, the flights of an imagination which abides not in their harsh, frigid councils, and the awakened hopes which are ever on the wing, soaring higher and higher towards the Infinite Good."

"Yes, and to bring them into this state," said he, " they must do something for themselves; and the first and simplest and most obvious thing is for them to unite to build a church. A common interest in this most worthy and necessary object may be an entering wedge to a higher and better communion between them. But somehow I have not leadership enough to marshal them into working order."

" I am glad you have not, for harsh guardianship, coarse

generalship we have had enough of in Christendom.   Let us, at this late day, come to the full knowledge of the higher spirit of our Lord, whose kingdom is one of liberty of action and equal responsibility for all, in proportion to each one's powers, opportunities and means, and that the pastor is but the teacher, inspirer, and guide of his flock, pointing to the living pastures of perennial truth, the sunny paradise of affection and high and pure sympathy; or perchance, the brave, disinterested and faithful shepherd who shall venture into the wilderness after the lost ones and bring them forth redeemed and penitent, for others of the fold to rejoice over with him, and protect and bless them so that they will not desire to wander from it again. Ministers now-a-days seem to feel that the salvation of every soul in their parish depends upon them though there are so many other means of enlightenment and guidance. While it is so, you may be sure the people will drag upon them with their full weight, it is so much easier in idea to be carried into heaven like a babe in one's bosom than to struggle upwards into it, step by step, like a true disciple of Jesus.   Unfold your arms then, let them hang down-wards their full length that they bear up no such lazy souls, and wear no robe, as friend Geiser would say, to which the unfaithful may cling and thus be smuggled into the courts above; for if they can show no title but *such* selfish dependence upon their wasting, yet faithful, untiring friend, they will surely be banished thence by their judge and yours."

"Well, I hope all will come right; I feel that if I could be the instrument of rousing them—not a few of the rich and mature in years and experience merely, but each and all, young men and maidens, the poor and the struggling to do this holy work, as an expression of their faith in, and love for God and their Saviour, that I should be satisfied to with-draw and leave them to the councils of one who could bet-ter express for them their wants and aspirations."

"Heaven knows who it would be or whether they have
any. But yes, they cannot be devoid of them as I know
they are real men and women, and not phantoms. most
certainly they are too prone to earth for that, and they seem
outwardly to possess all the characteristics of human be-
ings. Yes—O yes, certainly they must be human, for, as
I before said, they are our dear kind friends in private
life; but now I have it, they are under the spell of some
wicked genius, who, the moment that the great words—
God, Christ, Religion, the Soul, the Bible, are uttered
as to a society, are changed into 'spirits of the vasty
deep,' whose senses are so deadened by the element in
which they are condemned to live that they hear not, and
therefore come not up, as a matter of course, when the
sweet music of your heavenly piety vibrates upon the air.
They need the thunder, and lightning, and earthquake, those
coarser ministers of God's dispensation to men to reach
them in their low estate. *They* are the stern law, and
let it rule them if they would have it, for not even the
refreshing rain which follows the war of the elements,
which is like wisdom to men's minds, can they recognize,
much, much less the celestial dew, which is his love, dis-
tilled in this most gentle and ethereal form. Such is the
utterance of Christian truth by you in your most natural
and legitimate way, for to this elevation have your faith and
obedience lifted you. Had you stopped short in the first,
the Xantippe plane, you would be called great; for in this
is the world chiefly, and that of course is mighty in its
eyes which expresses themselves in a slightly ideal form,
but if ever you were in that, it was in the pre-existent state
if there was one, but not in this. You have climbed up
through the second period, and the benign spirit of Wisdom
has become one with you, and men see her not because
she stalks not about nor cries in the streets. But hand in
hand with Love, the heavenly pair modestly wait upon you
and point you ever to 'the well undefiled' of crystal Truth,

and you draw from it and dispense to those who are so many fathoms below you, that so few of its drops penetrate to their souls that they are not impressed."

"What a rhapsody! but I shall not dispute you. What husband loves not to be praised and idealized by his wife! *You* are my parish, my church, my—"

"Thank you for nothing. I'll be neither, I've long been jealous of both, and now you shall set them aside and admire and be at leisure, and make love to me in a more individual manner, and not as a necessary part of this provoking, stupid parish. Do you know that all this heart-ache and these disappointed hopes come from your false, unnatural notion of living for humanity and not for me?"

"My dear Lisbet, what do you mean? Are you turning tempter to warp me from the high duty to which I early dedicated my life? God first, and humanity next, has always been my motto. Then come other claims; *the me* must have the next share, else how could I accomplish the first, and then my own loved wife, and have I been remiss towards you, dearest?"

"Now you doubtless expect, after my rhapsody as you call it upon you and your preaching, that I shall most dutifully answer, 'O no, my liege lord and anointed husband! I am only too thankful for the droppings from the sanctuary of your divided heart. Shiver it into as many fragments as your swollen sense of responsibility sees fit; I receive the smallest iota of it with the most gentle and satisfied submission.' But no! I say again, I subscribe to no such falsehood of creed or unfaithfulness of life. You are quite in the wrong about this matter. My instincts have always rebelled against my position in your life's category of interests, and now my whole nature is up in arms to contend against it. I have spelled it all out and now I am going to give you a sermon from these words of your brother divine slightly paraphrased; 'God has hid away the

human soul in a *woman's* form that in finding it we may
rediscover our alienated and forgotten nature and rejoice
over the one that was lost more than the ninety and nine
who went not astray.' "

"What do you mean, my love?"

"Only that you are a tyrant and a hypocrite and a — no
wonder you stare, my archangel, who, all the women pro-
test, is the most beautiful, the most amiable, the most
agreeable, the most saintly, in short the most immaculate
of all mankind on this floating globe, and that I am the
most fortunate, the most blessed, the most ought-to-be-thank-
ful little woman, who is all but drowned in the ocean of her
husband's perfection! Pshaw! did they not serve old
Aristides right, whom all fools surnamed 'The Just?' I
wish I had been at Athens to throw in my shell of ostra-
cism with that single wise man who had got tired of hear-
ing him perpetually praised. He had doubtless been to
his wife and asked her how he was at home, and she had
told him some truths about him. Banish him, I say, and
that crabbed old Socrates, parading round with his impu-
dent questions and prosy old saws. Xantippe knew how
much they were worth, and she scolded him as he deserved.
I wish she had boxed his ears when she was about it, hard
enough for the tingling to come down the ages through
every husband's ears, seeing that most of us are restrained
by the idea that it is not ladylike to perform the deed, from
doing that same thing. Give him the hemlock, I say—the
hard, quizzing, conceited, tyrannical husband, who wickedly
married for the very worst reason that he could. O thou, so
called god, Esculapius! to whom the weak, mistaken, short-
sighted man sacrificed a cock after all his pretended
advance before the age, why could ye not have gone to the
rescue of that much injured and scandalized Xantippe—
wife of his I will not again insult her by calling her—
aud given her of your skill to mingle with her libation
some potion to soften his hard understanding for a true

12

idea of *her* to penetrate, that through his, thus enlightened mind, there might flow into his heart a pittance at least of the love which was her right, but which his philosophico, coldly moralistico, anything but tenderly spiritualistico nature denied her! O Xantippe! most injured, most to-be compassionated woman! here I erect a statue to perpetuate your wrongs, and thy delinquent husband shall kneel for thy pardon for his injustice and tyranny towards thee, and as thou wert a woman, and in that word dwells the very soul of forgiveness, when thou seest him thus humiliated and repentant, thou wilt raise him even to a higher level than thyself, that then, without injury to thy delicate sense of right and truth, thou mayst revere, as thy nature ever craves to do, him who when humble and tender, and not until then, becomes truly exalted! And so endeth the *first* head of my sermon; the moral of which is, that as your wife is a part of humanity, and God said when you married her that you should forsake father and mother and cleave unto her, saying nothing about parish and church, as you see; next to your own culture and salvation are you to devote yourself to her happiness and welfare, and in this way only can you twain become truly and emphatically one, and thereby be in harmony with God and his beautiful universe."

"Well, my dear, what am I to do? kneel for forgiveness or —"

"Wait, until I have finished my sermon. Pretty well too, for a minister, to speak in meeting! But I must ask you, however, if that is not well done? Now that is what the people would call great. Why can you not preach so to *them?* I am sure they deserve it enough."

"I will exchange with you the next Sunday, and you may add a little different collar and wristbands, as we preachers say to an old sermon, and give it to them hot and strong."

"Well then, I must go on to the *secondly*, and by way

of rehearsal, will imagine myself in church. And seeing that I wandered from my subject, ('an uncommon event for a woman;' said Mr. Liebenhoff,) on account of the imperfect education which tyrant man awards to her, thereby condemning her to lamentable scatter-wittedness, I will again return to the forcible text: 'God has hidden away the human soul in a *woman's* form, etc.' And, my brethren, as she, the least sinful portion of society, through your generous regard for her moral and spiritual welfare, and especially that she might become a meet, obedient and adoring subject of her lord and master, has by means of books, pictures, conversation and the ministration of the word applied especially to her, as also by the laws and institutions of our country been happily reduced to a very submissive condition; I will address my discourse entirely to you, hoping that you will be equally docile in the reception of this great truth, as she has been in listening to the homilies daily afforded her by your disinterested sex."

"You are getting personal, my dear! They will tell you, as they did me, that you will break up the society."

"The same answer is not yet worn out, "let it break up then, if it is made of so flimsy materials."

"And, first, I need not dwell upon this basis of all religions, the great and sacred idea of a Supreme, Intelligent and Parental Spirit, except to remind you that as of old it was reiterated again and again, that it dwelt not in idols made of wood and stone, in either the human or animal form, so neither does it any more, when converted into banks, warehouses, or any of the forms into which *business* is transacted or *money* made, nor even in any great man, whether Pope, Emperor, Noble, or Genius. Therefore I will pass on to the next clause."

"*Secondly, Hidden,* etc. A very significant word, my hearers, informing you of what you have not sufficiently considered, that a woman may possess more than what you with your pre-occupied attention and narrow judgment of her duty and destiny had thought possible or necessary, and therefore indicating that she was created for some wider and higher purpose than simply to be the minister to your pleasure or honor, or even comfort and solace under your heavy labors and responsibilities in the great cause of doing good. For, my brethren of the priestly order! of whom I see some among you, did it never occur to you that while you are dispensing the bread of life to multitudes of souls outside of your homes, and being the sympathizers, guides, and chief laborers of society in matters pertaining to their moral and religious welfare, indeed their willing drudges and servants of all work, from the chosen one of expounding to them the Holy Word and leading them onward to the celestial gate, to every imaginable secular errand which they may impose upon you; did it never occur to you, I say, that while spreading your sympathies over creation, and calling upon her likewise to keep even pace with yourself, that *her* Innermost in the . meantime either remained unawakened and sterile, or else became preternaturally excited without being justly responded to by you who have all humanity to cater for? She therefore goes moaning and shrieking through life till her intense and bitter cry for the natural and necessary food of her being has caused even the angels, who dwell in the nearer presence of God, to stand aghast at her cry."

"A pungent discourse! Spare me, I beg," said Mr. Liebenhoff.

"O don't take it to yourself! Pass it to your fellow-hearers as is the usual custom."

"*Thirdly;* 'The human soul in a *woman's* form.' My brethren, we feel no disposition to deny you the possession of intellectual strength; that element which is sometimes called talent, that power of fixing the attention upon truth, of holding it up as if it were a crystal before the mind's eye; viewing it on every side deliberately and patiently, until you have drawn from it all its possible deductions.

Nor do I deny you the practical power of subduing to your dominion all the ruder forces of nature and making them subservient to the well-being of man. But to the feminine soul, my hearers, must be awarded *par eminence*, the possession of genius, that divine inspiration, which enables her at a glance to pierce to the very heart of the truths which, by diligence and hard labor, ye slowly attain unto; and though from time to time, this faculty may show itself in full blaze in your sex, it is because that they are invested in a larger degree than is common with the feminine element. But the woman's soul, when nurtured by holy love, nourished by truth, led and imbosomed by nature, made strong and faithful and tender by obedience to the Christ, and ever bathed and invigorated, and inspired by communion with the Infinite, stands forth with no peer, call me not profane, but I repeat, *with no peer*, as the most glorious and beautiful representative of God in the world; for through her plastic, docile, and confiding nature, He is able to reveal, if not with more clearness, yet with more graceful and winning beauty, than through the more self-sufficient and unyielding man, his designs in the development of the races. And when, as the mother of infant humanity, she moves among you, mild, tender, and gracious, do justice to your better nature and give her your tenderest veneration; for even the angels clasp their hands and gaze reverently upon her and say: See how, under her loving care, the bud of immortality will bloom sweetly and fairly until it is garnered with us into the paradise of our God!"

"Any more, my dear? for I am sorry to say that I grow sleepy."

"You always do when you don't preach yourself, and some say that you are a little drowsy then, you know; so you must bear with my first imperfect effort. Courage! I have got fully half through, I do believe."

"*Fourthly;* 'That in finding it we may re-discover our alienated and forgotten nature.' Upon this head it is necessary to say but few words; for it is very evident that man cannot lose sight of the divine in one large portion of creation, and that so important a part as its better half, and blasphemously imagine that he is to appropriate its precious wealth to his trifling or injurious tastes, or at best to his selfish consolation, encouragement, and use, without fearful deterioration and loss. For all God's children rise or remain in limbo, or fall together through the mysterious sympathy which binds them in unity; and when one suffers physically, intellectually, or spiritually, all creation groans and agonizes with it. Therefore, my brethren, listen to this, my asseveration, ponder it and let it sink deep into your hearts, and thenceforward have a radical, perceptible, and most potent influence over your principles, sentiments, characters, institutions and laws, that woman has an *individual, independent, and responsible soul*, subject only to the God who created it, worthy of the highest, broadest, and most delicate culture which may be brought from every part of the universe, to aid in its perfect and harmonious development. And by means of this essential and heaven-ordered work you will arrive, my poor, ignorant, and purblind brethren, at this very evident and joy-inspiring truth, written upon your own natures it is true, and repeatedly revealed more distinctly all through the six thousand years of the world's existence, but which, lacking the clear glance of her genius, and still more, her obedient will, you are yet in doubt of, or practically, at least, deny altogether that you also are the possessors of the same great gift which I here announce in the loudest tones awarded to me, that *man as well as woman has an immortal soul*.

"*Fifthly;* 'And rejoice more over it than over the ninety and nine," etc. Yes, my brethren, when this glad truth is once and forever established, then will the world begin to stride with long steps in the march of advancement. For see you not its grand significance and tendency, the sublime value it will give to every human being, and the fearful consequences of marring, in any way, either by sin or oppression, or wrong of any kind, this great handiwork of God, and the necessity and privilege of aiding in educating and training this child of the ages, this heir of eternity? In this glad work let the male and female soul enter with joy and thanksgiving; let the feminine part of the Gospel be henceforward acknowledged, and great will be their mutual reward."

"Pretty good for a first attempt! You will improve if you practice."

"O! I have a great deal more to say upon the same theme, but the people would vote me a visionary and fanatic at once, so I spare myself and them. Here endeth the first lesson!"

CHAPTER XIV

"O friend! my bosom said,
Through thee the sky is arched,
Through thee the rose is red,
All things, through thee, take nobler form,
And look beyond the earth,
And is the mill-round of our fate,
A sun path in thy worth."—EMERSON.

"MY own Zoë, how neatly you are dressed and how sweetly you look," said Hilda one afternoon, as she entered their apartment just as the former had completed her toilet; "are you going out?"

"Yes, to my dear Mrs. Liebenhoff's; she told me to come and see her whenever I liked to, and that I might run up directly into her room, and if she were gone out I might make myself at home among her books and medallions and pictures until she returned; and I know she meant every word she said, for I can tell

"The true soul very well,
Without book or bell."

"And it makes you happy, don't it, love? Well, I am glad you have found another mate to rest your sad eyes upon once in a while; for mine, I well know, are such dancing, twinkling orbs that yours don't get from them much of the repose they plead for. I shall not be at all jealous of the quiet parsoness. She will be a nice little cushion for you to lean against; but when you want life, enthusiasm, and love of the strong order you will come back to me."

"You don't know Mrs. Liebenhoff, Hilda, for—"

"Bless me! don't fire up in that way for a trifle, for I give you fair warning, my Titania, that be duped as you may, you shall not lead me to believe there is a beauty or a heroine of romance in that ordinary little face and figure. Fall in love with her as much as you please and rhapsodize her high qualities, I see nothing in her but a nice little minister's wife, very quiet under the heavenly influence of my dearly beloved friend, her husband, who is a great deal too handsome and interesting and learned and everything else for her mediocre passivity. (She takes both her hands and lifts Zoë's face towards her own.)   I see I have swept you into the indignant mood and objective case, to be governed by none of my analysis of her style, type, sentiment, or covering.   But, my precious pet of a brunette with the sweeping, silken eyelashes, and the raven-winged hair, how pretty and fresh she looks!" and she stooped and kissed her forehead.

"Yes, I am trying to save my soul by what seems a prime article of Miss Ingemann's creed—a clean white skirt every other day, faultless gloves, and gossamer hose. It is rather a hard way of climbing up into the third heaven of her affections; I have very little faith that I shall succeed, for so far it is scrambling up two steps to fall plump down twenty, as I did to-day."

"Why how?" said Hilda, looking anxious.   "I thought you were getting rapidly into her good graces for the last fortnight.   Do tell me what has happened."

"Well, my best Hilda, after your remarks about my dress and habits, I determined to make an effort to be very orderly and proper, and as papa about that time sent me some money, I purchased some necessary articles of apparel so as to be as new all over as that figure in the shop-window up town, who every morning as she turns by clockwork, seems to say with a smirk, 'See how handsome I am, please to copy me and look as stiff and unhuman as I do.'"

13

" That you intend for me, because my dress stands out so full to-day, but this hair-cloth will yield in time. I don't want to look like a Grecian statue, you know, which is pretty in a book, or in a gallery of the fine arts, but not in life, it has such a draggled appearance."

" I know, I have made no complaint. The greatest inconvenience of it is, that one has to circumnavigate the globe to get around you, which seems a waste of time and steps you know, when one goes for a glass of water or a pocket handkerchief; but that is not to the purpose. To return—"

" I could not afford to have so much washing done, so I thought I would do some of it myself before the family rose in the morning, and I asked Annette, the cook, if she would be so kind as to allow me to do so. She is very good you know, and she told me that as I was not strong, that she would do it for me; but I could not consent to that, because she has to work so hard. So I told her we would change, if she pleased; I would make her breakfast cakes and she might be my laundress."

" And those nice muffins, and fritters, and other goodies were yours then?   I wondered that Annette's genius should flower all at once in the culinary line, for she is wanting in skill usually.   But how did you learn, pray?"

" It requires nothing but common sense, care, patience, and a cook-book to make good cakes, and if one has a delicate sense of taste and smell, it is all in one's favor.

" Affairs went on very smoothly for some time; I had a nice, funny hour with Annette in the kitchen-yard with the fresh morning air blowing upon me, and her to crack jokes with, and to pet me as nobody does, in this cold north world but you, Hilda, and I shone out like the sun in my freshness and cleanliness as you so often tell me now-a-days."

" And have you smoothed down your hair with the sad-iron, my roly-poly, or what has come over your ebony locks to quell them to such becoming obedience? They really look like smooth and dutiful Christians, and not like Pagan fury-emblems, darting at one from every point, as they used to do."

"Don't you see this tamarind seed band, which my own devoted, loving, ever-thoughtful mamma, daughter of the sun and southern cross, sister of the trade-winds, and wife of the earthquake of the tropics sent me by the last ship? That is the Delilah which has subdued them to such docility, my friend, nothing else would have had such power."

"Save me from its magical influence," said Hilda, throwing up her hands and starting back with affected terror; "you were such a witch before, that I had thoughts of getting Mr. Liebenhoff to bring his Bible and prayer-book and attempt to lay you. But now, I am afraid you are beyond the power of them all."

"The Bible! that is my wand, my horoscope, my talisman as you ought to know by this time," said Zoë, taking a small copy of a Testament from her pocket and pressing it to her breast, and looking upwards. "*Lay me*, do you say? it rather carries me to the heaven of heavens, where I ever, ever thirst to be dwelling." And she remained rapt for a moment.

Hilda looked on with a mingled expression of awe, anxiety and fun. The latter prevailing, she touched Zoë's chin with her fan, saying, "Please to descend to the history of batter-cakes and clean hose, for you left them both in limbo, and it is but common justice to release them."

"Well, as I was saying, matters went on very well until yesterday morning, when I discovered by Miss Ingemann's conversation in an adjoining room, that she had learned from Annette all about our bargain. She was not angry, but on the contrary, I caught enough of her conversation, (for I was taking my music lesson, and had to be a listener against my will,) to know that she thought she had found

out what I was fit for, and that it was a pity to spoil a good
cook by laboring so hard to teach me the studies and ac-
complishments of a lady, and that she was going to encourage
my becoming an adept in the business, by permitting me to
spend more than my usual two hours a week in household
occupations.   Then at dinner, (you were away and did not
hear it,) she smiled upon me most graciously, and praised
in an undue manner, some tarts which I had made; and
the tea-cake last evening, and in short made me feel so all
over like a little pastry-cook and nothing else, that I was
angry, mortified and overwhelmed with confusion."

"You should not be so sensitive, child! Miss Ingemann
meant to be kind to you then, why could you not love her
for it instead of feeling so badly about it?"

"It is the last time she will be kind, I think, even in
that way," said Zoë; "for this morning as I wished my
white Josey to be clean to wear this afternoon, I went into
the kitchen again, and while Annette was doing it up, I
made a ' Charlotte Russe' for dessert, and thinking over my
mortification, I forgot some of the ingredients, and not
having my wits about me, I had no skill, and such a mess
as I prepared was a sorry sight to behold. Miss Ingemann
ordered it away from the dining-room before the family
assembled and cast a glance at me, as much as to say,
'You spiteful creature! you did this purposely,' and
I verily believe she thinks I did, in revenge for her
praising me, for she saw that I was not pleased when she
did so."

"O no, darling! she can't be so unreasonable. But do let
her praise you, Zoë, even for such things. I like the article
so well that I shall never quarrel with it, not even with
downright flattery if it is laid on ever so thick. I flourish
under it like a green bay tree, you see. To-be-sure, if it
were not for my adorable saint, Zoë, to whom I ever kneel and
look up to, as my patroness and example, I know I should
be spoiled, but with her image ever in my heart to shield

me from evil, I gather in the good gifts of this wicked world and make the most of them."

"O Hilda! I wish I were good for anything for your sake, but I am not; and if I ever for a brief hour forget it, such praises and such cutting rebukes, as Miss Ingemann gives me, bring the sad truth back in full force and utterly discourage me. O! what am I fit for in such a world as this, where everybody seems strong and happy and at home but me?" and she leaned her head dejectedly on her hand.

"Come, my willow, let me tie upon your topmost bough this rosebud of a hat, which will brighten up your drooping pensiveness a little. There, puff! (fanning her with force and at the same time blowing upon her), away, flutter into the arms of your paragon friend, the Liebenhoff feminine. You are welcome to her if you leave me my 'Aladdin,' my 'Correggio,' my spiritual 'Frithiof Saga,' 'the Minister of the children of the Holy Supper,' the Liebenhoff mascu-line. I wonder you do not fall down before him; he really looks so much like the Christ that hangs there before us."

"Hilda!" said Zoë.

"My dear, don't suppose I confound the conception of some, I have no doubt, very human artist with our Saviour himself. It is not wicked to speak so of *his* work, espe-cially if I do it with a very sorrowful face, is it? my apostle, (drawing down her features). Good-by, I will come at twilight and walk home with you."

"I don't like to hear such trifling reference to anything connected with our Lord; but good-by, I will wait for you."

(*Hilda alone.*)

"The shadows deepen around her when I had flattered myself they were clearing away a little. What is to be done now? I am tired of being a 'medium' between heaven in the shape of Zoë, and the world in Miss Inge-mann and people in general. Our dear Lord must see something more of good in me than I have ever been able to discover, to give this precious little soul so much into my keeping so far as to shield her from utter misery on the world's side, or on the other to prevent her dissolving into the heavenly sphere before her time. But as she grows older she is too much for me in both directions. I am not ready yet to be transfigured and find myself behind the vail at merry seventeen. I want to enjoy myself in a lively, human, coquettish way with flesh-and-blood belles and beaux, so when I find that she is carrying me into too rare an atmosphere for such sinners to follow, I lift up the valve for the gas to escape, and down my balloon falls. Then on the other side, I am so tried by our teacher's prejudices and the girls' mean notions of Zoë, caught from her, that I don't know but my temper will be spoiled, and that would be a pity, seeing I am such an angel. Heigh-ho! I know well that I was made to be as joyous as a butterfly all the day long, and if the wicked world chooses to spoil the handiwork of my Maker, by making me sad and anxious by their treatment of Zoë, why they must take the awful consequences, that is all. But one gleam of light there is in the direction of the minister; for I rely more on his wise and kind friendship than on anything his wife may do. So I desire to be thankful for so much."

When Mrs. Liebenhoff returned from her walk in a distant part of the city, she found Zoë reclining on her couch looking very intently upon the face of a Sybil, which hung on the opposite wall. She presented so perfect a picture of luxurious, dreamy, passionate orientalism, redeemed from its sensuous character by the pure Madonna-like expression which was natural to it, that she paused in the doorway to gaze upon her. Finding that she was utterly absorbed by her own reverie, which might outlast her capacity of standing, fatigued as she was, she advanced and stood over her.

"And can you really find it in your heart to pardon me

for walking into your air-castle and shivering it into atoms as I have done? It was a beautiful structure, was it not? And now that it is demolished, how very bare and uninteresting the world and all of us who remain on its site look! Come, my little architect, lay aside all your moonbeam implements, and gossamer frame-work and spider's-web materials generally, and let us have a good, sensible chat together," said she.

"Pardon me for my freedom in lounging thus. I fear I exceed the bounds of your kindness," said Zoë, rising and smoothing the pillow.

Mrs. Liebenhoff tenderly bade her welcome. "O no, no, dear," said she, "the couch is not damaged at all by such indulgence, nor by making it the scene of your subtle masonry; for twenty castles, no heavier than the one you were constructing, would not injure it at all by their pressure; but are you quite sure that *your innermost* retains its integrity as well after this intoxicating occupation?"

"I don't know—I fear not; but I am ashamed to say that I am good for nothing besides. I am different from every body else, and—and—the fact is, I don't like the world as it is—I never did, and I don't think I ever shall—so I just build and live in one of my own. If I were made like you, my dear madam, and could do everything in its season, and be contented and happy all the time, I should be *so* glad, for I really do not know what is to become of me in this practical world. You know that I am of Oriental descent, for I have lately discovered that fact, and I have a right to be dreamy."

"Zoë, it is not because I am so unlike, but that I see in you the reflected image, as it were, of my youthful self, that my deepest heart yearns towards you as it does. I seldom speak of my interior life, for it has ever been so hidden with God and his Christ, that it answers not to the call of any feeble or faltering sympathy; but for you, my darling, who are approaching that perilous period, 'the

parting of the ways,' which divides childhood from woman-
hood, I am impelled to reveal to you some of its story, hoping
that it may serve as a kindly hint to you."

"O, thank you, dear Mrs. Liebenhoff; how favored I
am!"

"I, too, am an Oriental," said she, "in temperament
and mental tendency, and formerly I marveled, that with the
breath of the Sirocco wind sweeping through my soul, with
every pore of my nature thirsting like the banyan tree for
the dewy moisture and copious showers of sympathy, affec-
tion and intimate companionship, I should be planted in the
snowy north, where the pulse beats to an even tenor, and
a preponderance of physical life saves from the intensity
of existence within. But as I grow older and interpret
more clearly that wonderful human nature with which God
has invested us. and glance with steadier vision into the
life within life, soul within soul, of this great universe of
his planning, and my being like that same plant of multi-
tudinous unity from its center spreads out indefinitely and
roots itself in the common soil, only to spring up again and
again to absorb the all-enlightening sun's rays, and drink
in the fertilizing offerings of the clouds, I seem to myself
no longer peculiar and solitary, but as *one* most emphati-
cally with the great company of my sex all over the world.
The chief distinction is, that through God and the myste-
rious ways of his Providence, there has been burned into
my soul a deeper impression of its wrongs, a wider know-
ledge of its character and its wants, and a higher sense of
its aspirations, than is awarded to all. And as these would
but consume me by their excess, and burst my very being
asunder by the cry which they bring up from its depths,
did I not utter what is in me, it seems an intimation that I
should do so in the ways which seem truest and best to
me, though I yield with the deed the most precious privi-
lege of my life. For to the shrinking soul of the true
woman, publicity is ever most painful, and nothing can

compensate her for making merchandise of her thoughts which have been a highway only between herself and the Infinite, but a purpose which is paramount to a merely selfish advantage and enjoyment, though these may be the greatest and purest of which we are capable."

"And are you going to write a book, dear Mrs. Liebenhoff?"

"Yes, and I cannot but hope that it may be an aid to you, Zoë, in the discipline of your mind, which, in its chief characteristics, seems so much like my own."

"O I know it will; but in the meantime, please tell me more about yourself, just to me, a little simple girl you know, who likes her own secrets kept too well to betray any of yours;" and she nestled close beside her as she said this.

"Now I am not going to begin as the biographers do, ' I was born in such a place,' etc., but shall rather take vou for the subject of my story, and *I* shall point the moral," said she, throwing her arm around her.

"I am so disappointed," said Zoë, "for it can't be entertaining with such a foolish, uninteresting heroine, with no beauty even to recommend her. Please skip the story and give me the moral."

"What an uncommon young woman, to prefer prosy moral to a pretty story! I have great hopes that it *will* be interesting with such an original subject to deal with. Here it is. ' Far, far away, away from over the great ocean, there once came to this land a little sun-browned Ethiopian, with the touch of the same artist hand upon the waves of her hair, and with teeth, of which, the elephant, kneeling to her mamma before her birth-day, begged her to carve some for the Zoë which soon was to *be*. For, by that name, which means life, said she, shall my darling be called, for, from the life of our Father in Heaven, its father on earth, my life and the life of the universe, shall she be fitly created. And so one bright morning there was joy in the household, for Zoë had descended from the Heaven on high, and to their eyes the ray of light which was its car, justly provided, still rested above it. O, sweet were the visions of the blessed young mother! O, tender the glance of the dark, thoughtful father! And gentle her dreams of the lisping companion, who should fly o'er the sea-beach with feet like birds' pinions, and gather with her the bright shells of the tropics. But big were the hopes of the strong, manly father, that she should honor his name by her beauty of character, and the lore which could only be gathered afar.

" 'And so one strange morning, when the rain deluged the household, though a star in the East shone brightly above, which the father interpreted to be Zoë, returning in her lovely young womanhood, she set sail for the land of her exile and discipline, which was to give her the glory which was to gladden their souls.

" 'Our Zoë, weird-being, grows apace, with two magnified eyes, one which looks backward and homeward, straining to catch glimpses of the emerald isle of the blue Caribbean, with its perennial life and deep-dyed vegetation, of its quivering sun, love-smitten with its beauty, and wedded for aye, to this *Saint of the Cross.*

" 'But more eagerly than all, does she pine for the arms of her own loved mamma, to inclose her with tenderness and for the lullaby song of her father at even, to hush her to rest.

" 'The other glance is upward to the heaven of heavens for its light, which but dimly is granted to her impatient expectations and feverish cry.

" 'But Zoë, my darling, drop your eyelids and strain not your orbs to pierce the blue vault for the—' Thus saith your God,' to be written upon it, nor listen for the audible summons to the work of your life, and still your heart-yearnings for the dear ones at home.

" 'But what shall supply to the fancy-fraught mind the

food of her being, the aim of her life, and inspiration to labor. Simply the duty which lieth the nearest, and every good word spoken by all who surround you, no less than the Scriptures and prayer to the Highest, for he has made you, my own, with more than two eyes—with a being wondrously varied, and to glorify him by its flower-like development is your first obligation.

" 'Yet be not too selfish in acquiring the knowledge which is to open like a key, this beautiful nature, for we are bound to each other by a mystical chain, and to preserve it in its lustre and smoothness, we must ever be brightening it by some fresh object of sympathy, and what can be better than to study and express to each other by deed more than word, the beauty and excellence of the dealings and works of our God?' "

" Thank you for the lesson, and for my birth history which I knew not before. I will write it to mamma in my next letter, it may be new even to her. And now for the moral!"

" O Zoë, if you would only remember and heed it, how glad I should be, but I see in your eye, that your imagination more than your reason and sense of danger are affected by my Tale! Nevertheless, you shall have it, and though you are too much preoccupied by your gaze backwards and forwards and into the realm of fancy into which you have grown, to regard it, yet like the seed sown by the wayside, it may some time spring up and give new life to your being."

" For this is its essential truth, that woman needs strength as well as beauty, and tenderness, and aspiration. For lacking this, she is like the ship in full sail upon the wide and fearful sea without a helm to direct or ballast to steady her motion. Like the eagle soaring to the gates of heaven with an eye that can gaze without blinking upou the centre of Infinity itself, and yet without the sure-guiding foot and the weight acquired by the mingling with the earthy and commonplace, she will turn over and over with absurd gyrations in the atmosphere, causing the groundlings by turns to wonder and adore, only to laugh and deride all the more when, draggled and torn, her wings lie soiled in the dust and her clairvoyant eye is dim in bewilderment or death. And this saving force, this power over the imagination and fancy, those beautiful but perilous pinions of the soul, can be gained only by patient toil, watchful care, and self-crucifixion. Give up the reins to them and you are lost, perhaps for aye. Keep them in check, bring up the conscience, the reason, the power of labor, the sense ' of awe and love of the Infinite and of humanity into harmonious correspondence, and no eye of earth is strong and clear enough to see into the future glory, even of your terrestrial being, while Vestal and Sybil, prophetess and seeress were but meagre types in the ancient times of the celestial glory of womanhood, thus exalted by the complete action of Christian truth and the self-discipline it enjoins. The genius of her tender, imaginative, sensitive soul requires the sweep of all the choicest of creation to nurture it, and when these come at her bidding through daily exertion in gathering the wealth of the past and present, contemplation and glad conformity to all the higher laws of our Creator, like the flower which blooms into loveliness and fragrance by a higher will than its own, like the coral which builds its worlds by a law superior to itself, though through its obedience it is permitted to bloom in instinctive and conscious life at its summit, so does she go gladly on in the way of his appointment, and Poetry, Painting, Music, and Sculpture, ay, and even Philosophy and the orator's gift become but playthings in her power.

"O glorious!" said Zoë; "how can I be all this? It is the ideal of my life, the more than wildest hope of my brightest day-dream."

"Not simply by dreaming and aspiring, nor even by purifying your nature at the perennial fount of truth, nor even by the prayer of your most saintly hours, but by hard labor, by dutiful performance of every duty which is nearest you, through every season of your life."

"The great Thorwaldsen told me as much when I was a little girl. I have never forgotten it, but it seems as if I were disobeying one law of my nature while obeying another, to do all the duties which Miss Ingemann imposes upon me, so I get puzzled."

"What do you mean, Zoë?" said Mrs. Liebenhoff. "I know that your teacher is of a rather stern nature, but l had always supposed her a woman of high principle."

"O yes, she is most truthful and conscientious. We have grown up under her care with a hatred of everything false and unworthy; but she is very rigid in her decrees towards every one alike. For instance, she thinks mathematics a prime discipline of the mind, and we all have to take such awful doses of it. To Hilda it comes natural to calculate, and she says it has done her giddy head-piece, as the dear girl calls it, a deal of good; but I have no talent for it, my head aches, my heart is discouraged, and I become utterly frantic over my hard problems, and Miss Ingemann I verily believe thinks I am *non compos*, and I can't but think treats me accordingly. Did you like to study Algebra, ma'am?"

"No, my dear; it would be a sight to see the regiment of artillery, cavalry, and dragoons who could conquer the citadel of my tower of intellect and hang upon its bruised and battered walls, as I am sure they would be, a banner with a problem in Quadratic Equations well solved, for a symbol of victory. No, no, judge my *mens* by its capacity for algebra, and I am minus altogether."

"That is really encouraging. I wish Miss Ingemann knew it. We should get on much better together if that study was permitted to go by the board, for I am a dreadful trial to her in this respect, and she to me no less, to tell the truth. I dream of her some nights as a guide-board to heaven, with puzzling sums all over her, which I am to work out truly or lose my chance of salvation."

"I will speak to Miss Ingemann," said Mrs. Liebenhoff; "or rather, I will request my sister, Mrs. Körner to do so, who is a favorite with her. I have never got into her good graces, not being *prononcée* enough for her taste, I believe. A few words of suggestion from her, will perhaps influence her to change your studies a little. She knows that Lina has always loved you."

"Thank you," said Zoë, looking rather doubtful however about the result of this interference.

"Do you like history, Zoë?" continued Mrs. Liebenhoff.

"I like to pick plums out of it, here and there, in the shape of the rare characters of men and women and striking events, but I hate accounts of wars and battles which make so much of the history of the past, and in fact, I think there is a great deal too much said about very stupid, uninteresting, and very wicked people, whom I think our Lord would have put quite in the back-ground in his estimation had he known them," she answered.

"Yes, the chief thing which interests me in history, is what is called its philosophy—the showing as it were, the thread of God's Providence running through all time, with the light of his loving care resting over and working with the affairs of men, ever bringing good out of evil, and causing all changes and revolutions, no less than the more slow and silent weaving of the warp and woof of events together, to tend slowly but surely to the accomplishment of his benevolent and harmonious plan in creation. If a historian aims at this as a chief end of his labor, and especially if he recognizes in Christianity the great moral and spiritual power which is to solve all the difficult problems of humanity, so far as they can be solved in life, and to bring light out of darkness, I am placed in sympathy with him at once; but if he merely piles up masses of facts without recognizing these truths, I may find his book a

useful granary to gather needful materials from, but the
man interests me but slightly, and I have not full trust in
his work.

"Have you any more moral to my story for my edifica-
tion?" said Zoë, looking up archly at Mrs. Liebenhoff.
"Please give me the whole of it."

"I think you need it, for you are not converted yet to
my unpalatable doctrine, so I repeat: repress your imagi-
nation until your other powers are strong in proportion to
the elevation and extent of its flight; for, Zoë, we women
need to throw out every anchor that we have, to save us
from drifting into the whirlpools that would swallow us, or
upon the strands where we should bleach out our lives,
like the ghost-flower, and only in dying reflect the faintest
rays of the descending sun. For no Gospel is truer than
that she may be born in that securest of retreats, a home
in middle life in a rural district, under a father's eye apos-
tolic and yet fitted by his sagacity and purity to guide her,
with a mother (how can one speak worthily of her tran-
scendent worth?) gentle, pure, and loving — in the highest
sense simple, far-sighted, and wise, in the very centre of a
circle of brothers and sisters most kind, disinterested, and
affectionate, with but few incidents to vary life's serene
monotony, making but one pilgrimage into the high world
of conventionalism, affluence, and comparative luxury, and
that one relieved, ay immortalized to her mind and charac-
ter forever, by contact with exalted excellence, dignity,
high intelligence, and beauty — with a marriage of affec-
tion, in which the most generous freedom allowed her is
only equaled by the joy with which every fresh develop-
ment of her powers is received; childless, it is true, but
this scarcely regarded as a want by one to whom quiet in
the inner life and the opportunity of unoccupied com-
panionship in all his pursuits with the beloved one, is so
indispensable; with friends and objects of interest sufficient
to employ, enrich, and beautify her life above the common

lot; and yet, Zoë, *and yet* so much greater is the soul than its accidents, so exacting has God made it, in at least the feminine form, that, while it falls short of one good of its own being, and from its out-look sees the majority of its sex, wandering bereft and forlorn, miserable by their exposure and ruined by their fall into sin, shame, and delusion that, Niobe-like, at one time she is turned into stone and anon the shrieks of the Pythoness and the wailings of the prophets express for her all too feebly her sense of her woe, until she sees that, under God, she is to be an instrument of their relief and uprising, when there rushes through her being such a full tide of bliss as is known only to the elected of God. O Zoë, trust not to the uncertain, deceitful imagination, but labor, strive, pray for the strength which is needed even more for the perils of its seasons of joy than of its sorrows."

"And you never dream, madam, though from what you say, I know it is your nature to do so?"

" Listen to my teaching and ask not for my practice, that is your part, dear. It is hard to expect me to do both, and you neither," said she, laughing.

"Ah," said Zoë, " and you are one of the false preachers who cry aloud and point for the people to go up the stony hill-path, while they turn aside into the opposite flowery one. O fie!"

" I will at least say this in justification of myself, my little accuser, that through the whole year I do my best to act up to my own rule, while spreading my life over the thousand objects of care and interest which come within the sphere of a woman's life whose husband lives for the public weal, and I take only now and then a flight into the beloved, fancy-world, though through all its toiling hours and busy scenes come up visions of this same couch at this luxurious time, when our few, fervid days of summer give me a fitting excuse to shut the light out to the point of mystery, and I lounge and revel in dream-land

for a brief time, as it is the thirst of my nature to do
And you need not think that I have not my reward; for the
little grub which lieth patiently at the base of the earth-
pyramid, working out in silence, amid scorn and a sense
of degradation, but with patience and trust, the appoint-
ment of its Maker, is rewarded at last with its beautiful
butterfly being. Slowly and tremblingly she creeps up
over one green leaf and orange flower to another, until at
last she reaches the summit of the shaft, when gladly she
opens her purple and starry wings to the light, and what is
so bright and so gladsome as she? For it is with no vain
presumption that I say it, that after a childhood weighed
down by unnatural mental anxiety and premature care, fol-
lowed by a stormy and perilous youth, at times nearly ship-
wrecked among the floods, then scorched by central fires,
and anon withered and seared by the sterility of the arid
deserts of life, through all of which I strove to be faithful
and true, I am now, not rewarded, Heaven forgive me if I
ever, for a moment, conceived the idea of such ingratitude,
but inconceivably, immeasurably, unmeritedly blessed with
childhood, youth, and middle life in one, and through his
abundant aid who endowed me, I have the control of every
faculty of the nature he has given me."

"There comes Hildal" said Zoë.

"Good evening, madam," said she, as she entered.
"Pardon me if I interrupt you. The servant directed me
to your room."

"Welcome to *my* sanctum; you are already familiar to
my husband's, I believe "

"Yes, madam, I have that privilege. Is Mr. Liebenhoff
at home?"

"Yes, and here he is; come to give an account of
himself, I ween, for disobeying me. I ordered him to be
quiet as he is not very well; and here he dares to return
to me with the dust upon his feet of every street in the
city, to say nothing of what he gathers in the hovels he

14

visits. I shake off mine," said she, stamping as she stood
before him, "as a testimony against such undutifulness,
and give him a boxing into the bargain."

"That I can at least defend myself against," said he.
"But I will try and not be too savage towards the wife, lest
1 should alarm and disgust these young marriageables with
the holy bonds."

"Marriageables! Heaven forbid for these eight or nine
years at least," said she. Spare them as long as possible
from miserable servitude like mine. See my chains and be
pitiful towards me, ye tender young hearts," said she, catch-
ing up a wreath of flowers and holding it up with mock
despair in her face, and then, quick as thought, throwing it
over her husband's neck and leading him along by it.

The girls laughed, and then said that as twilight was
deepening they must return home. After affectionate
adieux and repeated invitations to come again, they de-
parted.

"How funny Mrs. Liebenhoff is," said Hilda. "She is
so different from what I thought her. O I shall like to
visit her. Let's go next week again."

"Yes, we will," said Zoë. "But I like her for other rea-
sons than her fun." And she became silent and thought-
ful, and heeded but little the continual chatter of her
friend as they walked homewards.

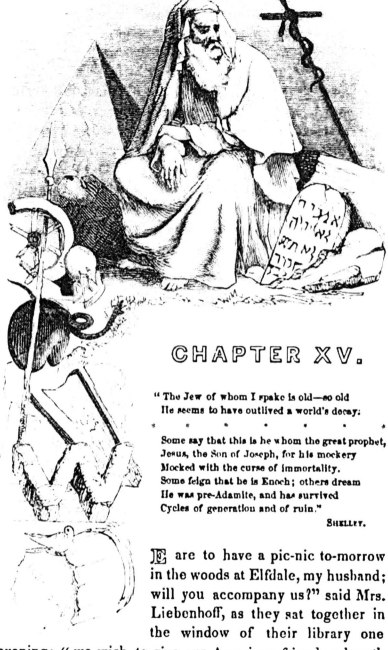

CHAPTER XV.

"The Jew of whom I spake is old—so old
He seems to have outlived a world's decay:

*　　*　　*　　•　　•　　•　　*

Some say that this is he whom the great prophet,
Jesus, the Son of Joseph, for his mockery
Mocked with the curse of immortality.
Some feign that he is Enoch; others dream
He was pre-Adamite, and has survived
Cycles of generation and of ruin."

SHELLEY.

E are to have a pic-nic to-morrow in the woods at Elfdale, my husband; will you accompany us?" said Mrs. Liebenhoff, as they sat together in the window of their library one evening; "we wish to give our American friends a breath of the delicious odor of our pine-woods, and a glimpse of our country life at this halcyon season. You *will* go, dear, will you not?"

"I cannot, I am sorry to say; I have much to do about this church matter you know; our vacation comes soon, and I wish to have all settled before that time. Go you and enjoy yourself, and my play shall be by-and-by."

"And after that moving discourse of mine, you can find it in your heart to tell me all this without a blush! I see you are just like other sinners of the common clay of the world. You agree that the preaching is all very good, and you mean to repent and be converted—O yes, certainly, nothing else, but not until you have committed the very last sin, which seemeth good to the perverse nature within you. Pray heaven, it may not then be too late to turn from the evil of your ways," and she looked upon his pale face with solicitude.

"What a crooked stick of a husband she has got, has she not? I wonder how she happened to take him to lean upon; does she not repent of her bargain, the little wife?"

"Too little crooked is the difficulty for this naughty world; I thought I had proved that to your satisfaction in my memorable sermon. Why, I do believe you have forgotten it! How discouraging to be a preacher! But, as I was saying, if you walk through life so erect, like a tall white pine tree, you will blow over, or break off, or be torn up by the roots in some unlucky gale or other."

"*You* are not a willow precisely; your sap has too much exhilarating gas in it for that, for though you may droop once in a while, before I can get across the room to comfort you, ten to one, you have played some trick upon me, and are ready to meet my condolence with a laugh in my face."

"It is all out of sheer compassion, I assure you. You have so many 'live vidders,' as Sam Weller calls them, and forlorn elderly maidens to console, and tempted, endangered young girls to keep out of harm's way, and young men's harum-scarum ways to straighten, and old men's bitternesses to sweeten, and the wounded, bruised, and out-of-sorts generally to heal and set right; to say nothing of being chief purveyor for the community at large in their worldly affairs, that I long ago made up my mind to resign all claim upon you."

"Who brought home that nice market-basket, this morning, full of the delicacies of the season, to say nothing of a pretty bouquet of flowers and a Cape of Good Hope shell into the bargain? How unhappy I am to have such an ungrateful wife!"

"O, of course you must eat something under all these inflictions, else you might fail of strength, and flowers and shells, and pictures, and such things, I am going to live upon in the future; I don't believe in eating, we think too much of creature comforts. Thank you, my dear husband, for everything of beauty you give me, and they are not a few; each leaf, petal, and full-blown flower, and tint of the shell is suggestive to me and nourishes my higher life. And as for pictures, they are my quartos and folios now-a-days."

"I am afraid you *will* grow willowy upon such ethereal food. Pray put this doubtful nutriment, for the *corpus* at least, between good, substantial slices of bread and butter, by way of sandwiches, you know; I really cannot spare you yet."

"Well, anything to please you; but don't be alarmed about losing me, I am going to be like the yew tree, that grows and grows until it seems to be past living, and you are on the point of cutting it down as a dead incumbrance, when lo! it makes a crook and out it shoots again all as fresh and new as ever, and thus it does indefinitely. Don't you see some new sprouts in my pericranium now?"

"Yes truly, but that is nothing new. You have been growing younger ever since our marriage. I must tighten the reins and disturb your happiness a little, or I shall

have upon my hands 'the child-wife' which Dickens writes
about. But it is bed-time, especially if you go into the
country to-morrow."

"Yes, tighten the reins, please do; I want more op-
portunity of curvetting and prancing than you give me.
Wouldn't I show my paces?"

The next morning, bright and early, the little lady was
up, spreading bread with butter for sandwiches, cutting
cake, and collecting from her storehouse the various dain-
ties which northern women make a great point of accumu-
lating for special occasions, if not for daily use. To see
the generous provision she was making, one would incline
to dissent from her assertion that she was going to eschew
creature comforts; and her husband, as he passed her on
his way out, hinted as much, adding that the source of the
new shoots of the yew tree was no longer a mystery.

"A truce to your insinuations," said she; "Zoë Carlan is
my especial charge to-day, and I am going to try to add
some pabulum to her physique, or she will go off some day
in cloud and vapor. She is the most dreamy little thing
ever inclosed by mortality. I thought in my zeal I could
make her common-sensible and contented with life in one
or two interviews; but no such thing. I believe I have so
far had exactly the contrary effect upon her, and that is
not the worst of it either, for she carries me back to my
foolish youth so completely by her great weird-like eyes,
looking over, as they do, into 'Borrooboola-gha' continu-
ally, that ten to one, I shall find myself there with her,
careering over the desert upon my Arabian steed with
Abdallah by my side, telling me of his feats with his forty
thieves, and whispering of our evening rest on the oasis by
the side of the fountain, under the cocoa-nut palm-tree
and —"

"Whist! the little wife, what is she talking about?" said
he, stooping towards her and raising her laughing face
to his.

" O just giving you a hint that I am a part of your parish that needs looking after a little as well as the rest. Good-by," said she, tying on her bonnet, and taking her basket on her arm. " I told Zoë I would call for her on my way to the public conveyance. If we don't return before midnight you may know that we have dissolved into thin air, and to-morrow morning when you visit your favorite Cala-canthus you will find me there before you, in the shape of a heavy dew. Until then, adieu."

Arrived at the carriage-station, they found Mrs. Körner and her children, Miss Dahl and Miss Meldan, friends of hers, the two American young ladies, Miss Holberg and Mrs. Castonio, a favorite friend of Mrs. Liebenhoff, who, with Zoë, Hilda, and herself, including baskets of every shape and size, bursting with refreshments, filled to somewhat more than the point of comfort the well-sized vehicle.

Just as they were leaving the city, Mr. Körner's bright face appeared at the window.

"Here you all are I perceive. Success to you! Good-by, darling," said he to the youngest, who, with outstretched arms, was petitioning for his attention.

" You will come, dear, will you not towards evening?" said his wife.

" If I can; but don't expect me too confidently, I have so much to do. Fare ye well," said he, kissing his hand to them as they drove away.

' Widows indeed, if not widows in name two-thirds and a half of the time!" said Mrs. Körner. " I have got a plan for making a general conflagration of the notaries' offices in the city. Will you each turn out with your torch on the occasion, my friends? The signal shall be: 'Down with *business;* up with reasonable and religious good works.'"

" You are fortunate if you have no religionists who put a technical meaning to that term," said Jenny Hale, "and cover with opprobrium, as they do in my country, the sect to which I belong, for believing in their importance."

" What do they believe in?" said Miss Dahl, " bad ones!
Then their cry would be — Down with Odin; up with
Loken !"

" I must do them the justice to say," said Jenny, " that
they would not own to that watchword, but that is really the
practical effect upon our countrymen. Loken *is* let loose
in every direction, as every morning newspaper shows in
black and white, and I attribute his rampancy to the domi-
nant church and self-styled evangelists keeping him before
the people so continually in their sermons, putting him too
nearly on an equality with ' our Father in heaven,' horrible
to say! and especially insisting upon it that we are all his
subjects—that we are made so that we must obey him
whether or no, unless a miracle is wrought upon us to pre-
vent it—and that our more than probable destiny through
eternity is to burn up forever, without consuming, in the
bottomless pit. Now, if that would not have the effect to
exalt his pride, his expectations, and increase his power
over us, if his black majesty *really does exist*, at the same
time that it tended to make us powerless against his arts,
I leave it to the true, simple-minded, sensible and devout,
to determine."

" Come," said Theresa, " I put my veto upon this doc-
trinal talk; I have too much of it at home; I am tired of
the very sound of anything that smacks in the least of Cal-
vinistic dogmas. It is blasphemy in the worst sense, their
Druidical belief. ' Belay that,' as the sailor said to Father
Taylor, in his chapel, when he was dealing it out in a
somewhat mild form on a Sunday, 'give us something
about Napoleon Bonaparte,' or anything else as opposite as
possible."

After a pleasant drive of five miles, the party arrived at
the wood where they were to encamp for the day. It was
composed principally of pines, hemlocks, and firs, although
beeches, oaks, and other forest trees were intermingled,
forming a full and grateful shade from the fervid heat of

the sun. For his summer's reign in this northern latitude, though short, is powerful, and all the more yielded to by the inhabitants from being so distinct from the nature of his sway at other seasons of the year.

There they met a party of their country friends, and after the first friendly greetings, the chief object seemed to be for each one to make herself or himself as comfortable and happy as possible. Mr. and Mrs. Pendleton soon arrived in a britzska.

"What a lovely spot!" said she, as she alighted. "These fragrant pines, and this assembled group, with their costumes fitted for the occasion, remind me so much of home, only with this important difference, I did not, as is my custom there, get up at four o'clock in the morning to prepare for it."

"Veterans in the service of society always get their reward if they wait long enough," said Jenny Hale. "Please make the most of this respite from your long campaign in the warfare between *chicken-salad* and *chopsticks*, your *flowers* and the *Floras*, to say nothing of *ice-cream* and *screamers* in the shape of all the children in the neighborhood."

"O horrible!" said Theresa. "Save us from such detestable puns, I beseech you."

"Bad enough to be good, are they not? But you should kindly encourage my first attempt. I will seat myself by Miss Dahl. She will have a fellow-feeling for me. She must have made a beginning sometime though she shows such facility now in this species of wit."

"What a beautiful piece of embroidery that is you are working!" said Mrs. Liebenhoff to Miss Meldan.

"Yes, it is a traveling-bag for a young friend, who is to be married soon; I am willing, so far, to weave a thread into the destiny of the fair creature's future. Farther than in some such way, I shrink from going."

15

"Then you don't believe in match-making any more than I do," said Mrs. Liebenhoff.

"No indeed, I have seen too much trouble from such sources to attempt so dangerous an enterprise. Let each couple pair themselves, I say."

"No one but the Highest is equal to it in my opinion. He who has tempered each of his children according to his own sense of beauty and fitness, alone knows the adaptation of one to the other," said Mrs. Liebenhoff.

"Then you believe that matches are made in heaven?" said Theresa.

"All true marriages are," said she. "All might be in the best sense if we would have it so, but there is great infidelity on this point as well as everything else connected with our highest life."

"How is a body to know?" said Theresa, "if her marriage is ordained? I desire light upon this subject, for I have a feeling that I am fated to be dreadfully taken in, in this awful business. The very thought of it makes me frantic. What is your rule for knowing? Do you find it written in the Bible, chapter and verse? or are you impressed, as the spiritualists say? Do tell me, for pity sake."

"I have no rule for any one but myself. Mine worked well for me, but it might not for you; so you don't get it with all your urgency. That is my own secret, but you cannot convince me that my marriage was not ordained above. There are quite too many rules of life in the world and too little of acting up to the highest *spirit* of our nature and God's requisition. The great thing is to reach an elevated plane of thought and feeling, and then most of the perplexities of life would be solved. But where is Zoë?"

"Wandering off alone," said Hilda; "shall I follow and make her return?"

"No," said Mrs. Liebenhoff, "I will walk with her a few minutes."

She found her standing perfectly still, looking at a large spider's web, which was woven from branch to branch on the dead limb of a tree above her head.

She started on seeing Mrs. Liebenhoff, but was reassured on finding it to be no other than her friend.

"What strange creatures insects are!" said she. "They seem to me a sort of revelators, if I may so speak, of our fortunes, and in consequence, impress me with a kind of awe."

"And what does 'Mrs. Hairy-leg spinner' deign to announce to you of your experience or destiny? That you are to be very industrious and practical; that you are to build your own house, and keep the larder well provided?"

"O no; but, that as she sits solitary and despised in the centre of her world, so am I alone and peculiar in the sphere in which I am thrown; and yet God alone knows if we are not equally with others living truly according to his will."

"I think, dear, if the spider could speak, she would tell you that you informed her of that fact quite as much as she you. However I am not quite free from superstition, as it would be called, about a thousand such things. I have not made up my mind about them, and perhaps never shall in this world at least; for, in a universe of infinity, how can finite beings expect to know everything? Much must necessarily be indefinite, and here comes in our glad privilege of trust, faith in God and his Providence, which is much better than going to spiders to have your fortune told. And, Zoë my love, pray combat this idea which I see is fixing itself in your mind that you are peculiar. It is pernicious every way. You will, through it, grow morbid, unnatural, and unhappy. I don't like *peculiar* people, they are so self-conscious and disagreeable. Come, let us return to the company."

"I dislike to, they stare at me so; I look so different from them one would think I was an ourang-outang, to see them gaze upon me. It is as much as I can do to prevent playing some odd trick or other when their eyes are all upon me. And I must tell you that one sunny day, just at the opening of spring, Hilda and I walked to the outskirts of the city, and while she ran aside for some purpose, I sat down on a stone to wait for her. A group of children gathered around me, and there they stood with staring eyes and open mouths. I had just eaten an orange and had cut the rind round into strips. I put one of them to my eye for a quizzing-glass and grinned at them with all my might. You would have laughed to see them run. 'It is the queen of the dark Elves,' said they, 'run, run, or she will carry us into her kingdom under ground, where we never shall see our mothers again!' I thought Hilda would have died laughing, when she returned just in time to witness the fun. She actually rolled upon the ground, and she had her best pelisse on too."

"Well, we are never satisfied in this life," said Mrs. Liebenhoff. "It would be a great convenience to me to have a more distinct character than I have to *my* face; then I should not, so often as I do, have the trouble of telling my name. To my butcher, my baker, my grocer, and the shopman, I repeat it over and over again, when I direct packages to be sent to me. Latterly, I have formed the habit of saying, when I enter the presence of persons that I have not seen for the last six weeks, 'Mrs. Liebenhoff, ladies, how are you?' and to gentlemen, who have sat at my board and received, with the utmost graciousness, everything in the way of hospitality I can grant them, when they meet me abroad, a bare portrait, without the setting of my house, and to my cordial greeting, answer, with an indifferent look, 'You have the advantage of me, madam: I don't recognize you,' I simply say, 'O, ay; I suppose so,' and pass on."

"I should have known you, after my first introduction, if I had met you in Timbuctoo," said Zoë.

"I have no doubt of it dear, simply because you have another style of measurement than the superficial one in vogue. But here is a new arrival."

"Do you know all these people?" said Zoë.

"Yes, more or less, enough to bow to them, though some of them would not say the same of me for reasons aforesaid. That full-faced gentleman is Mr. Calthrop. I have called at his house when riding into the country with mutual friends; I just bowed to him and he looked wonderingly at me, as much as to say, 'Who is that common-looking woman? She could not have bowed to me.' However, that is his affair, not mine. It was proper that I should be civil to one whose hospitality I had received."

"Who is that sweet-looking woman near him, talking with animation to Miss Meldan?"

"It is his wife, simple, artistic, and loving. They rise each morning after a twelve years' marriage to a prolonged honeymoon, and as they wander, hand in hand, around their beautiful grounds, they drink in with appreciating eyes the beauties of shrub, tree, cloud, sunlight and shadow, and thank the good Giver of their varied blessings, with pious and grateful hearts. If they are in fault, it is that blessed with wealth, culture and health, they feel too little their obligation to return in the direction of their fellow-men the benefits which flow to them from God. She says she feels nearer to Him through communing with nature than through humanity. It may be so; we need to bathe our spirits in the silence, solemnity, and loveliness of its beautiful scenes; yet it should be but at intervals, only to return more fresh and enthusiastic, to labor for the world's good; for only in proportion as we do our full part towards its renewal and advancement, are we saved when in our retirement from an aimless dilettantism, or a selfish, or perverted life. In the very Eden in which we have thought

to ensconce ourselves away from all the defilements of life,
shoots out the serpent-head of evil, and alas! his trail winds
itself gradually through its holiest works, showing that
humanity in ourselves, no less than in our kind, is greater
than nature, and only as we grasp the idea of the height
and depth of its vastness, and are inspired to labor for its
full manifestation by removing from it the crust of selfish-
ness and wrong, and every species of narrowness, can we
have a just feeling of self-satisfaction and be saved from our
most dangerous enemies, our unoccupied selves."

"And who is the tall gentleman with the full brow, talk-
ing with Mrs. Petersen?"

"It is Mr. Keutsch, an influential man at court."

"I observed he looked as if he expected you would
greet him farther than by a passing bow. Do you not know
him?"

"Yes, he has been at our house, but I shall not trust to
his memory to recollect me. My bow was for his speaking
manly and courageous words for the independence of
Schleswig Holstein, which so few of our noblemen dare to
do; I honor him for that."

"Who is that gentleman walking with Miss Carden?"

"It is Mr. Henshom. Don't they enjoy dissecting the
last new literature and philosophy together? and they do it
in pretty good style too, only that they are too minute in their
criticisms to suit me. My scissors, which I use in that
line, are not over-sharp, for I have an instinctive fear of
damaging the *interior spirit* of life and its simple expres-
sion by cutting and hacking right and left, as some do.
When I find *that* to suit me, I am rather blunt in my per-
ception of inferior faults. Many a young Miss in her
teens has overthrown and ridden right over me, when
mounted upon her exegetical pony and running a tilt
against the religion, learning, science, and art of the past
and present times, besides crowning one author with im-
mortelles and completely extinguishing another in the

same breath. I sometimes amble along with my mode-
rately-paced nag for a brief moment or two, until I see what
a fearful campaign it is going to be, when I turn aside
quietly into the first green wood near, which offers a slight
but refreshing illusion to the senses, and then I let the
poor, mortified animal browse a little before I return home
to shut her up in the stable until the good God relieves us
from the sharp perils of these dangerous times, where
nothing is sacred enough to escape being picked to pieces
by our critics."

" Do they visit you?"

O yes, Miss Carden is my friend, earnest, intelligent,
and religious. She only needs to see more clearly that
the study of books is not the sole enlightenment of life,
but that when one has accumulated such stores of know-
ledge as she has, and acquired her discipline of mind, that
if there is a different sphere from any which she has yet
occupied, open for her, it is the very one most assuredly
which her soul needs, in which to bring up its flagging,
more passive power, so to speak, and lay to its proper level
the watchful, critical, exacting intellect.

"As for the gentleman, we know each other—no we
don't—and yes we do again. Not so well, however, as if
he were not born in the last century, and I quite far along
in the present."

"O you jest, madam!"

" No, he is nearly a hundred, that is in his opinions,
which are conservative to the point of the admiration of all
staid old nobles and dowagers, who look very suspiciously
upon any quickstep in the march of progress. Still I am
undecided again. What has come over me as well as him-
self? He has been speculating theologically and philoso-
phically, and his ancient basis is a little shaken. I see it
in his face, his manner, and his curt style of answering the
most simple and innocent questions, as much as to say,
' You are going to look me through, are you? You don't

seize upon my secrets.' I wonder if when he goes to his home far away, he will sit down by his beloved mother and say, ' you taught me to be good when I was a little boy, and the same instructions, hallowed as they are by every thought and memory of you, dearest mother, stand me in good stead in my manhood; but as my mind grows, there are opening upon me vistas through which I look, half fearful and half joyful and dimly discern, as I think, higher truths than have been familiar to me of yore, in the distance—and now, my best friend, tremble not for your son, if with prayer, with the Scripture, and your counsels to guide me, I venture into what may seem to you dangerous paths; for, through Christ, I trust to be guided safely to the light and seize, through a high conviction, upon these glorious verities, and bear them as trophies of my soul's warfare with intellectual blindness and error to your feet, my mother; when together we will bless God for that great good of our being, a pure, unadulterated conception of Christianity.' In this enterprise may heaven speed you, my old, middle-aged, young friend.''

"How bright and well Mrs. Petersen looks to-day! I wish she liked me; I think I should love her so much," said Zoë.

" You must speak to her frankly and cordially when you meet her, my dear. You do not often see her, and then you are so shy that she has no opportunity of knowing you, occupied as she is with her children and many other objects of interest. But her brightness and willing sacrifices for the pleasure of her friends, are not the true gauge by which to measure her physical vigor or her soul's equanimity, for she has had a great sorrow and has heavy cares; and though, to the superficial eye, she may seem to pass through them unscathed, yet there are abysses in our nature which, young as you are, Zoë, you are fast learning, may be stirred to their deepest and blackest extreme, and yet convey no echo of the hoarse and fearful

roar, which rises and swells and subsides in the hearing
only of the Infinite, revealing to mortals the tumult below
only by the brighter rainbow hung over the spray of its
floods.   What matters it if no human sympathy can pour
oil upon the troubled waters to smooth them to peaceful-
ness, if through their commotion comes all the more grate-
fully the still small voice of God, our Father, whispering
of rest and reward in that world where 'there is no more
sea?'   But here is Miss Holberg."

"I come to share your bank with you if you will
allow your tête-à-tête to be broken in upon, Mrs. Lieben-
hoff."

" O certainly, with all pleasure.   Is it not a pretty
tableau opposite—the ladies with their fanciful costume,
and the children with their heads wreathed with leaves,
dancing on the green?"

" To say nothing of the grave relief to the butterfly scene
which the gentlemen present," said Miss Holberg.

" Yes, but I am falling mightily in love with women in
these days.   They seem beautiful to me in every way, and
I have many, many questionings with myself about their
position in society as it is."

" Unfortunate for me to come upon you in this particular
mood of yours, as it is of one of the other sex I wished
to speak to you.   I hear you are taking lessons, in one of
the oriental tongues, of a Hungarian Jew.   Does he speak
the German language correctly, think you?   We wish for
a teacher in our school."

" Yes, so far as my ear informs me, he does; besides,
his character inspires me with so much confidence that I
do not think he would attempt what he cannot do very well;
and it has been his chief medium of intercourse with his
countrymen since childhood."

" Is he married?"

" No, he has lived too busy and turbulent a life for such
quiet happiness.   From his student life, he entered heart

and soul into the Hungarian revolution, from which he has
borne away some honorable scars."

" Does he know Kossuth?"

" Yes; he is his intimate friend and profound admirer.
He says, rising as he does so, and with emphatic tone, that
he is the noblest being on the face of the earth. He jour-
neyed at an inclement season, over a long and tedious way,
to apprise him of the traitorous designs of Görgei, gathered
from his own observation, and begged him, for the sake of
Hungary, to concentrate the power of the kingdom more
in himself. But Kossuth, true to his Christian and repub-
lican principles, refused to appropriate to his own person
a dignity and rule which, to his high ideal, was inconsistent
with strict justice to his compatriots."

" And so Hungary fell! I think he had better have been
a little more commonplace and sensible, and done what
most generals would not have hesitated to do in his place."

" So Mr. Seüll thinks under the circumstances. But I
do not; and the world will yet see that, as there is a Su-
preme Arbiter above, such unflinching devotion to a high
sentiment, though apparently it may result in disaster at
the time, will bring about in the end a higher good than
any that could be gained by a most conscientious departure
from it."

" Well, we shall see. There is not much evidence of
it as yet; but to return—how old is the gentleman? for un-
married and young, are a combination that would shock
Miss Ingemann in a German teacher of young ladies."

" O anywhere between five and five thousand! the latter
age I am inclined to think. He must have sojourned with
Abraham, though I am sorry to say he is not quite his equal
in faith; he is twin brother to Joseph, as he shows in
various ways. Moses and he were special friends, though
he would have had too much self-possession to have broken
the two tables in a passion. Pity he had not intrusted
them to him in coming down from the Mount. He was

prime minister of David, and privy counselor to Solomon; but in the reign of Hezekiah he broke out in a new place as Isaiah, and I will just add that he says that he did not exactly describe our Saviour in his fifty-third chapter. That had special reference to the Jews in their captivity; but this he knew through his prophetic foresight that something very great and good was to happen to the world, and that it came in Christ and his religion."

"What form did he assume next?"

"That of Jeremiah, and uttered his memorable Lamentations over Jerusalem. Next he was in gilded captivity with Daniel, till, for his disobedience to the wicked commands of the king, he was thrown into the den of lions; but being master of the magnetic art he put them to sleep, and was taken out the next morning unscathed, to be made more of at court than ever."

"What next?"

"He was John the Baptist, and prepared the way for the coming of our Saviour; which mission accomplished, he magnanimously confessed the superiority of the Messiah to himself, and was, you know, put to death by Herod for his moral boldness in reproving him for his sin. Soon after this he appeared again on the earth in the form of a little Jewish boy. He was early left an orphan and subjected to the cruel guardianship of a miserly Pharisaical grandfather; was educated first for a rabbi, and was deep-dyed in the superstitions of the Talmud, but broke loose from the bondage only to fall in the course of ages into the no less Gentile superstition of Calvinism, through which ' wild woods ' he groped his way to the light partly by the aid of German theology and philosophy, but much more through the pure truth of the New Testament, till after all his peregrinations and transformations he stands forth to the world as John the Baptist again, but of the more spiritualized and glorified dispensation of our Lord. In short, my friend, he is the Wandering Jew *par excellence*, not the vulgar, stale idea of one so much written about, who scoffed at our Saviour on his way to the cross and was condemned to an everlasting life on earth as his punishment, but the true, sublime, all-suffering, all-sympathizing, all-conquering, and at last purified and Christianized Israelite, who is to bring the millions of his countrymen wherever they may be scattered and peeled and ground to the dust into the light, joy, peace, and full satisfaction of Christ's kingdom. I doubt whether his eye is yet opened to the view of his glorious destiny; but I know it, and rejoice that it is so. Do you not think I am fortunate in the choice of my teacher?"

"Perhaps you can bear up under such a marvelous history and experience, but I fear that he would set the girls crazy, especially Zoë here. He would just suit her fancy, but I should fear for her sanity under his administration."

"O do engage him, Miss Holberg! I know I should learn of him faster than ever before. Try me, please," said Zoë.

"I think you had better," said Mrs. Liebenhoff. "I have noticed that he has a very father-Abrahamic way with young girls, and a distinguishing characteristic of his is moral- force, and power of inspiring his pupils with the same, which, with his fidelity, and last, but not least, his very natural and true method of instruction in the languages, insure him great success."

"I will tell Miss Ingemann, and she must do as she pleases; but I must say I have some misgivings with regard to some foolish little heads," said she, pressing Zoë's to her face affectionately.

"Come," said Mrs. Castonio, running towards them, "you have given me no opportunity of chatting with you to-day, and now we are going to partake of our refreshments."

"Take a turn through this little grove with me first,"

said Mrs. Liebenhoff; and arm in arm they threaded their way through the fragrant pine wood.

"I have something to tell you in return for your confidence. I, too, am writing a book as well as yourself," said she.

"O, I am so glad," said Mrs. Castonio; "now we are more than ever sisters, having a like interest to occupy us. Do you love to write?"

"Yes, it is a great pleasure as well as relief; but the publication is the worst of it. Awful, is it not, to see fragments of one's most precious self, flying hither and thither, and gossiped over and laughed at and picked to pieces by the self-styled wise?"

"Yes; but one always has the hope of doing good and conferring pleasure, and that compensates for such annoyances."

"Yes, certainly; and I have made up my mind to put the finishing touch to the salvation of mankind by my Tale; that and the Bible are to be *the* books henceforward. None of my friends seem to believe it; they speak of it like any other common work, Göethe's, Schiller's, Oelenschlager's, etc. Only to think of such presumption! But never mind, that makes no difference. We shall see what we shall see;" and they laughed at her ambitious designs upon immortality.

There was much merriment over the multiform repast, especially the Gammel cheese made among the mountains. Mrs. Pendleton liked it, and resolved to carry some home on her return; while Theresa said it was hateful, from the strong taste of the yellow flower of which the cows ate abundantly, in the season of its manufacture, and which imparted its flavor to the milk; and as for carrying it home, she should not permit it to go on board ship, lest some Nipon, or Loken, or the king of the dark Elves, or some other one of their heathen deities or sprites, should smuggle himself into it and sink them all in the deep.

At the beautiful hour of twilight they turned their faces homewards, with many expressions of thanks and good-will to those who had contributed to their enjoyment by their assiduous attentions, and as the shades deepened, they sank into the silence and thoughtfulness which so well befits this holiest season of the day, the dividing line between busy labor and anxious care, and the rest and hush of quiet, holy evening.

CHAPTER XVI.

"The mathematics and the metaphysics,
Fall to them as you find your stomach serves you.
No profit grows where no pleasure is ta'en.
In brief, study, Sir, what you most affect."—SHAKSPEARE.

A few days after the event of the pic-nic, a group of the pupils of Miss Ingemann's school were together in one of the recitation rooms, from which their new German teacher had just departed, leaving them at leisure for the rest of the afternoon.

"Have we not caught a Tartar now?" said Adelgunda Heiliger, who was given somewhat to indolence. "We shall have to tread the exact line with him I see, or there is no knowing what will come to pass. Dearee-me, where is my book? It frightens me to think how I shall have to study to come up to his high ideas of what can be done."

"Yes," said Freya, "and the cool way in which he says, 'you will read so far for the next lesson, and in six more you will have finished this; and in three months you will be able to do so and so,' is quite admirable for simple maidens to behold. It actually takes away my breath to think what a race in learning we are to run, to say nothing of my neck's aching at gazing upwards at such a mountainous height of superiority. A Tartar! say you, why he is Hercules himself, only instead of a club he wields the vocabularies of all the languages which scattered the people at the tower of Babel."

(183)

"Nonsense," said Rinda. "The idea of trying to make a hero of nothing but a despised Jew. I wonder that Miss Ingemann should employ such a person. I do not think my papa will wish me to take lessons of him. He is very particular about my associates in every respect."

"A *despised Jew!*" said Zoë; "how strange to speak so contemptuously of that nation of which the most perfect being that ever walked the earth—our adorable Lord—was one, to say nothing of lawgivers, prophets, and apostles, who gave glory to the race! I don't understand it."

"Did not the Jews crucify Jesus, and don't they deserve all the contempt and punishment that can be heaped upon them?" rejoined Rinda, in a coarse and angry tone.

"Our Saviour said, ' Father, forgive them, for they know not what they do,' before he died, and even while suffering the death-agony; and it is not being much like him for men to harbor revenge and heap obloquy upon them *eighteen hundred years* after they committed the deed," said Zoë.

" Jew, or Christian, or Hottentot, I care not," said Hilda, "he is a splendid fellow. His forehead, eyes, and mouth are quite faultless. His nose, to be sure, might be chiseled a little more like Apollo's and not suffer in appearance."

" That is the remnant of the Jews' stiff-neckedness. It comes out in this shape, you may depend upon it," said Zoë. " Cosmopolitan as Mrs. Liebenhoff says he is in his sympathies, attainments, and power of adaptation to different circumstances, he can't surmount the strange prepossession the race have for that peculiar nose. For the rest, I have seen many pictures of the Christ, with a much lower ideal of the high-toned and spiritual than a copy of his face, when illuminated by its best expression, would present."

" You put me out of patience, talking in this style. You will be falling in love with him next, Hilda Strophel," said Rinda Brandt.

"I look like marrying Father Abraham and the patriarchs downwards, don't I?" said she, dancing around the room with great glee. "No, I am going to wed a North American Indian and live on a bluff, such as I read of at Mrs. Pendleton's, overlooking the prairies, with the sparkling rivers running through them like silvery threads; with lakes gleaming like diamonds in the desert; with oak openings here and there on their borders; and the rank prairie grass waving, and thousands of gold and crimson flowers shining in the sunlight, through which sweep the herds of the terrible buffalo, and anon troops of mustangs make the welkin ring with the

16

sound of their galloping hoofs, and their neighings and snortings."

"I suspect you are too '*loud* a thinker,' dear Hilda, to suit precisely the young brave by your side," said Zoë. "*I* should fall into his own mood more naturally. As we sat dreaming and gazing at the shadows of the passing clouds, or the flocks of wild pigeons, or the herds of deer, or may-hap were startled by the young Chippewa warrior flying across the plain on his way to fight with the Sioux, he would utter in bass the guttural *ugh*, and I in softer tenor would echo *a —ugh*, and then sink into silence and reverie again; and when 'the chambers of our imagery' were filled to overflowing, we would speak out of our hearts, one after the other."

"Yes," said Hilda, "he would say to you, 'O Zoë, life, with the drooping eye and raven feathered hair! I have stolen you from the bondage in which you were inclosed, to dwell with me upon the wilderness prairie; and when I have, with my eagle eye marked the young bison for prey and dragged him as conqueror at my saddle-bow to my wigwam, then, my life, you shall have your right, and cook for your brave the tender flesh which is to strengthen him for the conflict again.'"

"And I will answer," said Zoë, "'Yes, my brave 'Eagle Plume,' joyfully will I share with you the toils of your way, and I will open the tender young corn from its sheath, and its sweet kernel shall delight and nourish your soul. And when together we have cared for the field and the wigwam, will we mount—you, your noblest wild horse; and I, my fleetest of mules, and the wind shall sigh after us as we leave it in the rear; and the hours shall speed to their swiftest the coursers of the sun, and yet lag behind; and the tempest shall in vain follow after us with its fury, for we will outspeed them all. And when we reach the bluff, I will descend from my daughter of the wild ass and mustang, who shall graze by my side, and I will weave with the quills of the porcupine, the beautiful moccasin, while you scour the forest and prairie again for our winter's supply. And when, weary and drooping, you return to me, with no trophies it may be, to lay at my feet, then sweeter than the music of the birds of the forest, tenderer than the hush of the evening twilight, shall my voice be in soothing you to rest; or again more inspiring than the breeze from the north, telling you to test your fortunes again.' "

"Ay, ay," said Hilda: "I could do all that as well as you. Give me the Indian, and you take the Jew. I think you are the very one foreordained for our teacher."

"*He* would not think so," said Zoë, "for he would have to hang his harp upon the willow again and sprinkle ashes upon his head anew, and wail for Zoë as well as Zion. No, no, I never shall marry."

"What absurdities are you dealing out?" said Rinda. "I should think you were both moonstruck. I declare I will tell Miss Ingemann if you don't hush."

"Come," said Hilda, "let us go to Mrs. Liebenhoff's. You know she wished us to do so before the arrival of her friends from Iceland, and this is the last opportunity we shall have. You go first, Zoë, please, while I finish practising my music lesson, and then I will follow you. I know you will be glad of a tête-à-tête with her."

Zoë hastened to the parsonage.

"Please to walk into 'my ladies' chamber,'" said Mrs. Liebenhoff from the window, as she ascended the steps and entered the room. "How are you, dear? you look pale."

"I am not very well: we are pressing on with our studies very fast, as we have entered upon the last half of the term, and I am tired of them—that is all. Miss Ingemann would think it laziness and want of interest if I complained, so I say nothing."

"Did Mrs. Körner speak to Miss Ingemann with regard to changing the study of algebra for some other more congenial to the character of your mind?"

" No, ma'am, I requested her not to. The fact is, my
pride has been aroused of late by finding that my teacher
was making up her mind that my fit destiny was to be a
cook, as she found accidentally that I had some native skill
in that way, which, added to a little care and patience,
made me successful in preparing a few trifles for breakfast
and dessert, and I was determined to show her that I could
do something in the line of her mathematical exactness;
so that algebra, geometry and I go into a pitched battle
every day."

" Which is the victor?"

" O the Chaldean and Arabian of course; how could it
be otherwise, seeing that I never was made to fight with a
parcel of ciphers and circles and triangles! Let them be
conquered by those who need them; I do not. I feel that
my warfare — if I have any — is to be a moral one, with
the evils of the world, and, therefore, I must furnish my-
self with moral weapons." And her face began to assume
the rapt and contemplative expression common to it in
repose—" but (rousing herself,) I was determined to show
Miss Ingemann that I could do something besides cook,"
said she, contemptuously.

" The culinary art is by no means to be despised," said
Mrs. Liebenhoff, " for on that depends very much our
soundness of body, and through that, our health of mind.
Besides, in middle life at least, and I will say in every sta-
tion, no one can be a lady—and that in my view, compre-
hends very much, even a high Christian character, with its
troop of sister virtues; a culture in every direction, commen-
surate with our opportunities; and manners, the natural
expression of a mind thus enlightened and a soul thus en-
riched;—I repeat, no one can be a lady who has not the self-
possession and grace which a command of the general prin-
ciples, if not of all the particularities of her menage gives
her. Without this power, the exigencies of life may haply
drag her down from a queenly height of elegance, delicacy,

artistic taste, and a soft and fascinating amiability, to the frantic perplexity of a weakling who has lost her household gods; to the coarse scolding of a shrew; to the unseemly capacity of a drudge, too ignorant to fill the unwonted station without complete absorption in this necessary but second-rate department of life; or to the querulous complainings of a grown up baby, whose wedded life, opening as it did with flowers, music, and poetry, may, through her own or her parents' neglect, end in dingy ugliness, vice, or insanity.   No, Zoë, despise no useful capacity, my child, however humble."

"But one does not wish to be praised for such things," said she.

"I don't object," said Mrs. Liebenhoff, "though I crave the privilege of modifying the kind compliments of my friends, for when they tell me, as they sometimes do, ' you make the best cake and pastry in the city;' then I say to myself, 'behold your reward for struggling with your dreamy and indolent temperament, which would have led you to lie hour after hour, with your head resting upon your hand, looking at a Sybil.'"

"Ay, ay," said Zoë.

"Longing to be one, and yet squandering the time and neglecting the means which would give you more than her mysterious power. Depend upon it, a common-sensible, practical, Christian woman, in the best and highest sense, is a great deal better and a more agreeable personage than any such one-sided peculiarity."

"There you are again."

"I am as bad as Miss Ingemann, am I not?"

"O no, no, ma'am. I always feel when with her—here is a person entirely exempt from the frailties and sins of humanity, and of course she can have no sympathy with poor, weak, guilty me. Let me hide myself from her faultlessness and intolerance of wrong. And so I do as much as I can. But with you I feel encouraged and inspired, and if

I had been very, very naughty I could lay my forehead upon your shoulder and tell you all that I had done, and that as you forgave me when I was contrite and sad, so also would I hope for mercy from our Father in heaven;" and her head drooped and her voice sank into the lowest whisper of pensiveness.

"Come, my little penitent, we will wait till you sin more than I know of before I become your father confessor. You shall be shriven, however, when that time arrives, I will warrant, so don't be despairing. Let us go into the garden."

They sat down under the shade of a tree in the little inclosure and resumed their talk.

"Don't you think it is very hard to get used to the world as it is? I really am afraid I never shall."

"Yes," said Mrs. Liebenhoff, "and more than that, I never intend to. My struggle has always been to preserve my principles and sentiments intact without bigotry or vain-glory; to lead a true and natural life in a very artificial state of society, and in the midst of mean and false customs, where a low standard of life and manners is set up; to walk with a pure and affectionate spirit among my fellows, with my eye fixed with unfaltering gaze upon the banner in the skies, upon which is inscribed, 'Liberty, Holiness, Love!' But it is a weary way of traveling through life. One has too little company on the road, and I thirst more and more for the sense of companionship in my highest thoughts, plans, and aspirations. I am tired of but half uttering what swells my heart almost to bursting, so I am going to make a bold stroke and try and bring the world up to my stand-point. Presumptuous am I not?"

"The world will think so; but you are blessed in the sympathy of Mr. Liebenhoff."

"O yes, and until lately I have left to him, through his preaching, to which I have ever listened with a more entire satisfaction than to that of any other man, to express for

me my deep sense of the need of our race for the Chris-
tian religion, and his conversation in social life, varied as it
is by the expression of the most cheerful yct fervent piety,
learning, and wide information expressed with an accurate
judgment and delicate taste, enlivened by humor and
sweetened by love, has more than compensated for my own
shortcomings in this respect.   But blest with his society
and guidance for twenty years, naturally contemplative and
retiring, it cannot be but that by snatches in my busy life,
I have seized upon scraps of the intellectual wealth which
is floating all around me.   And while occupied with a
thousand familiar cares, there has been good time for it to
be assimilated into my own being, and through the broad
sympathies which a docile and appreciating reception of
Christ's teachings gives to us, all the past and present
seems gathered to a loving embrace in my soul, and the
future, through the power of our faith, is, O! so glorious
to me, Zoë, that I pant for the time when the good God
shall vouchsafe to reveal it more clearly to men, for then
would they never cease to adore and be led by him."

"Therefore you write?   O, I long to read your book!
I know it will be what I most need to read."

"Well, I still trust that not only you, but many another
will read it, notwithstanding the dampers thrown over my
hopes from time to time by prudent friends.   Ay, that to my
sex of every class and condition, I may be able to express
something of their wants, and satisfy as far as an individual
may, their vague, yearning aspirations.   For to the woman
soul, with its ideality, its delicate perception of truth and
beauty, its fervor of temperament, its religious reverence
and trust, its glance of genius and its artistic insight, there
is needed another and a tenderer expression of interest, a
closer sympathy with her peculiar trials, and wiser sugges-
tions than men can give.   They need all this from one
who has, either through sympathy, imagination or reality
'trod the wine-press' of her life's trials alone, and through

God has worked her way to the light, peace, and trust, of believing in, loving, and adoring Him, in closer and more constant and familiar communion than seems common in this cold, intellectual age. One friend tells me, on reading what I have already written, that it will be suited only to the more refined and cultured classes, that the majority will throw it aside for the flashy tale of passion and intrigue. But I do not believe it, for I have an instinctive dread of cliques, which is strengthened every year by every principle and high conviction. I was born among *the people*, I have ever lived and been familiar with and loved them. I know them, I trust them. I see between the poorest, coarsest, and most uneducated, and the most favored only the differences which circumstances create, and often I long to fly from the gilded surroundings of the one to the lowly hovel of the other, for the comfort, suggestion, and hope which I find not in satin and gold, or in her who puts her trust in their superficial splendor. So that in my heart of hearts, I have an earnest that even the most ignorant, degraded, and wretched will be brought into sympathy with me through my pen, and will find in its flow some solace, support, and strength to relieve them from their woe. And if it can, like Ithuriel's spear, touch the great heart of struggling, suffering, aspiring humanity, crushed and bleeding as it lies under the hoof of the spoiler, and it shall start up, it may be, in its ugly nakedness at its thrill, O! then will I plead that, like maniac of old, through the spirit of Christ which it is my life's aim to paint, it may become clothed in the garments of virtue and holiness, and conscious of its restoration to its right mind evermore sit at his feet. And if the lowly and fainting ones find in my tale some nutriment, enjoyment, and inspiration, then am I sure of an audience with the stronger and happier, for life is ever in an ascending series. The germ of its best products lies deep in the common mould. Gradually the little seed swells, and enlarges, and bursts its envelope. It spreads its roots and sinks its foundation down towards the world's centre. It shoots upwards and expands its leaflets to the sunlight. Every element of nature and the direct smile of the Almighty watch over it and contribute to its growth. Slowly but surely, it is elaborated, expanded, and beautified, until trunk, branch, leaf, bud, and flower attest to his wonder-working hand in creation, and his goodness in spreading it so fairly for 'the healing of *the nations*.' In like manner, as God rears high its structure and transfuses its sap into the rude bark-covering as into every delicate vein of its flower-petal, so will I utter the best that is in me, either of mirth, of sadness, or high contemplation, and send it lovingly forth to the great multitudes all over the world, nor be impatient and distrustful if it makes its way slowly among them; for this I know, that even 'a cup of cold water' tendered in the spirit of our faith, refreshes and purifies, and thus yields its reward; then how much more the very spirit of one's best life's experience, hopes, and aspirations poured out of a burning soul?"

" Mr. Liebenhoff encourages you, I know."

"O yes, I never fail of sympathy from him; yet very wisely, as he thinks, he puts a check upon what he regards as excited hopes, for fear perhaps that I should grow elated and proud; and another friend thinks I need the discouragement of some 'hardhearted man of business' to moderate my expectations, so he very properly gives me his plain opinion. But how little do we know of each other here. Afraid of my being proud! Why, I have eaten little else than *humble pie* all my life, so that I am one great slice of humility! But in this condition of lowliness, Zoë, I have learned to see clearly that God is to be glorified and man exalted by ministering as we may, to the best good of mankind, and when we have been led by one path or another to the altar of self-consecration, and experienced the blessed fruition which flows from it; you

17

may as soon look to see Orion smiling with vanity ex-
pressed in his twinkling orbs, or the moon covering her
face through a weak self-consciousness, or the sun striding
through the heavens with a step of haughty pride, as vain-
glory in such a one.   For when we are led into full com-
munion with Him, then reposes the soul upon the will of
the Most High, without care for its destiny, whether it be to
be blighted like an untimely flower, to bask like the ephe-
meron in the sun for a day, or like the sturdy oak to stand
firm against the varied fortunes of centuries.   For to know
that we are in his hands is sufficient.   I have but little
anxiety for my story, but I *know* it will go."

"I trust it will not be like many books that I attempt to
read.   It seems to me that their authors have a great many
crude ideas, which they think much of and very recklessly
express.   Another person dislikes them, and gets angry,
and sends forth another book in a very unchristian spirit to
oppose the first, when ten to one, his own ideas are not
any truer; and so it goes," said Zoë.

"Yes, criticism, criticism is the spirit of the age.   We
have got beyond our soundings upon some most important
points, and need to plant our feet firmly by the side of
Jesus upon the shore of the great ocean of truth, and take
our reckoning anew, and then we shall live in and give out
the positive, and not forever deal in negations."

"It puzzles me to hear the philosophers and theologians
talk about what they call the essential doctrines of religion.
I don't find them in the precepts of Jesus, and they seem
to me very contrary to nature," said Zoë again.

"So they do to me, and most injurious also, as turning
men's attention aside from the pure, and holy, and bene-
volent life of the author of our faith, and subverting his
faultless rules which are to be our guide.   And to one
who, when young, acknowledged the authority of these, and
has ever found that they enabled one, as Jesus said they
would, to be like the house founded 'upon the rock,' upon

which the storms of time might beat in vain, the discussion upon these knotty points seems like the talk of the demons in Pandemonium, of whom the English poet writes, when they reasoned

> "Of providence, foreknowledge, will, and fate,
> Fixed fate, free-will, foreknowledge absolute,
> And found no end, in wandering mazes lost;
> Of good and evil much they argued then,
> Of happiness and final misery,
> Passion and apathy, and glory and shame,
> Vain wisdom all, and false philosophy."

"One evening last week, there was a long conversation between our German friend, Professor Henschall, and Mr. Lias. Mr. Liebenhoff, who has but little interest in the subject, chimed in, however, with his modifications, and Mr. Pendleton described to us the extreme ground which the prevailing sects in his country took upon these vexed questions. I sat and listened to the account of these abortions of the mind until the air about me seemed to become blue and imbued with a sulphurous smell. Flames of fire enveloped the forms of our friends, their tongues were like fiery serpents, and their eyes gleamed like coals from the furnace of the bottomless pit, in which their thoughts seemed determined to dwell. I fancied my garments were becoming scorched, and I trembled lest they would draw me into this terrible vortex. I rushed out and never was the sweet air of heaven or the bright stars on high so welcome to me. 'O beautiful universe!' said I, 'ye elder scriptures of God! roll on in your majesty and loveliness, and may our ears be opened to listen to your daily and nightly revelation, for the written Word has become darkened and deadened to the eyes of mankind. They read in it the gloomy and horrible doctrines of their own perverted minds. They see in thee, O Father, but the stern tyrant, the inflexible, cruel, and unjust judge of their own hardened natures, and thy all-abounding care to thy children in sending them prophets, apostles, and above all, thy

well-beloved Son to teach us of Thee, and thy infinite love,
and how we can become like Thee, they convert it into a
terrible *scheme* which steals thy abounding salvation from
all but a few. O horrible doctrines! O unfortunate world!
O wretched, bewildered, and orphaned mankind, wander-
ing through space, (if we believe their words to be true,)
demons by birth, nurtured in corruption and sin, and des-
tined to eternal damnation! O my soul, come not into their
counsels again!"

"But these are considered the great men of the age,
are they not?"

"O yes, strong thinkers they are called; too strong alto-
gether in their love of one particular figure of the New
Testament, in which fire and brimstone are prominent. To
us Orientals, Zoë, it seems very stupid in these mighty
Anglo-Saxons to make their creeds out of our favorite
tropes and metaphors, which are so abundantly scattered
through the Bible. That comes of making metaphysics all
in all in the exaggerated culture of the *understanding*,
which is the order of the day. They will have to come
round to our ground and acknowledge that the soul is
something more than a sharp iron spike, christened *intel-
lect*, to pry into things with. They have made a pretty
mess of creation with their narrow way of dealing with it,
and with human nature, that emanation from the Divinity.
Anything is invaluable to them that shines, if it is nothing
but a piece of old carbon, brightened up by staying under
ground a few centuries. No matter what a theory is, if it
is only brilliant and ingenious. Is it to be wondered at
that the deep, crystal well of truth undefiled, hides itself
from their shallow inquiries? And yet the most subtle
results of the mind are like a dead mass of matter with-
out it."

"But there are a great many seekers after, and teachers
of truth in these days, I should think," said Zoë. "Our
new master speaks of the benefit he has derived from the

study of the German philosophers and theologians of the present day."

" O yes, if people will get into the ' wild woods ' of dark speculation and skepticism through their dullness, disobedience, pride and self-conceit in this late day of our Lord's kingdom, it is well that there are moral Hercules to venture in and drag them out by the head and shoulders, all bruised and battered, and slay the hydra-headed monster in whose grasp they are struggling. Yet in a family, that is not considered the best child who, like a fool, is always running into mischief through rebellion; nor he the most agreeable member of it, who does nothing but drag him out of it and sour his temper, may-be, by continued castigation; on the contrary, that one is best, who buds and flowers gracefully, as God intended it should, through the pure counsels and example of loving and enlightened parents, who, through his docile obedience, are at liberty to leave behind the beggarly elements of our religion and go on to higher and still higher attainments in it. So in society, it seems to me that our Father loves and approves more of those of his children who receive, with a meek and docile temper, his instructions to them through his Christ, his greatest, truest, and purest messenger, comprised principally in his sermon on the Mount and his parables, believing implicitly in the good which he says will result from them, than those who stick in the crude thoughts of the heathen, who lived before his time, or who overlay the mind with the corruptions which crept into his church after it. For the Beatitudes are the nutriment which Jesus elaborated from all that was choicest and loveliest of the fruits and flowers in the moral and spiritual universe of which we are a part, and them he places before the ages, and by his life of benevolence and love, pleads with us to grow up into their sublime, and tender, and holy disposition, and live everlastingly. And where in them do we find the so-called ' essential doctrines of Christianity?' The *spirit* with

which he walked among men, from childhood to manhood,
which shone out in his obedience to his parents; in his
zeal in the search after knowledge and light; his true sense
of the use, which he was to make of his mighty powers;
his humility, his affection, his patriotism, which embraced
the widest philanthropy; and his philanthropy which in-
closed as its nucleus the most heart-melting patriotism,
when he foresaw his country's doom; his submission to his
inevitable fate, and his martyr-death, crowned, as it was,
with the clustered virtues of filial love, confiding friend-
ship, forgiveness of enemies, disinterested regard for the
penitent, resignation and trust—this *spirit*, I say, is the
more than nectar, of which that of the gods was but a fee-
ble type, which, by drinking of it fully and freely, will
make us sublime and godlike as himself. And where in
it do we find the assumption, the bigotry, the narrow policy,
the corrupt yielding to the sins of the times, the misera-
ble fear and distrust of God, the low ambition, hypocrisy,
deception, cruelty, and fraud of multitudes, in the so-
called churches of Christendom? The eye of the world is
not couched to see all this; but I have a living proof of the
truth of my sermon, which I fear has wearied you, in my
beloved husband; and here is a letter from that same.
Thank you, Carl," said she, as she received it from the
hands of the lad who brought it. " I have not told you,
Zoë, that he is absent for a few days. Run around the
garden, or anywhere you please about the premises, while
I read it."

CHAPTER XVII.

"Not like to like, but like in difference;
   Yet in the long years liker must they grow;
   The man be more of woman, she of man:
   He gain in sweetness and in moral height,
   Nor lose the wrestling thews that throw the world;
   She mental breadth, nor fail in childward care;
   More as the double-natured poet each;
   Till at the last she set herself to man,
   Like perfect music unto noble words."—TENNYSON.

HILDA practiced her music, a difficult piece from Wagner, and then set off in her usual bright mood to meet Zoë at Mrs. Liebenhoff's.

"I shall have a merry time I know. I am so surprised to find the little parsoness so full of fun. We laughed and chatted together on our way home from the pic-nic in the public conveyance, and I mean to have a second edition of the frolic."

Full of this intention, she was running towards the house when she caught a glimpse of Mrs. Liebenhoff in the garden. She ran towards her and found her with her husband's open letter in her hand.

"Ah, I have caught you in the very act, have I not? Is it so very charming to have a lover, which one has to meet by stealth and send messages to by craft, and in short to pine after in secret—the fascinating Cicisbeo?"

"What do you mean? what has come over you?" said Mrs. Liebenhoff, looking at her in amazement, really fearing she had lost her wits; but she saw only the water-sprite with her laughing, innocent, happy face, who seemed marvelously unconscious that she was saying anything offensive. She looked at her as if she would penetrate into her very soul, until Hilda was sober, surprised, and seemed as if she were ready to cry.

" Ah, I see," said her friend, " you have been reading some naughty book or other, which has sent your wits and sense of right astray. What is it, dear?"

" Only ' Indiana,' by George Sand."

" ' Indiana!' " said Mrs. Liebenhoff. " Where did you get it? Does Miss Ingemann know what dangerous fiction has superseded her matter-of-fact class books?"

" No, ma'am. Rinda brought it this morning from her home. She says it is one of her elder sister's favorite books, and she lent it to me for an hour or two in which I could very well run through it. Where is the mighty harm, pray?"

" In its leading you to trifle, as you have just done, with the most sacred feelings of womanhood, if in no other way, my dear Hilda. Read this sentence, and then talk to me of a Cicisbeo if you can. (She holds the letter so that she may see it.) ' Together have we borne the trials and quaffed the joys of our youth, each day made happier, and I trust holier by each other; and now that from the height of full middle-life we cast our horoscope anew, whatever may betide, whether sickness or health, prosperity or adversity, we know that we can, by the beautiful experience of the past, ever repose more and more upon each other's truth and affection, which shall be God-ministers to point to the virtues and joys of the heavens above.' "

" But ' Indiana ' had an old, cross husband who made her very wretched, and so she accepted a lover. Very wrong I know, but was she not to be pitied and excused, partially? Of course, ma'am, I was only in fun in speaking thus to you."

" O yes, I know, and I agree that Indiana, and such as she, are to be pitied, who, for a loving protector and guide,

find in their marriage only a jailer, harsh, coarse, and repulsive. But our fortunes are not altogether in our own hands in this world. Indiana was under God's care and discipline no less than her husband's rule, and only he should have severed the bond between them."

"Then you would bear everything from a cruel, heartless tyrant until God saw fit to take him out of the world?"

"I do not say that. There is a cause which annuls all obligation, because first broken down by the guilty husband; and it is vain to seek to keep united a one-sided bond. It is a contradiction in terms; but whatever betide, the wife is to keep herself true. What do I say! It is only for lawyers and courts to speak thus coldly and juridically of this delicate connection, or of aught that can sever it. To the pure and religious wife it has been formed by ' our Father.' It was He who saw how his child needed to be tempered, and trained, and through what trials or joys she was to weave her wings for the skies. If he judged her strong and good enough to place in her keeping one of his most faulty ones; it was that through holy marriage he too might become meet for his presence. You can decide, Hilda, whether she fulfills her trust when she abandons him for a lover. And what was *he*, pray, this *fascinating Cicisbeo?*"

"Why, a vulgar, vicious, disgusting fellow to-be-sure! Yes, yes, I see it was all dreadful, and I am ashamed of myself and of speaking thus to you. Will you forgive me?"

"When through marriage," said she, kissing her, "my Undine has a tender and more thoughtful soul breathed into her gladsome life, she will know better than to ever whisper to herself or her friends of *Cicisbeos.* But have done with preaching! I have already sermonized Zoë and sent her away for relief. Run and find her, dear."

They now returned and seated themselves side by side on the turf.

"How do you like my new hat, ma'am?" said Hilda, untying it and laying it aside.

"Very much," said she. "I noticed it the first moment you came, and thought it very becoming."

"Then if you *are* a pious minister's wife, you like pretty things, I see."

"Why not, pray? My eyes are set in my head very much like other people's, and I profess to have as good a taste as my neighbors. I always dress just as pretty as I have the means to, and always intend to."

"So do I," said Zoë. "I wish I could be clad as prettily as the violets and lilies are. God adorns them beautifully, and I do not want to be a blot upon fair creation in my person more than in my mind and character. I have become quite converted in this respect lately."

"That is right," said Mrs. Liebenhoff, "only do not let dress encroach upon higher duties and tastes; and the more the latter take the first rank in our regard, to the well-balanced mind does external ornament seem appropriate and harmonious."

"I am delighted!" said Hilda.

"I am going to dress well even when I am very old," said Mrs. Liebenhoff. "I shall not wear four caps and five shawls about my person, like a certain old lady I heard of the other day. It is more than my share, I should take up too great a proportion of room, besides looking like a formless heap of linsey-woolsey and cotton lace; and if I am a minister's wife, I am not one to 'wear a green ribbon and look very thankful,' not I."

"How old *are* you, Mrs. Liebenhoff?" said Hilda, with all simplicity.

"What a daring question to ask a lady of my age!" said she. "That is one of the legitimate secrets of a woman past twenty-eight. The idea of my revealing it, indeed! What crooked fairy possesses the little girl this blessed afternoon ? But rather than disappoint your curiosity entirely, I will deign to inform you that I have arrived at the ' everlasting now,' which Carlyle tells us of. I am ashamed to have been so long in coming to this desired haven, but here I intend to fast moor my lifeboat and never be drifted away from it. My sister, Katrina, who is a disciple of Spiritualism, says that there is no time in the heavenly sphere, and I see no reason why there should be here, especially to ladies of my mature years. My soul is a great deal younger than when it was born into this murky time-world, because now I really begin to see daylight ahead, which is quite rejuvenating in its effect, I can assure you; so I am just of no age at all."

"Good!" said Hilda, "only alas for the birthday gifts if that era never comes round!"

"O, I get presents, I can assure you, notwithstanding that I live in eternity. Do you see this beautiful opal ring, my husband's last present, given me not to tell of his inconstancy, but that with the changes of life our love will only shine with a more varied lustre? I like jewels, they are so suggestive. My whole pearl, for instance, which the little fish forms to cover up some harassing, injurious, foreign substance, inserted by accident into its shell. What a lesson to me to envelope my troubles with the covering of a beautiful resignation, which will enable me to float through life, injuring no one by my harsh contact, but to give out the gentle radiance of this precious tribute of the sea! My garnets; of slight value in money because plentifully abounding among the common rocks of the hills: all the richer for me, showing that there are bright virtues shining out abundantly from among the rudest of humanity. My more brilliant ones, set with little pearls, mean fervor and purity combined. I know some one by whose face I might place my sparkling bracelet and say: ' What an excellent likeness!' And so I might go on to the end of the catalogue."

"But you say nothing about diamonds," said Hilda; "I really feel that my pet ring is neglected."

"O intensely brilliant and sparkling and transparent, like the great lights of the present age, but with too little depth for me! Give me the pearl which has more soul than it displays to the shallow penetration of the day! 'Sour grapes,' you will say, as I do not happen to have one. I used to try to get up great admiration for the diamond, thinking that it had been elaborating since time was, in the lowest strata of the earth's formation, but when I read that it is found in the sandstone, and of course is the result of less time and cost, I lost my interest in it somewhat. Very splendid it is of course, but I can live without it—and if I were as rich as Crœsus I would not give the foolish thousands for it that some do."

"I met a lady in the street as I came here, who I am sure rouges; her cheeks were so delicately rosy, and I have seen her when she looked very sallow," said Hilda.

"Perhaps she was flushed with heat," said Mrs. Liebenhoff. "I never saw more than one or two in my life whom I suspected of having an artificial color. Did she look as if she were masked?"

"No; I think it made her prettier than without it," said she. "She used *rather* too much powder. To be artistically put on, it ought not to lie in lines but be suffused, so as to have the face look somewhat like a ripe peach with the down on."

The two other ladies laughed.

"Let me study yours," said the elder, "so that I may adopt your style, as I suppose you have got the right medium, being an artistic judge. Well, I shall take you for my model rather than Miss Lias, who puts so much on her cheeks as to make them stand out in quite bold relief, while her eyes, surrounded as they are, with a dark circle, are cast into so deep a shadow, that they look as if some one had dealt them a heavy blow, forcing them quite back-

wards. I wonder if they are receding to look after the
lady's brains. At any rate her process of beautifying her-
self has a *stunning* effect upon me, I can assure you. O,
Hilda! my fresh, fair and frank-hearted! give to the winds
all thoughts of the paint, plaster, pomatum, and powder,
for which young ladies in these days exchange their deli-
cate natural beauties, only to disfigure and destroy them
with these counterfeits. You are pretty enough without
them. I take the responsibility of flattering you thus
much."

Hilda rushed impulsively to the little fountain near, and
dipping her hand in the water, soon washed all traces of
the powder from her face.

" Good-by to the first gay deceiver which has had the
art to take me in; and I mean it shall be the last," said
she.

"I have not told you the news," seating herself, and
beginning with fresh zest upon another subject. " Mrs.
Gylich's wedding was yesterday. Only think! her husband
has been dead but eight months. To be sure she married
an intimate friend whom Mr. Gylich loved and confided
in. She was truly inconsolable when he died, for they were
warmly attached, and she was perfectly devoted to him;
but she is very affectionate, and is one of those who always
require some one to lean upon, and that is the reason she
married so soon, I suppose."

"And could she not wait even one little year," said Mrs.
Liebenhoff, " and devote it to honor and cherish his mem-
ory, and thus blend anew their separated, yet more than
ever united lives; for when the death-vail divides them
from earthly vision, who knows but a purer and closer union
grows up between them, even while they walk to the com-
mon eye so differently ensphered? And shall another
presumptuously step between these two souls, who were
everything to each other here, ere they adjust themselves
as God would have them, to an experience of a higher and

more celestial sympathy, growing out of the earthly and lasting for aye? Nothing would make me doubt so much whether this friend were fitted to succeed him in her affections, as his appreciating no better the holiest and tenderest feelings of a woman's nature than to thrust himself thus early between them."

"Zoë," continued Hilda, "says she cannot bear to think of second marriages at all, especially for a woman. She seems to consider it an unpardonable sin in her to contract one. Now there may be cases when it would be very natural and proper in my opinion. For instance, Indiana, who married an old, disagreeable husband, not because she loved him, but because her parents made the marriage for her, I think if he had died, and she and her lover wished to marry very much, they might do so, rather than for her to remain a forlorn widow all her days. Or, I will say, even if her husband were kind and she had loved him ever so much, if he chose to leave her and go to heaven, where, as everybody says he would be a thousand times happier than she can be here, marry again or not, I don't think he would be so selfish as to wish her to remain weeping till old age over his grave, while he, perhaps, was careering through the universe, seeing all the beautiful sights and hearing the delightful music with, perhaps, some fair young lady-angel, who knows? Now confess the truth, Mrs. Liebenhoff, could you not possibly be induced to marry the dear friend, and give the excuse, if you chose, that you were *so lonesome*, as they all do? Say, please."

"My dear," said Mrs. Liebenhoff, "we will drop the subject where it is. It is one upon which I am accustomed to shun all personal reference. I am satisfied with my present destiny, and I have no wish to make any future reckoning upon this point."

Hilda looked crest-fallen and Zoë disappointed, but after a pause the latter insisted with more confidence than was usual to her: "You said the other day, dear Mrs. Liebenhoff, that you were accustomed to live through many scenes to which we are liable in life, by imagination and sympathy, and that thus you had often prepared yourself for great emergencies. Why not this for our benefit?"

"Well then," said she, with a rapid utterance, "who am I, to say that I would surely do or not do this or that in the future of a world in which God notes 'the sparrow's fall' and numbers the hairs of our heads? I have long since learned that such presumption is rebuked, by having done exactly contrary to what, in my impetuous youth, I avowed I would, and yet at the time, it seemed God's will. It might be the same in such a case. But of this, I may venture to be sure, that I never would link my life with another, divided as it would ever be to me, unless he had a nature broad enough, and a culture elevated enough to share with me each high and holy feeling, awakened by the changing experiences of life. Unless he would say in spirit, if not in words: 'I ask you to cover up for me no precious memory, or crush no natural wish to blend the name, and spirit, and deeds of him on high in meet and loving harmony with our own most consecrated acts. Together will we stand by his grave, and as I see your faithful remembrance of him, I gather fresh surety that you will be true to me, and as you have done your full duty to the deceased, so no shadow shall be cast from his tomb, and no lament come sighing from over it to darken our marriage-day, or blend its discord with the sweet music of our bridal fête.' For when nature, religion, and love combine to weave themselves into a flower-garland and crown the brow of the true woman, there need be no fear that the different spheres of her earthly life will jostle against each other in rude and painful collision, but her heart will be more than broad and generous enough, and her soul too full of melting tenderness for *him* to fail of finding in its smile the heaven he pines for."

She looked up as she finished and saw Theresa Ingalls

standing a few steps from her. She had heard her last remarks.

"A fresh breeze from the west!" said she.

"Welcome! and brush away some of the cobwebs which are sticking about these little girls' brains this afternoon. They really are too much for me with their astonishing surprises and unexpected questionings. I should think *you* had been dealing with them. At any rate, I will pass them over to the strong-minded young American, for they quite upset my equilibrium," and her face assumed an anxious expression unusual to it.

" You don't pretend to say that you find any man, living or dead, worthy of all *that* sentiment, do you? I think less of the German and Danish gentlemen, if possible, than I do of ours. Indeed I think I shall be ready to fall quite in love with them in toto when I go back; they seem to me so much more chivalrous and truly wise and refined, and in advance of yours in their judgment of us. To decide by what I have seen of a woman's life in Europe, it seems to be considered that, in general, she fulfills her mission when she cooks, sews, keeps the house, and tends the children; or if there is especial magnanimity and great desire to award her her full rights, she is to have a privilege commensurate with the whole length and breadth of her capacity, viz.: to make herself as pretty and agreeable as possible for his supreme and selfish pleasure, or if he happens to get into trouble (of course she never does) he gives her full liberty to devote her life to his *comfort* and *solace*. What wonderful condescension!"

" I know it is very much so among the majority; but the time will come when it will be seen that a woman's clear insight and quick moral sense are to serve as a barometer to warn society against corruption and sin; that her veneration and trust are to be the weather-vanes to keep the proud, speculative intellects of men in the direction of clear and starry skies; her charity and love are to enfold and keep warm the heart of the world, which otherwise would be forever imbittered, estranged, enraged, crusted over with selfishness, or blackened by tyranny and wrong— those dragon's teeth from which horrible seeds spring up the armed demons which ravage the earth—and her artistic genius is to be the element which is to beautify, enrich, and glorify life. This is to be done first through her own ascendency of soul, and then by its natural action within the sphere designed for it by its Maker. In accomplishing this, her legitimate work, she will indeed include in it every proper and needful household duty, but above and beyond these, there will be spheres for her occupancy, which will save her from a weak and degrading dependence upon man, whose love, and protection, and sense of her value to him are not up to the requirements of her nature or the commandments of God. Thus she will become the queen of realms never dreamed of by poets or foretold by seers, where she will reign in the true spirit of all dominion; even in that which giveth glory to the Almighty through her every developed and purified faculty, that he may be all in all. But there is the auspicious queen of night, the evening star; the dew is falling, let us go in."

18

CHAPTER XVIII.

THE island of Iceland, of which Mrs. Liebenhoff was a native, was discovered by Naddod, a famous Norwegian pirate, who was driven hither by a tempest about the year A. D. 860. Just before this period, Harold, the Fairhaired, had extended his dominion over all the petty kingdoms of Norway, and deprived the inhabitants of that liberty and independence which they had previously enjoyed. The consequence was that multitudes of their best and bravest emigrated to the various islands in the neighborhood, but to none so much as to the more distant and larger one of Iceland. Here they hoped to be in security from the rule of the oppressor; nor were their hopes disappointed.*

In little more than half a century the Icelanders formed themselves into a regular republic on principles of the most perfect liberty, making a wise distribution of the different powers of government, enacting laws admirably adapted to the peculiar circumstances of the nation, and by their natural genius and love of liberty combined their interests

---

* For these facts, see Henderson's Iceland.

and energies in support of a political system, at once cal-
culated to protect the rights of individuals, and inspire the
community at large with sentiments of exalted patriotism.

For four hundred years they maintained for the most
part this state of freedom, and when, at the end of that
time, they became tributary to Norway, and afterwards
were connected with Denmark, they were still permitted
to retain the spirit and the government of a free people.

The remote ancestor of Mrs. Liebenhoff, who emigrated
to Iceland at its first settlement, was head officer of one
quarter of the island, which was divided into prefectures
or sheriffdoms. He was at the same time, as was required
that he should be, a minister of religion, and upon him
devolved the care of the temple and preservation of due
respect for the rites of worship. His descendants had,
with more or less of intermission, occupied the same station,
and her father had retained it, with great satisfaction to the
community, for a period of nearly half a century up to the
time of his death, which occurred a few years before.
Thus born and nurtured among a free and religious peo-
ple, she grew up breathing insensibly their best spirit, and
in a home where narrow means contended daily with wide
opportunities for the judicious and benevolent use of large
ones, in which the dispositions and habitudes of both her
parents harmonized much more with the dispensation of
what is commonly thought sufficient by the more affluent,
than with their own small yearly pittance, it followed that
the most rigid economy in deed, though seldom alluded to
by word, was the order of the household. To meet the
various exigencies of such a life and preserve an honorable
independence from pecuniary embarrassments, the child-
ren, a goodly number, were inured to hardy toil and a
careless freedom from reliance on any of the luxuries,
which by many in the same station of life were considered
indispensable.

Living in a rural district, she shared the employments,

the sports, and the means of culture of the country people, and in a severe climate where the greater part of the year the inhabitants are confined within doors, she grew up studious and contemplative. It is well known that the advancement of the Icelanders in science and literature has been of no inferior character. At a period when the darkest gloom was spread over the horizon of Europe, they were cultivating the arts of poetry and history, and laying up stores of knowledge which were not merely to supply posterity with data respecting the domestic and political affairs of their native country, but were also destined to furnish very ample and satisfactory information on a great multiplicity of important points connected with the history of other nations. To this a wonderful combination of circumstances proved favorable. The Norwegians, who first went over to Iceland, were sprung from some of the most distinguished families in the land of their nativity. They had been accustomed to listen to the traditionary tales of the deeds of other years and had frequented the public assemblies where they saw the value and importance of knowledge. Their mythology and the wonderful scenery of their native land were favorable to the cultivation of poetic genius. The art of writing was for a long time little practiced, and in order to transmit to posterity an accurate knowledge of important events, history assumed the garb of a poetry peculiar, underived, and national in its character.

The fame of the Skalds or poets of Iceland was not confined to their native country. They visited the courts of Denmark, Sweden, and Norway, where they were received with the highest honors; and the Edda, which comprises their most important poetry, and the Sagas their historical compositions, chiefly reliable for their truth, though occasionally wreathed with beautiful fictions, were dealt out to the admiring ears of their entertainers and reaped from them a rich reward..

Thus, though the native of a bleak, barren, and frigid island, scarcely noticeable as the eye runs over the map of the more extensive and prouder countries of Europe, Mrs. Liebenhoff, it may be seen, grew up encircled by no mean environments.   Naturally of a poetic and imaginative cast of mind, she found no lack of excitement for these prevailing traits in her quiet and secluded home in the literature of her own country, no less than that of other lands which flowed in from time to time at the call of eager seekers after knowledge among the more cultured of her people.

The natural wonders of the island, too, had a powerful effect upon her training.   Here were burning mountains and eternal glaciers, rivers of lava, boiling springs and floating fields of ice, bringing from regions far to the north their intenser cold, and their wild, strange animals, where the sun is too feeble in its rays to dye their furs.   Here was displayed also on a grand scale, the Aurora Borealis, those mystic heavenly lights, now flashing out in the horizon, with a more weird-like lustre than the lightning, to disappear and be seen anew, blazing far up in the zenith, extinguishing the north star's steady light, and putting to the blush the fervid planet Mars by their blazing stare into his face, and their eccentric whirligig around him.   And when the dogs would howl and moan at the ghost-like music which accompanied their wondrous dance, she too would bend low with her protecting arm about their necks, and feel a suffocating sense of awe and dread, which made her cling to them in strange companionship.   For, to the gentle, loving woman-poet, the sublime and the awful are soon wearisome and overpowering, and she longs for the warm sunlight and tender shade, and sweet dews of evening, which may bring to her senses the distillation of flower, fruit, and tree, and hush her spiritual nature to the repose of silent communion, in which she can hear the "still small voice" of God in the holy of holies, which he has fashioned within all outer courts, even in the sanctuary of her own soul. But where in her cold clime, in which summer is but welcomed ere it is flown, where nature seems in chaos, whole regions lying blasted as it were, by the scorching fires of some evil demon, and where centuries must roll on before they put on the garments of loveliness which reflect the benignity and mercy of a God of these attributes, could she find the home of her yearnings? The occasional terrible devastations by volcanoes and shipwrecks, and the various hardships of life in a rude and sterile country kept her sensibilities painfully upon the stretch. Lacking the energetic, demonstrative qualities of the other members of her family, who were ever efficiently employed in deeds of useful benevolence, in which, it is true, she shared, though only in the quiet way suited to her disposition, she all the more sought for refuge amidst gentle scenes, and for a scope for the longings to do good consonant, at the same time, with a generous nature and very retiring habits.

To the Bible she resorted for the glowing home she desired, and the perfect ideal of her youthful aspirations. There she found, not only her way of duty and the path of peace, which comes from the sense of forgiveness, and the hope of eternal life through the knowledge of God and immortality brought by Jesus; but besides all these, the most subtle and satisfying food for her poetic being, the richest storehouse for her gorgeous fancies, and the fullest treasury of feeling with which to feed her craving, impassioned nature. So that it came to pass, that in the usual catechetical exercise of the Sabbath morning, when, dressed in their simple *best*, the children would gather around their pastor to answer his questions from the Scriptures, with her brief reply to " who was the first man, and where was he placed," there welled up images of living, paridisaical scenes, and of lovely innocence expressed in the perfect form of the first man and woman, which painted themselves

all the more enduringly upon her ardent artist-soul that
they never were expressed. With Noah, she entered the
ark and swept with the floods over the wreck of a drown-
ing world. With Abraham, she sojourned; rejoiced with
Sarah, and wept with Hagar over her sense of injury and
desolation. With Moses, she led the Israelites through
the wilderness towards the promised land, and shared with
them their varied fortunes through the ages, as conquerors,
as rebels from Jehovah, and captives in a foreign land, as
freed from bondage, and as, with mingled feelings, they
builded the walls of their temple anew.

And with their history came breathing over her, even
during the most chill and dreary Icelandic winter's night,
the waving of palm-trees and of the cedars of Lebanon,
the gurgling of the fountain, more precious than the gold
of Ophir to the weary, dusty pilgrim of the desert, and the
savor of manna to her hungry nature. And with each inci-
dent of historic life, and every scene of nature from the
hallowed East, came blended as of yore the " Thus saith
the Lord," to the acts of her present life and her dreams
of the future. As she flowered into her full youth out of
a many-sided, interior experience, needless to dwell upon,
and Jesus, the faint ideal of her childhood, became the fixed
pole-star of her maturity, little by little came out in full
relief the perfection of his character, in which no quality
stood out too prominently, leaving others only indicated,
but in which all were in just proportion, making the
whole full, round, and harmonious. As one great man
after another rose and set in history or in society around
her, wielding power for a brief period by some one over-
grown development, she clung the more closely to the
Leader of the ages, understanding through others' de-
formities no less than his own transcendent superiority, the
reason of their imperfect appreciation of him, and why, by
some he was deified, and by others denied. Then came
the resolve, which grew stronger and stronger with years,

first to live out her own conception of him as revealed to herself, and afterwards through her imagination and culture, to represent it, weaving into her fiction thoughts upon the position, and wants, and destiny of her sex in the civilization of the day; for in the uprising of the feminine element did she foresee the restoration of the world.

Married as she was most happily after the period of her early, stormy youth to a man of an intellect, character, and heart rare in their truthfulness, enlargement, and tenderness, she found in him the guide and example to aid her in her secret life-wish, and deemed herself blessed in a companionship with him through a broad range of her being, though into its intenser life his calm, and clear, and equable soul was never spontaneously led, and of which, therefore, on account of her reserve on points where she was not instinctively met, he had but little cognizance.

Mrs. Liebenhoff and Mrs. Körner were now in the happy reception of a visit from their relatives from Iceland, two sisters and a brother-in-law, with their children. After some playful dispute between the sisters, the parties were finally arranged to the satisfaction of both, and a pretty equal division made of the guests between the two mansions.

Mrs. Hansen, one of the guest-sisters, the next older to Mrs. Liebenhoff, between whom there had ever been a strong affection and sympathy, though in some respects very different, had lately become deeply interested in the subject of Spiritualism. This wide-spread delusion, if such it can be called, had taken its rise in America, but as spontaneous movements among masses of people are almost always simultaneous in different regions, showing the magical sympathy ever existing between the great family of humanity, so in Europe it was beginning to attract much attention. Mrs. Hansen, a woman of a strong, healthy mind and physique, with no predominance of imagination, but with an exact, practical intellect and of a high-toned, deeply religious character, had been led, by curiosity in the first place, to investigate the subject. After a few experiments, too well known to be repeated, to bring herself, as is supposed, into communication with the spiritual world, she had been astonished at the developments made to her inner life and its increased wealth and enjoyment thereby.

As the two sisters were sitting together the day after their arrival, the subject was introduced.

" It surprised me," said Mrs. Liebenhoff, " to hear of your being a subject of this mania, with your sound judgment to keep you right."

" Do not call it a mania," replied Mrs. Hansen; " for it seems to me the only true life, this close intercourse with the spiritual world, which is granted me."

" I do not feel disposed to deny its truth yet, any more than that of many other subjects which come up at the present day. I simply wait for further data and a stronger light thrown on it thereby, before I determine its reality. But this much I must say, that we are very ignorant of the nature of our minds, and still more in the dark upon the subject of Inspiration, the way in which we are influenced by the great Spirit of the universe; and as yet I have seen or heard nothing well authenticated which convinces me that a new mode of communication is opened between us and heaven."

" How can I account then for my power of writing involuntarily of what had never before entered my mind, and of receiving from different spirits, from our brother's for instance, information which I knew not from any other source?"

" Have you never had any false or mistaken information given?"

" Yes, the spirits are candid, and say that of earthly things they have not sure knowledge; so they sometimes mislead, and in one instance I was induced myself to take steps for the recovery of property which I found not in the possession of the person with whom I was told it was "

19

" Have you always communications from the good who have departed?"

" No; one evening I was conversing with your friend, Helenor, and I was telling her of my high estimate of her character while on earth, and the good I had derived from it, when my arm was sensibly twitched. I turned, and was addressed by a low spirit who rebuked me for flattering thus, saying, it would make her vain. 'And who are you, friend?' I said. He spoke the familiar name of Heinrich, who died soon after our venerable father. He said he had through all these years, been wandering in the lowest sphere, and knew not how to rise. 'Can you not say, God be merciful to me a sinner!' 'That is it, that is it,' said he exultingly—and so much power have these words had upon his state that he has already risen to the third sphere."

" I do not think you gain much by enlarging your society, if he is a specimen of your spirit-acquaintances. We all know the blessed effect of penitence without such a revelation."

" That is an exception to the general rule. But it is impressed upon me, that I must write."

She takes pen and paper, and in an unexcited manner, writes a page and reads it to Mrs. Liebenhoff. At the conclusion, she said, " Now these thoughts are new to me. I never even dreamed of them before. They are not mine, but your friend Nora's."

" And yet, they are in perfect harmony with Katrina Hansen's mind, character, attainments and usual mode of expression. It would require a warping of my judgment to believe these thoughts the product of any one but yourself, guided in the usual mode by the good spirit which is ever about us, helping our infirmities. One may easily be deceived upon this point, until we have much self-knowledge. Our thoughts come to us we know not how, or from whence   To the truth-loving, who has faithfully used all possible means of instruction, whose mind through mental culture, charity and a devout spirit, has been put into communication with nature, humanity and God, all these great ministers stand ready to do her bidding; and when hushed to quiet, earnest labor, they come freighted with their best to wait upon their priestess, to her the fire which burns within her may seem that of a vestal, or an angel spirit, while it is the natural but none the less wonderful result of means which the world in its spiritual deadness designates as common."

" I am disappointed. I looked for sympathy from you, Lisbet."

" And you have it, my beloved sister. Heaven forbid that it should be wanting in any experience of your life, when yours has ever been so full, so generous, and more than appreciating for me. But by keeping my judgment cool and uttering my distinct convictions, we both gain more than by any weak, yielding sympathy."

" O, certainly; and now what theory contrary to mine have you to offer me, for you may be sure of its receiving my full attention. Your remarks just now do not convince me."

" I must commence with a few words upon what I consider the connection of the Supreme Being with our spirits, if it will not tire you."

" No, certainly, I wish to know the result of your own thoughts upon this engrossing subject."

" I feel that the union of our souls with God, is regarded too much as a technical and narrow thing. It is thought that he at one time, inspires more than at another, and that to some persons, he is partial in the bestowal of the great gift of his spiritual influence; arbitrarily endowing them with a clearer insight into the glorious working of his universe, and a closer intimacy with his divine counsels. But this seems unworthy of his greatness, and a reflection upon his goodness. To me, God is the Sun of the moral and spiritual universe. His beneficent light pervades all space, and his parental love is the warmth, life, and fructifying power by which all creatures live, move, and have their being. In nature one object absorbs and another reflects the rays of the natural sun, according to their essence and quality, and nothing on the earth's surface remains unaffected by its radiance, in a greater or less degree, according to its capacity of reception. So with humanity, according to each one's obedience to the laws of his being and the requisitions of the spiritual universe, is he a recipient of God's light in his soul. If *that* temple for its indwelling is marred by sin, or darkened by ignorance, or contracted by the vail drawn across its portals by bigotry, intolerance, or narrow prejudice, and incrusted by pride, selfishness, vainglory, and Pharisaic self-satisfaction, then but an imperfect enlightenment reaches the spirit enshrined within, and it gives out in consequence but feeble, flickering beams for its own guidance or the world's advantage. But if through our fidelity in using God's abundant means of grace, we, who are made to reflect his image, keep the portals of our souls wide open for the reception of his inspiring spirit, then are we blessed with its full flow, for his measure of its gift is stinted only by our self-inflicted incapacity of receiving it?"

"Then you think the inspiration of Jesus differed in degree only, not in kind from that of other beings?"

"That is all. In his pure soul there was no obstruction to the true light as it came from God, and therefore he is the enlightener of the world. No other one has shown a like obedience to the conditions of this inspiration; therefore the mingled light and darkness of men's counsels."

"But what has this to do with communications from spirits? These ideas of yours annul no such possibility."

"No, very true. As on earth we gather suggestions from other minds of the past and present, so there seems to me *no* impossibility that we may from the spirits beyond the vail. Provided the great fact of spiritual influence is established, and men waken up from their earthliness and vice, the medium of that influence, if it be good, is comparatively of small importance. This however is my own experience. From one cause or another adhering to my spiritual constitution, needless to comment upon, a large part of my being has found hitherto no expression, even with the nearest and dearest. Do not think I complain of this; I simply speak of it as a fact. The capsule which incloses and ripens the seeds which are to perpetuate its life, may be long in maturing, or in finding a fitting soil in which they may germinate; but it bides its time, and finally it opens, and the ripened germs are scattered far and wide, where every element stands ready to perfect its life-work. Thus with me. But in this half isolation, weighed down at times by imperfect fellowship, think you I would seek to slake my longing, even at the fount of an archangel's pity, or a seraph's sympathy? No, no. By the great privilege taught us by our Christian faith; by the sublime power we have of mounting to the Infinite himself, where alone the soul may find its home, its refuge and its inspiration, I am led to desire no lower revelations. When weary of the world's babble, and sick at heart of its folly and blindness, I fly to solitude and God, shall my most sacred moments be broken in upon by some vulgar spirit's interruption? Excuse me, Katrina; but we are accustomed to speak plainly to each other."

"Yes, but if you could be useful to it!"

"If it heed not the greater light which we are accustomed to think floods the higher sphere, I should distrust the timeliness of my interference. But you always were a missionary of good to the unhappy here, and if you have found a new sphere of doing the same work, my sister, I would be the last to throw cold words upon your enterprise."

" How do you account for the strange phenomena con-
nected with this subject which we hear and read of on
every side?"

" I cannot explain them.   There are some strange mani-
festations from all accounts, though I have never seen
them.   But this I know, that there is great ignorance, as I
have said, prevalent upon the philosophy of the mind, its
natural workings, and its union with God.   The imagina-
tion, too, has great power over the multitudes; and besides
this, it is a subject fruitful of opportunities for fraud and
charlatanism, and there has been an abundance of these
connected with it.   It is interesting to me chiefly from its
showing so conclusively that the spiritual nature will vindi-
cate its supremacy, though at first it may do it in strange
and awkward fashion.   I trust that more light will be thrown
upon this interesting subject, and that through this upward
movement of humanity, when explained on rational and
Christian grounds, the age may take a long stride in the
march of true progress.   I have a set of subjects which I
call *the indefinites.*   I cannot decide upon their truth or
falsehood in my present state of knowledge and character.
So I patiently wait, leaving my mind open to what truth
may be granted to my candid inquiries.   This is one of
them.   I neither believe nor disbelieve the wonderful
things I hear, but making great allowance for extravagances
in this new theory, I feel that it is to lead to some truth relat-
ing to the spiritual connection between all beings of the past
and present, and with our Father in heaven, which we
have yet not fully understood.   And for the rest, I trust in
the progress of the human soul, and will not seek to tear
open untimely the bud of God's events, but wait for the
natural method of the flowering of his truth on earth.   For
your calm, well-balanced mind I have no fear of fanaticism,
but hope that through it some light may be elicited, which
may be serviceable to us all."

" It greatly elevates and enriches my life, and I marvel now at the contentment of others, whose thoughts are bound chiefly to the earth; and yet I feel no lack of interest in it, but on the contrary a purer and stronger one."

" I am most happy to hear it; only keep your mind open to new convictions and nothing but good can come from it. But the danger to the masses is that they materialize heaven by low conceptions upon spiritual influence rather than exalt the present. Fanaticism is always dangerous, for it burns the soul with the unholy fire of earthly passion, while the subject thinks himself within the very gates of heaven. Then we do not need new mediums between us and God, so much as to take to heart the teachings of Jesus, which ever point to direct communion with him. The world is prone to idolatry. At one time, it deifies one set of objects and then another; it is so hard for the human mind to soar to the centre of Infinity itself, and yet from thence alone shall we bring home our choicest blessings. Pray heaven this Spiritualism be not the Fetichism of the nineteenth century, but may lead on to a higher development, and to a more natural and universal union with God and his Christ than the world has yet known."

" Here is your manuscript, dear Lisbet," said Mrs. Hansen; " I have kept it concealed as you desired, only showing it to one or two persons in all these years. On looking over it of late, I have felt that you must have written it under spiritual impression. Good morning for an hour! I will call on Lina as I promised her."

(Mrs. Liebenhoff takes the manuscript in her hand.) " Yes, here thou art, poor, yellow, old, young offspring of my heart and brain! Twenty-one years ago I penned thee with big hopes distilling from thy every syllable. To me how much more was involved in every line than met the cold gaze of those who passed thy pages lightly over. But disgust and loathing followed at thy imperfect art-expression, and so thou wast sent into obscurity. (She runs it over.) I had forgotten almost its every incident, and now I see it was but the embodiment of rules I laid down for my life's observance. (She reads.) Pretty well, Lisbet, written as it was more than a score of years ago, and I am not so very, very old even now. Why verily, the doctors of divinity are still groping in the muddy waters of their dark theology, while a simple country girl worked her mind clear of the dross of dogmas, and pierced the very core of Christian truth, and fed upon its marrow! And has not my soul thriven by it? Read the early and the later Tale, and which is the more youthful in tone and spirit, though a greater acquaintance with life, literature, and character gives to the last the varied and dramatic life, which the other so much lacks. What a sermon! The story but a thread to hang grave thoughts upon, but its principles laid down for a life-guide, not less condensed and clear than my maturer life could furnish. I rather beg pardon of the aforesaid doctors that I did not publish it for their benefit; they plunge and wallow still in such dark, muddy pools. I will lay thee tenderly aside, for thou wert the healthful dewdrops exhaling from my soul after the exhausting, gory sweat drawn from it by its life-battle with the powers of evil without and the grim fancies and horrible fears, magnifying the errors of its youth within, conjured up by the so-called Christian, but in fact heathenish theology, whose malaria lurks even in homes whose inmates strive to attain and teach the perfect truth of Jesus. O! come the time when Paganism, with its bonds and terrors, shall be laid low in the dust forever, and Christianity, the mild, clear, joyful genius which can alone lead on the ages to their glorious destination, shall be seen as it truly is, and its rightful sway be given it! Shall I dedicate it to my young class of girls, who gather around me on every Sabbath, and thus give it to the world? Compressed here is the truth I have sought to teach them, and exemplified by the few ideal characters naturally adopted by a young maiden new to society and its checkered life. It may be that to many a young heart working out life's problem, it may hint of the reward awaiting the faithful and patient laborer. But no; I shrink from this effort of my timid, fluttering youth being thrust scornfully by or sneered at by critics, who measure by superficial rule and Gunter. For the work of my maturity, I care not; but thou at least, my firstborn, pale, spring floweret, shalt have a gentle euthanasy, and therefore I, thy mother, consign thee without a sigh to the shadows of oblivion!"

During the visit of the relatives at Copenhagen, the two sisters visited with them the different objects of interest in the city, and among others, for the gratification of the children particularly, the museum. There they met an unfortunate woman, an attendant, and it may be, a part of the show, who called forth their sympathy and interest. Mrs. Liebenhoff, who had a nervous dread of monstrosities, tried to evade her, but hearing her, in conversation with her brother, utter the sentiments of a pure and resigned spirit, she conquered her repugnance and approached her. The woman fixed her eyes upon her and asked if she wished to have her fortune told? Impulsively she answered yes, then hesitated and half refused; but at length crossed the Sybil's hand with the required piece of silver and seated herself beside her. She took a pack of cards and slowly passed them through her hands, reading at the same time the number upon their surface, and as she said, the book of Mrs. Liebenhoff's experience. She suggested to her her prominent traits of character and mind, and also some of the most striking events of her past life, and then looked into the future and told her of its destiny. She did not insist upon the truth of her prophecies; spoke of the art as an entertainment to herself and others, and ended by saying; "If the events of your future life prove my words true, you will remember and think kindly of her who foretold them." So they parted with a mutual friendly interest, Mrs. Liebenhoff to her home and the Sybil to a distant country, from which she said she never should return.

Her friends gathered around her again, for she had not permitted them to be present during the interview.

"Good luck, Lisbet?" said Mr. Hansen.

"O yes, plenty of money, that is good fortune, is it not? and I shall not have to ask my husband for it either," said she.

"Children in flocks, I suppose?"

"O yes, of course; twins and all, more than I can manage."

"What *did* she tell you, dear?" said Mr. Liebenhoff.

"A wonderful fact! how could she have known it; that my husband tenderly loved me? She must be a conjurer truly to learn that!"

"But, joking aside, did she really startle you by any unexpected revelation?"

"Truly then, she did. Events in my life which I have not thought of for years, she spoke of in the most matter-of-course way. When I asked her how she performed the art, seeing her do nothing but read her cards in a dreamy manner and look with some attention in my face, she touched her head and said, 'It is partly in my brain.'"

"'And you consider the gift as a compensation for your misfortune, do you not?' said I to her.

"'Yes,' said she, 'it brings me near my kind, and they remember me with tenderness;' then looking again intently in my face, she said, 'You have a lively mind, full of fancies, and you love women.'

"'Shall I write a book?' said I.

"'Do you wish to?'

"'O yes.' She read her cards. 'O yes,' said she, 'you will write three.'

"The poor unfortunate public! thought I. 'Will they be read?' said I, anxiously, 'for I never like to lose my labor.'

"'I told you,' said she with a tone slightly impatient, 'that you had a lively fancy,' as if that were a sufficient answer, and then began to count the money; five hundred, nine hundred, and so on, until she seemed tired, and then ended with, 'You will have plenty;' and then, but with no leer, she added: 'And you love men too.' She then played with my bracelet as a child would do, looking confidingly into my face from time to time, when I left her to rejoin my friends, she at the same time going out, each looking back to find the other gazing at her until out of sight."

" Is that all?" said Mr. Körner.

"All that I shall tell you now," said she, thoughtfully. " It has given a new phase to my thoughts at any rate. Was it through magnetic sympathy that she possessed herself of floating images which, at some period of my life, have been in my mind? If so, it is wonderful enough; or does God impart to her, through some peculiarity of constitution, the power to read futurity? Verily, ' there are more things in heaven and earth than are dreamed of in our philosophy.' "

" She was impressed, no doubt," said Mr. Körner, with a sly glance at Mrs. Hansen. " What is the world of women coming to?"

" Two of them, to say the least, are getting quite off my track," said his wife, with a face of solicitude.

" Lina, my dear, do not be anxious about Katrina, so as to enjoy her visit to us less because she is investigating this subject of Spiritualism. Who of us are calmer than she? If she is mad, it is with a method most serene and self-possessed, and I promise you that I forswear all means to place myself in communication with ghosts, black, white, or gray. No, no, there are enough of stupid, impracticable people on this earth-sphere for my equability of temper, and I find it rather doubtful whether one falls among better ones in the other. So you need not fear me."

" I am told," said Mrs. Hansen, " that the air of your

city is so impure that the highest order of them cannot breathe its impurities."

"Heaven defend us from the lower ones, I say!   Katrina, that convinces me that I am right in seeking spiritual communion only with the Highest, for then I am sure that aid and inspiration will ever be about me.   His parental love and all-surrounding presence are no less in the dense, polluted city, than in the purer breath of the green fields or fragrant forests, provided we keep our souls open to their influence.   To him I commend myself rather than to the dainty spirits whose interest for us is graduated by more or less of carbonic acid gas.   That is too much like our petty aristocracy, in their decisions of who are good enough for their refined companionship.   Save me from such contracted sympathies, say I."

And she left the room, swinging her bonnet with an absorbed expression of face quite usual with her.

CHAPTER XIX.

"Nor do I know how long it is,
For I have lain entranced I wis,
A weary woman, scarce alive."

"But vainly thou warrest
For this is alone in
Thy power."—COLERIDGE'S CHRISTABEL.

AN extract from Mrs. Liebenhoff's work, entitled "The Way:"

"Here cometh my Hebrew teacher of the Hebrew tongue," said the pastor's wife of Reykiavik, as she heard his step upon the staircase which led to her husband's study. "Verily these crooked characters and this inverse style of reading backwards instead of forwards, agreeth not well with the spirit of my 'Tale,' which

(229)

is onward and still onward, casting no vain, regretful looks behind, but ever pressing for the goal of the New Jerusalem, that city in the heavens, which is to be brought down to earth, and its temple for a universal faith to be rebuilded by a woman.   Verily, again I say, there is too much of the dust and odor of the ages past upon the language to assort well with my aspiring contemplations.   It does not crush, but for the time being, so confines and thwarts them that their flutterings to be free disturb the order of my soul and make it like the caged lion, tramping to and fro within his narrow prison, more piteous to behold than his most dangerous rampancy is awful.   I will tell him that I must relinquish it and only read with him the French language."

He approaches the door which is wide open, and she is standing directly in front of it with her eyes upon him, but at which he nevertheless knocks and stands until he is bidden to enter, when he bows profoundly.

The lady aside: " Truly a most oriental mode of entering the presence of the royal sex!   But it is all very well. As women are henceforth to take the lead in life, I am glad that one man's manners are on the whole up to the idea."

" Good morning, ma'am; I come to you in the sublimest possible mood.   After my wanderings of ages and the multiform experience of fifty centuries' existence in which I have ever, with a child-like eagerness, clung to some fond dreams of personal happiness, I have resolved to cast them to the winds and live for Truth alone."

"A very sensible and pious resolution, and I rejoice that resignation, that plant, it would seem, of tardy growth in the harsh soil of a man's nature, has. at length flowered in yours!   With women it fructifies almost spontaneously; the soil, if not so *strong*, being more mellow and pervious to skyey influences.   Nevertheless I congratulate you. Better late than never."

" But lo! a strange phenomenon attended the stern sacrifice!   As with a struggle such as divides the soul from our

corporeal part, and with a gasp of agony I flung them from
me; amazed I saw come trooping towards me the angels
of Hope, of Joy, of Peace and Victory, bearing in their
hands their different symbols, and attended by cherubs,
scattering from golden vases the flowers and perfumes of
the heavenly sphere, so that where I looked to travel
henceforth in the rugged path of self-renunciation, I found
it strewn with roses, and the sweet, heavenly company
awaiting to attend me."

"O yes, that is of course the natural result of yielding
up one's blind, selfish will to the guidance of the wiser
one of the Supreme. Plod on patiently five centuries
longer, and I have no doubt that then this truth will be
thoroughly stamped upon man's nature; that God never
intended that we should live in an exhausted receiver, but
in this living, boundless universe, every part of which will
minister to his health, happiness, and highest good, pro-
vided we journey through life in parallel lines with his
harmonious appointments. Now that you have schooled
yourself to submission to all evils which may await you in
particular and the universe in general, it may be the most
fitting time to announce to you the painful intelligence
that I shall for a time deprive you of the felicity of admin-
istering to the stupidity of a preoccupied mind. I relin-
quish the study of Hebrew for the present."

"I cannot listen to your determination for a moment,
madam. Allow me to use the privilege, which my position
as an instructor gives me, and earnestly insist upon your
continuance of the study." ·

"Your urgency is of no avail, sir. I have sublunary
reasons sufficient to determine me, and besides this, I am
bidden through a friend by the spirits beyond this time-
vail, to keep my mind perfectly passive. I wonder if they
think to *impress* me against my will? I defy them. So I
shall relinquish the study."

He fixes his eye upon her and says emphatically: "You

will please read these four pages; you will have no diffi-
culty in doing it. Keep your mind passive, and this tongue
of Eld, the great medium of God's subtle influence over
the ages, shall enrich your life by its possession. And
what a mine of wealth does it unfold to the waiting soul!
Not through the vulgar, school-boy notion of plenary inspi-
ration, as if each line and word were a magic spell to keep
the darkened, timid mind in fetters that it go not astray,
leading it into idolatry of ink, parchment, and letter-press,
no less gross and still more crushing to human nature than
that which deifies the elements, the fruits and flowers, the
sun, moon, and planetary bodies, and the ideal of man and
woman; but through its spirit, which is in perfect harmony
with common sense and reason. As in my passage through
the ages I paused in Greece and Rome, and took note of
their Deities—Jupiter, Minerva, Mercury, Juno, Bacchus,
and Venus—and thus saw these their thoughts expressed
to the eye in their almost living, breathing works of Art,
though to worship such seemed most unmeet to me, to
whom the one true God has been revealed, yet was I glad
that to any people it was permitted to reveal in its perfec-
tion the wondrous handiwork of God, the human form, the
living temple of his image here on earth. And as I gazed
upon the Muses, beautiful representations of poetic woman-
hood, to whom is given in keeping some great Art to teach
and to transmit to coming humanity, I rejoiced that such
broad glimpses were permitted to these early times of her
high mission here below. Surely, thought I, when cometh
the brighter light promised to my people, men will see
clearly that those earth-gods are but the types, the reflec-
tions, the imperfect embodiment of the great idea of a
universal Father, all-wise, all-present, joyous, beautiful,
and loving. And when the truth of the Messiah shall
flower in lovely woman, a tenderer grace shall sit upon her
brow than any that adorned these Muses; for endued with
the true Christian spirit, home, through her affections and

fidelity, shall be her shrine, from which shall arise her worship to the Most High, and the hearts of her husband and children be the Lares to which she will award the tribute of her life's devotion."

"There has been a failure somewhere, for we are not so much in advance of the ancients as we ought to be, and as the whole spirit of Christ's teachings taught us to expect either in religion, morals, intellectual culture, or physical development."

"No, the ascetic element so rife in eastern countries, whose deities are monsters, whose nature is to blast more than to bless, has ever mixed with Judaism. As soon as Christianity left the bosom of its founder, in whom dwelt perfect love of God, invigorated only by a healthful, inspiring awe, it mingled in his imperfect followers' minds with this dark stream flowing from the perturbed, bewildered minds of Jews and Pagans. The Catholic Church, so called, by its penances and cruel, abominable restraint upon much that is innocent and beautiful in human nature, and by its bold assumption, in which glares the spirit of Lucifer, not beams out the encouraging glance of meek, disinterested, freedom-loving, liberty-giving Christ, has perpetuated this degrading principle. And not less grievous and wicked, but more insidious and life-crushing is the same in the prevalent Protestantism of the day, dubbed Calvinism, self-nicknamed Lutheranism, or with the presumptuous title of Orthodoxy, rolling like a sweet morsel its self-assurance under its blistering tongue. For it has by its worse than heathen dogmas darkened our earth's atmosphere, set it awry upon its axis, wheeled it aside from its proper orbit, so that the moon's dark side is turned towards it, the spots upon the sun are so magnified to the world's eye by their false position as almost to conceal its beams, and the planetary system and the stars seem not to shine by their heaven-appointed light, but have the lurid glare of Hell upon their spheres. O! it is awful that this perversion of the great

20

good of life, this connecting, binding link between man and God, Religion, should be the chain and manacle to force him to tremble, and it may be curse, while he grinds out his daily degraded life in the prison-house of his spirit's bondage."

"Yes, bondage it is, as the faces of its willing captives indicate; for they are full of unnatural lines and sad grimaces, as if heaven were to be propitiated by the disfigurement of his most perfect work, 'the human face divine.' I was looking to-day at some representations of the Nine Muses. They were beautiful in their full, harmonious development, and their expression of serenity and joy, as they stood with the emblems of their art in hand, indicating both their mission on the earth, and the delight it gave them to fulfill it. I then turned to a volume on Sacred and Legendary Art, with delineations of the Christian saints, martyrs, priests, and principal nuns of the middle ages. These, almost without exception, had the downcast, anxious, agonized expression of poor victims to the wrath of some avenging deity, and I closed the volume in disgust and sorrow that a religion so full of joy, peace, bright hopes, thrilling memories and glad anticipations should thus be represented by its believers so as to make the unthinking and superficial say: 'See how much better humanity throve under the former than the latter faith!'"

"Yes, and I range myself side by side with those whom you call shallow, and say that the idea of religion given by these ascetics, through assuming to be the only recipients of God's truth, is lower, as it is more unnatural than even the excesses of the old idolaters, inasmuch as love, joy, and free abandonment to nature, though it may merge in lust, is better than hatred, persecution, hard-hearted, Pharisaical assumption, the sneer of bigotry, and selfish love of power. If either of these were the only true representations of Divinity on earth, I go back to the ancients "

"Nay; but there is a strength of will, a command over

the baser passions, an invigoration of nature attained by those who believe in Christianity, even if mingled with the popular theology, unknown of old.   The stern law is necessary to hush the lions and tigers of our souls to due obedience, before the singing birds and flowers which Christianity developes in us, can find a safe, fitting bower and garden to chant and bloom in.   The simple majesty of law is sadly smothered by false traditions, it is true; yet for all that, there is more of it still in action to nerve us than the ancients had.   Were there no sins and persecution, no bigotry and assumption then?   History is not written aright if these were not rampant, even worse than now."

" Look at Sebastopol; read the list of its hecatombs of slain; measure the humanity of Protestant England, who suffers thousands of her best and bravest to die rather than overstep a miserable conventionalism; see Catholic France lying so low within the toils of the spoiler as to suffer its life-blood to be daily drained that its tyrant may, concealed by the smoke and din of the battle, forge her chains more surely; and say, whether the asceticism of the nineteenth century has more of the love of God and humanity in it than the mirth, and free scope given to nature by the Pagan idolatry."

" O, but does not a protest, never heard by the ancients, arise from the universal Christian nations against these horrid butcheries, set on foot by a few selfish despots, whom Providence, for inscrutable reasons, permits to wield powers which they shamefully abuse?   And this protest will be heard, for it is the last war ever to be waged again by Christendom."

" Do you believe it?"

" Most sincerely."

" Meantime, I wage my battle against the dark doctrines of the prevalent theologies.   Born into this my latest transformation under the Talmud's rigid sway, nurtured, nay half starved, body and soul, by a grandsire, Pharisaical,

covetous and cruel, whose dire conformity to false tradi
tions made his whole nature like a pool, stagnant and
fetid; my being would have been poisoned had it not been
for one backward glimpse, half faded but ever cherished
of a most sweet and saintly father, who died before my
infant eyes could fix themselves with steady glance upon his
reverent face and form.   That gleam shed on my pathway
from his angel-sphere conducted me to Jesus, in whose
perfected truth I saw the flowering of my people's faith, the
consummation of the law of Moses, for which *that* was
a preparation and a prophecy, and *this* the seal of the sig-
nificance of all its rules, and rites, and ceremonies.   So
that in early youth the Christ became my ideal of human
perfection, and this gradually led me to become his fol-
lower.   But after groping through a dismal Jewish boy-
hood, it was by no flowery paths that I have reached what I
believe his simple truth.   For into the ' wild woods ' of the
superstitious, popular theology I plunged where there is but
a doubtful glimmer of light here and there to tempt the
wanderer on his journey.   But on and on I waded through
thickets of speculations, through briery paths of discour-
agement and doubt until I found the elevated plain where
beautiful Truth stands fully revealed, beckoning me on and
on towards the source of its Eternal spring."

"And now, having inflated yourself with this sublime
element, balloon-like you are sailing from one nation to
another down the ages, dispensing as is needed of this
ethereal gas with which you and your car are charged?
Does not Father Time get tired of seeing you following
his footsteps all these years?   He is more lenient to you
than to me, or he would scowl at you and say: ' Don't
think to defy me, look at the wrinkles upon your face,
signs all that my sickle is sharpening to reap you low.' "

" I defy him until I have given to the world proofs of
their gross idolatry in worshiping the *letter* of the Bible in
no less than one thousand discrepancies within its pages,

showing how vain it is for men to trust their salvation to
anything so shifting as human language.

" You will not be understood.   The Priests and Levites
will say that you are an infidel and scoff at Revelation."

" Let them say whatever their bigotry and lust for power
suggest; if these motives prompt them to reckless denun-
ciation of all utterance which squares not with their pigmy
rules.   To God I commend my cause, who knows that it is
not because I love the Scriptures less but more, that I
seek to tear from their simple majesty all lying preten-
sions, patched upon them by foolish, ignorant men, that they
may stand forth as they truly are, the *record of a revela-
lation to be studied, judged of, and obeyed with the same
reason and common sense wherewith nature, man, the
earth and its concerns, and our own characters and actions
are weighed.*"

" I hope the world will be ready to read your book, for
it is sadly in need of its truths.   It likes the positive, how-
ever, better than the negative; for its feelings and imagi-
nation are in advance of its reason and religious principles,
so it is careless of laying its foundations deep on the rock
of truth, but is forever putting new turrets to its apex, and
thus it topples over continually."

" Yes, the positive truth is to save the world, but before
its basis is thoroughly established, it must see clearly what
its enemies have been in the past, and conquer and lay
them low in the dust.   This is my present work."

"And I take the positive. Can I not, presumptuous
woman that I am, lend you a helping hand in your hard
drudgery. Supposing I advertise your work in the Tale
which I am writing, so that if it should fail of descending
far down the vale from its own lack of the life-principle, its
memory may still be perpetuated through mine.

(Aside.)

(" He frowns, I see, at that. What being in the likeness
of man, though he have the wisdom of the ages, ever

thought a woman could do anything for him but cook, sew, please and *comfort*, and amuse him in some humdrum way?)

"For I write for nothing less than immortality. Or do you intend to outlive the world and keep fast hold of your book in your peregrinations, and so secure its life?"

"I know not what may be before me. I live for truth, and take no anxious thought for the future. But in dreams of night, amid the hush of the city's roar and tumult, when my clairvoyant eye is couched by the subtlest element of nature, and under the greenwood tree when time and space are annihilated and I live in the eternal Present, there come to me visions of cool waters in the distant future, bathing my feverish, aching brow—glimmerings of ambrosia fit to nourish the divinities, freed from all corporeal substance, and sweet visions of the peace of God shed upon my weary, suffering heart of eld, yet ever young in its sense of agony and striving with itself and the all-present powers of evil. I will be patient, yet I know that happiness will, in the end, lift her coy face and smile her sweetest even on me."

"I hope so. It would be nuptials worthy of publication: Married, the Rev. Everlasting, Restless, Suffering, Wandering, Unbelieving Judæus to Miss Serene, Loving, Quiet, Gospel Felicitas. The blissful pair have taken up their abode in the Valley of Christian Contentment, and the world rejoices at its own relief from his sad aspect and his low mournful cry about our dwellings of the 'old ra-ags, ra-ags!' of Judaism, no less than at their joyful prospects.'"

"Good morning, madam; I will return to-morrow at this same hour and hear you read your lesson"

(*The pastor's wife alone.*)

"Verily a strange mixture of all the ages is this weird, mysterious man, and for this he interests me. My truant fancy, ever striving to release itself from conventionalism, has full sweep with one whom no age, country, or narrow sect can bind; and yet, with the freedom breathed from a rarer atmosphere than what envelopes other men, he preserves a strict integrity of mind and manners. My husband has his female friends, sweet, gentle, loving souls, who have grown up within our heart of hearts, some of them in the sacred inclosure of our home. We love them both alike; for jealousy! why it is. a word not known in our vocabulary, so trustful are we of each other; and when they meet and part from him, it is with a sister's and brother's kiss of welcome and farewell. And they write to him, 'So glad were we to see your dear face again.' But I have had no friend of his sex with whom I could think aloud, and though a broad sweep of my being is met by his, not all is exercised. For his life is full of grave cares and labors, and though with marvelous power he frees himself of the dust and cobwebs of the study when he comes to me; yet soon he hies away to scatter his sympathies and gather an unnatural weight of solicitude from the multitudes, who find no friend so gentle as he to listen to their woes. And so it happens that while the world's anxious, sorrowful ones pour into his ear their tales of bereavement, sickness, or mayhap worldly trials and vexations, and never in vain, my soul goes ranging alone through perilous paths of questioning and denial of what the sages have settled as finalities; and Fancy, its butterfly, now flutters in dangerous proximity to the sun, scorching its gauzy wings, till scared at its dizzy, solitary soarings, it crouches low, dimmed and disconsolate, folding its pinions, and sighing for the dull, dark safety of its imprisoned, grub-life, then spreads them with a bolder, stronger sweep to gather sunlight and fervid heat from upper regions, which even his pure eye has not yet penetrated.

"But this man of the ages has been there before me, and I see that into these regions we can soar in meet companion-

ship. And now, were I a young, undisciplined girl, and did
not love my husband with a strong and true affection, and did
not *know* that he was given me by my Maker who read the
temper of his child, and fashioned its fit training and due
measure of earthly love, and if I had not long ago given
all feelings not intended to be met by earthly friend into
his keeping, who, with interest, richly has repaid me, then
I might suffer a crude and a foolish sentiment to usurp the
place of the true gold of a wife's love and duty. But
strong in the might of God's support, my love, and clear
perception of the beauty of the right, and direful con-
sequence of wrong, let me, through imagination, gather
some truth for the well-being of others less favored than
myself. Let me, if I may become the interpreter of my
sex and keeping fast hold of the anchor let down from
heaven and fastened deep in time, cast a clear and steady
gaze into the awful pit, ten thousand fathoms deep, where
lie buried the virtue and happiness of frail women, beguiled
and led astray by the bewitching cant about twin soulship,
psychological completeness of sympathy, sealed marriages
and spiritual wifehood, Cicisbeoism, and all other deceitful
forms of breaking a commandment written on our hearts,
and in God's word by him who made us singly, as well as
gave us into each other's keeping in social bonds. And
now I will reason, as many an unfortunate must do, before
she oversteps the line of duty to herself and God.

"My husband regards me not, or if he does, it is with
such cool indifference and rude sense of ownership, that
my soul is starved for sympathy or blasted by injustice.
Here is his friend, who has leisure, gentle manners and love
for my society, and wooes my confidence by his religious
aspirations and high-toned thoughts. He seeks my friend-
ship; gradually hints that we have tastes in common not
shared with me by my more busy, practical husband, pro-
poses a spiritual union, which shall lift us to the third heaven
of purest bliss. Gradually grosser thoughts steal unawares

upon me. The laws and customs of society war against the natural love of tender hearts. Was not Jesus lenient to the poor, lost woman, while he rebuked her accusers, no doubt steeped in the same guilt themselves, but, as now, mean, base, and profligate enough to seek to cover their own shame by exposing and scorning hers? But in the Holy One she found a friend; and shall not I in this my life's extremity?

"And so she falls *low, lower, lowest* in the scale of our humanity. O woman, flower of the earth, if virtuous, fruit ripest for the skies, whom, if wicked, thy keen, wounded sense of the ruin of the angel in thee drives to demoniac madness and fierce desperation! let me unravel for thee, my poor, tempted, deluded sister, the tangled skein of thy troubled, flying, fascinated thoughts, and in few words point to the remedy.

"But what is this strange feeling that steals over me, as if my being were parting asunder? Can it be death, and I in fullest health but now? Or can it be that the weird man has dared to throw over me the subtle influence of magnetism; me who have shunned all drugs of narcotic and alleviating influence, so that my spirit might be free and natural in its workings?—over me, whom mingled disgust, pity, and indignation have long since driven from all haunts in which its daring votaries exhibit to the gaping multitude—some, their power over the individual will, and others, their weak submission to those who wield the powerful element. Let me bethink myself. Yesterday, in the absorption of our lesson, I recall to mind that, for a moment, my robe came in contact with his arm. And could he thus transmit the potent fluid? And in the afternoon my half hour's siesta was so profound that I seemed to have slept through ages. I remember, too, his frequent calls upon my husband; some strange tale to draw him to his dwelling; some cabalistic secrecy attending it; some unwonted questionings of my tale-telling. Has he *dared* to

21

exercise his magic on *me*, God's child and nature's protégé, whose principles and whose instincts alone have guided me since the first day they laid me in my mother's arms within this earth-pale, sealing upon my infant brow their baptismal mark, the blazing star? Has he dared to attempt to mingle his being by the mesmeric touch with that of *my husband's wife?* Does he know how much this means— *my husband's wife?* Even this. Of all men on the wide earth, *he* is the only, only one whose love, whose due sense of power and of my right, whose claim upon my affection and obedience have been so justly balanced that I have been allowed a true development, and thus with only him I could have lived in wedlock and not be prostitute. This I learn through the marvelous power of a sympathy with other minds, known only to her, reposing in nature's loving arms, who, while she broods over her as the dove over its young in cooing accents, tells her her secrets, while mother and child bathe in the eternal, benignant smile of 'our great Father.'

"I tread upon your power, thou impotent conjurer! get thee behind me, Satan! you offend me by your pretensions and miserable attempt at despotism! I'll breathe the open air. Come, ye breezes, and blow from the top of Lebanon's mount and cleanse me from the unwelcome gift forced on me by thy country's degenerate son! I tear my robe from off me, and cast it into the purifying waters fathoms deep, that it drown out its sinful participation in the deed. I faint—I die. Come, my husband, and fold your protecting arms about me, and let me sleep against your heart-pulse that it may hold your own away from the Death-angel's grasp, whose chilly breath comes faintly to me through the portal, half-opened by that tampering Jew."

(*She sleeps.*)

The next day the Pastor's wife, pale yet resolute, awaits the magnetizer's usual visit.

(He enters.)

"Good morning, madam. You are surely ill."

"It is the truth. Ask me not the nature of my disease, for I mistake me, or ye know it well. Confess, sir, that you used the mysterious influence, you wield, to magnetize me."

"I did. There are different temperaments so naturally attuned, that by the influence of the subtle magnetic fluid strange harmonies may be awakened, so that two beings become blended into one. In our sentiments, and tastes, and life-experiences, so far as different ages justify, there seemed a wondrous unison, and for a reason which now I will not name, I sought to ascertain the extent of our dual unity. But some resistance has come between us, unaccountable to my weird vision."

"And you dare to confess all this to me, your equal, ay, your superior so far as a teachable spirit which gives clear insight into the laws of life can make me so? You, who have fought for your country's freedom, who plead the captive's cause, and defend the oppressed, can stoop so low, it seems, as to seek to cast your spell over a trusting woman's soul and person, and try to read her secret thoughts by a mean trick of jugglery!"

"I stand condemned; what farther say ye?"

"I grant ye an intellect, critical, inquisitive, and subtle, an artist-eye, and a poetic soul, with learning gathered from the deeps profound of eastern science and western schools of rare and curious knowledge, and an insight into the souls of men with power to wield their sympathies seldom attained; but into that of woman ye have read no farther than the alphabet, and one, who claims the title to be *Psyche of her sex*, pronounces you a *hypocrite*, inasmuch as ye in the same hour seek to enlighten and to darken, to free and to enchain, to awaken her to larger views of nature and its Author and to drown her in a sleep imposed by your unlawful tyranny. But I discard your power."

(He rises to leave.)

"Madam, our usual order is reversed. I stand the instructed, and you the teacher are. I acknowledge my mistake."

"I do not decide against your character by a single untoward action. I wait to see if your errors be not the consequence of a defective training, of an early, superstitious faith, the brambles and briers brought from the 'wild woods' of false theologies, sticking even to one who strives for the highest truth; but if ye ever repeat the attempt to subdue my will, to reveal my mind to your too curious scrutiny in this unhallowed way, and above all, to make my pure, noble, and loving husband the puppet of your capricious will in this design, I'll scorn you like an imp of hell. For I would as soon clasp hands with a fiend and turn my face straight towards the under-world, as carelessly to join myself by means of magnetism to one whom I had not, by long and tried companionship, read through and through, who did not use the power invested in him with the same holy sense of responsibility with which the Christ performed his miracles. And know this, O presumptuous man! that for the amusement of a passing hour ye may wield an influence given you to bless with, as a temptation and a curse to some one who, sad and solitary, climbs up a steep and stony way; who in glad innocence may yield a hand to one who seems able to lead her across life's precipices, but who, instead of replying to her confidence, throws her among the lions. Beware, beware of the evil that lurks, as it may seem, in flowers and music, and may, like ravenous beasts, tear your own soul if not another's."

(He moves with sad and repentant aspect towards the door.)

"I leave you. Forgive the injury, forget the lonely wanderer who, from no baseness, but a pure desire for a spiritual friendship hitherto denied him, sought through a means, by God appointed as I deemed, to win the blessing from you. For in starlight visions in the desert, it was revealed to me that, far west of Sinai's heights, I should discover the twin complement of my soul, and this sign of dual unity sealed between us should be the test to guide me to her. This I found in you. Mother, sister, wife are all denied me, and miserable that I am! this more ethereal boon I have now lost by a too eager grasp. Farewell!"

(*She rises.*)

" Do we understand each other?"

"Ay."

"And do my words seem just and reasonable to you?"

" Even so."

" Then we will give the usual sign of friendship, (clasping hands), and you will be a brother in the same great cause to which my husband and I have pledged ourselves, a safe inmate in our family, a friend to rely upon, not a wizard to guard against."

" I pledge myself."

" And now we know the meaning of a *spiritual friend. ship*, which shall liken us to the angels of God in heaven *A common zeal and mutual labor in the great cause of humanity and truth; sanctifying all life's aims, labor, mental culture and beautiful tastes;* holding in unbroken unity and awful sacredness, the ties of husband and wife; superadding it may be a third, companionship in open faith avowed and with his full approval, in which each shall draw from the other all that is loveliest and rarest from our souls, while the triennial chain shall never rust in either link, but grow brighter and brighter unto the perfect day, when there is neither marrying nor giving in marriage, but all are as angels of God in heaven."

CHAPTER XX.

"'Tis to create, and in creating live
A being more intense, that we endow
With form our fancy, gaining as we give
The life we image, ev'n as I do now."
                                BYRON.

(Mrs. Liebenhoff alone.)

"I hear the voices of Lina and Mr. Körner coming up the yard. I will read this chapter of my Tale to them, and see if they approve it. They give me right cordial encouragement in my work, but tremble a little for my free pen. I fear that this will startle them—Hilda and Zoë, too! and better still, the little three-year-old. You are welcome, friends; be seated, pray. And seeing

that my larder is unfurnished with dainties for your refresh-
ment, shall I give you a tit-bit from my romance? or are
you not in the mood for it?"

"O yes," said all at once; "pray give it us."

"I like to see your progress; go on, you will be read,
never fear," said Mr. Körner.

"When are we to be immortalized, dear Lisbet?" said
Mrs. Körner, "for I see your fashion is to serve us up for
the benefit of the public."

"Yes, I am acting upon your motto, ' make your friends
useful as well as ornamental.' Do you feel damaged
thereby?"

"O no! I like myself very well, idealized as I am. But
are you sure that every one you dress up in this way will?"

"I have not asked them. They must get used to it.
My revelations are nothing to what will be made of them
at the day of judgment, when we shall know as we are
known. Won't that be a glorious time?"

"Ha, ha! a woman's heaven that, where her curiosity
will bo fully gratified. But why don't you imagine charac-
ters, or take them from a greater distance? Novelists
usually do, I believe," said Mr. Körner.

"O you and a few others are good enough for me; only
tip you off with a little glory here and there, excepting
you, however, who do very well just as you are. But paint
people at a distance! What a question? Did you ever
know an artist stand a thousand miles off from the subject of
his sketch? You think I am a witch, do you, brother mine?
Imagine, create characters! What a wicked thought! God
only does that. What are you thinking of? I must use
for my story what he has made for me, and be very thank-
ful that he allowed me to be born and to live with such
interesting people. So you may consider yourself as pre-
destined to shine in this way from all eternity; for I am
compelled, by the exacting spirit that strives within my
little person to write a book, so here you all are."

"What you just now said reminds me," said Hilda, "of what Miss Ingemann told us yesterday, that women were not creative in the character of their minds, only imitative; that men were the inventors."

"Worthy of Miss Ingemann's farsighted wisdom! Excuse me, Hilda. She is not the only one in these hard times whose cold, steel point of an intellect pierces the eyes of their *souls* out so that they live and grope about in mental and spiritual blindness. Is not that a paradox? There is a certain volume somewhere, which says 'that men have sought out many inventions,' and don't speak of it as much to their credit either. I agree, they are *very inventive.* It is enough for the women to imitate, combine, arrange, group, and show off to good advantage, by the gift of their idealism and common-sense, the materials which a good God has strewn abundantly around in life, history, and nature, and in that way they stick to the *truth,* which is what we were made to live for in this universe. Men want to build a world of their own, and so they set about *inventing,* and they make poor work of it, seeing they cannot fly out of themselves, or get entirely away from the rule of their Maker, try as hard as they may; but they have contrived thus much, to turn the world topsy-turvy with their abortive attempts at *creation.* But the women will set it all right in time; let them have free cope."

"But when is this happy revolution to be made? for I suppose you date it from the publication of your book."

"O! of course. That depends upon my publisher. I see he dreads to throw up the reins of government himself, as well as to see them drop from the hands of his fellows, so he delays. If he were not a man of honor he would, I fear, burn my manuscript; but being such, he contents himself with keeping back my proof-sheets, telling me something like this, that my Tale is not of much account. But I will now give you my last chapter."

(She reads it throughout.)

"Lisbet, you frighten me," said Mrs. Körner. "What does this mean? Were you thus insulted by your teacher?" (looking very serious.)

"My dear Lina, you are as literal as I was the other day when you asked me if I had 'Bacon,' and I answered that I had some in brine, when you meant the great English writer! No, surely not, to my knowledge. You still look doubtful; then, for the first time in my life, *I swear* that he has ever treated me with the respect due from one Christian to another. Why, you make me blush that it can seem possible to you that I should be treated thus. My husband never doubted me in his life. Don't you see my drift? I had to write a chapter upon some of the new notions of the day—magnetism, psychological twinship, etc., etc., and I naturally wished to make it a little thrilling, and I have a foolish fashion born with me, of thinking in petty dramas. So I just wrote down one of them as it bubbled up in my mind, and it frightens, when I thought only of amusing you. For *you* do not need the moral. I am sorry."

"But really I think you are too hard on Mr. Seüll, an exile, and alone in the world, as he says he is."

"An *exile!* well, all the better. It gives him an opportunity to make new acquaintances. *Alone, aloney*, he says, does he? I had hoped there was one man in the world of sensibility and genius who did not fancy himself *peculiar*, but would take everything in the shape of trial and training as a matter of course, as it comes along—in short, who begins life, expecting nothing, thinking he deserves but little, and then whatever favors come to him he regards as so much clear gain and is thankful accordingly. I hope, at least, he did not berate the world, because, forsooth, it did not *appreciate him?*"

"His conversation squinted that way once or twice; but he did not enlarge upon the subject."

"Do you think Mr. Seüll is self-conceited?" said Hilda.
" Rinda does."

" Not particularly so. All men are, you know. Of
course they must be from their self-imposed position, having
arranged themselves since time was, on an elevated plat-
form, with the women all below, who are bidden to look
up to them as *superior, stronger, more creative, indepen-
dent, worthy to receive due wages for their labor, the fa-
vored recipients for all the wine of life,* which froths to
the full brim."

" While your sex are destined to cook, *sew for,* and *com-
fort* them, that comes next," said Mr. Körner. " Lisbet,
you are falling into *cant;* don't repeat that again."

"No, for you seem to have learned the lesson. But,
seriously, I except you *almost* entirely. And, as for my
husband—"

" He is not self-conceited," said Hilda.

"No, not much—a trifle so now and then. But I
forbear to check him, for he is so faultless now that he
half loses his transcendental labor, preaching to this de-
generate age. So don't tell him, Hilda, for he would imme-
diately set about reforming. I don't like perfect people,
and I am sure the world is not good enough for such."

" But this Mr. Seüll, Lisbet, I don't quite like his giv-
ing you lessons," said Mr. Körner. "A Hungarian, a
countryman of Kossuth, your demigod; rather dangerous
for my enthusiastic little sister. What does your husband
say?"

" My husband! Surely he asked him to teach me
Hebrew. Why, he lets me do just what I please, and in
return I take every hint from him as an inspiration. The
other day, I dared to differ from him upon some verbal
matter in my 'Story,' and wrote it according to my taste
rather than his; but I lie awake nights about it, and so I
have got to hunt it up, for I have forgotten it, it was so
trifling, and change it according to his decision. That is

what wives do, who have their freedom. Don't hinder
Lina, if she ever takes a fancy to be *strong-minded* and
have her rights, for only so will she give you yours."

"As every right brings with it a duty, I have as many
now as I can respond to," said Mrs. Körner; "I do not
wish for more."

"Mr. Seüll speaks of his critical work to some of our
young men, the young elect, as you and Theresa call them,
and they make themselves merry about it and his numerous
corrections," said Mr. Körner.

"O! I suppose so, of course. No doubt *he* would come
in for a share of their ridicule, as nothing escapes their
carping criticism. He has not had time since he came into
Anglo-Saxondom to learn to be ' as wise as a serpent,' as I
have, with the brilliant but shallow spirits of the time, and
keep his generous designs for humanity for those who would
deem them not fanatical, but pitched to a tune higher than
the contralto voices around us can express; designs which
will swell the song of the millennial day, and be the *common*
sentiment of souls made glorious through truth. So much
do I distrust the judgment of any clique, who sip daintily
here and there at every new rivulet which bursts out from
hillside or glen, gathering a few sparkling drops to glitter
upon their pericraniums, leaving the great ocean and the
mighty rivers where they could learn their own specific
gravity, and be humble, and gather from their generous
depths to fill their belittled souls, that when they utter
their shrewd dicta, I turn instinctively to the opposite pole
of thought for the probable sanction of the truth revealed
to the docile pupil of the ages. Jesus not only gathered
up the knowledge and wisdom of all time to guide him
and prepare him to be the Christ, but paused at the rites
and symbols of his people—those sure landmarks by which
to judge the fidelity of discipleship to the good, the fair,
and beautiful—ever the same, standing before us in contrast
to the shifting waves of speculation, which make strange

inroads into the solid earth-banks. Such has been this Hungarian's course, ever breaking the fetters cast about him, deeming of little value the already attained, so that with strong grasp, he reaches after the truth beyond, while sign and ceremony give to his poetic soul the refining grace denied to those who, mole-eyed, see not their great significance. Look on this picture and then on that, and note well that the one will be revealed as the poet-critic, the child-philosopher, the Christian hero and patriot, and inspired divine; while the others, banished from the pinnacle on which an unsanctified imagination has self-exalted them, with penitent, willing hearts must return even as far back as the *two tables* for the religious strength of character they lack. And then it will seem plain to them, that sinking all petty differences of opinion, it is better, shoulder to shoulder, to do our part, to bear the ark of God along the centuries, than to slink away to fondle and hug to souls, into whom leanness enters more and more, an *ism*, an *ophy*, or an *ology*."

"As for Mr. Seüll, I fear not his displeasure for being made a victim by an illustration, indited with the intent of doing good, for he is Hungarian, which means noble; a Jew, which means acute in reading hidden meanings; a Christian, which makes him universal; and a German, which means *gemuthlich*—so much that is rare and excellent that it cannot be translated."

" You have a high opinion of him, Lisbet. I have failed to see all this in him," said Lina.

" Yes," said Mr. Körner; " these foreigners one knows but little about. You may as well be careful in trusting them."

"A foreigner, say you, and one of your own countrymen! That is like you Germans, forever talking of dear fatherland and sighing for the reunion of her principalities into one glorious commonwealth, and yet doing nothing to effect it. You do not wish for freedom nor reunion, else

you exiles would band together more in the expression of
a great central sentiment, even Christian toleration and
good-will.   Instead of that, you stand far aloof from each
other with a microscope in either hand, so that you need
not miss a single point of difference between you, gather
ing all such together to build a high wall of separation,
preventing all cordial effort in laboring for Germany."

"What is the use of trying for anything; it would do no
good, and only make us miserable, by stirring up useless
regrets," said Mr. Körner.

"You have no faith, more than our physician and good
friend.   It is not every one who, in seeking medical aid
can summon Poet, Philosopher, Reformer, and Doctor all
in one; and yet, of what use is all this glory, for when
my husband is ill, though I know he has beautiful boxes
of *Idealistic Pills*, which I dare say would cure him, so
little faith has he in their efficacy, that ten to one, he does
not give him salts and senna, or filthy calomel and jalap,
pah!   So it is, I fear, with his treatment of his country.
He gives it the bitter dose of sighs and tears, and keeps
the heroic to himself.   I see I shall have to take the matter
in hand.   I dare say I shall do more for your fatherland
than either of you, with all your wailing."

"Go on.   It may be that you will, I'll not hinder you."

"Who is your illustrator?" said Mr. Körner, turning
over a blank-book, in which were specimens of his art.
"He seems to have genius."

"That figure of Tyranny," said Zoë, "is very spirited
and expressive; how did you find one to suit you so well,
in this department of your work?"

"O! in true woman's fashion, Zoë; just as you would
have done.   In one of my prowling excursions about the
city, in which I drop into this picture-shop and that toy-
store, looking for suggestions here and there, and every-
where my truancy happens to lead me, I was walking
along Dritte-street, and I chanced to look up at the third

story of a building, and saw this sign—Lovie, Landscape
Painter, General Illustrator, and Designer; Bauerle, Artist.
Thinks I to myself, that is just what I want; an Illustrator
for my 'Way,' so I began to interpret. Lovie! so far, so
good. If a man has moral courage enough to call himself
thus in these times, when 'Hatie,' 'Fightie,' 'Slan-
derie,' 'I am-better-than-youie,' 'Down-with-youie,' are
the favorite cognomens, he must be the right one for me.
'General Illus.' etc. Surely if he can touch up the
universe in general, with his art, he can my little book:
better still—'Designer!' Then he is not a mere copyist
with no ideality. Heaven deliver me from such! Another
recommendation, 'Bauerle, Artist!' If his partner pre-
serves enough of the scent of the pine woods and green
fields when he gets to dry, dusty, legal Dritte-street, so as to
remember to call himself the 'Bower,' it is all I need.
I'll forthwith mount skyward. So I did, following one
staircase after another, until I saw the name repeated on a
door at the end of the passage. I knocked and entered,
without waiting for it to be opened, not exactly knowing the
etiquette of business-houses. One young man sat at a table,
writing or drawing, with his hat on. 'That must be the
'le Bower,' thought I, 'he keeps it on as a symbol, lest
he forget his rural name in these brick walls. The other
at his desk, a pale young man with gentle mien, arose to
greet me.

" 'Mr. Lovie?'" said I.

" 'That is my name.' "

" 'You illustrate books?' "

" 'I do?' "

" 'Will you mine?' "

" 'I will.' "

" 'And give me lessons in drawing?'"

" 'Even so.' "

" 'Please call at my house to-morrow morning.' "

" 'At eight o'clock?' "

" 'Precisely.' And so with a few more words, showing some ignorance on my part, of technical rules, we separated. The next day he came, with a little fear and suspicion in his aspect. I imagined, as he was bidden to mount the staircase at such unwonted summons, but which were dissipated as he found me no deluding cheat, and he does my work promptly, gladly and with appreciation as a Poet-Artist should, which proves to me that my mode of doing business is a very good one."

" Ha! ha! ha! But, my little sister, that is not quite the thing. Why did you not let your husband make the engagement? It is more proper for him to settle these matters for you."

" No, not while you and all the other strong men in our parish pile most of your religious work on his shoulders, until I see he begins to totter under the cruel load. I am not the one to add to his labors more than is possible, but am going to take care of myself. Three hundred and fifty husbands, wives, and children are too much for one man, even if he were the grand Sultan of the Turks. I vacate the spiritual harem and walk independently henceforth, until a better order of things is established. Besides, Mr. Liebenhoff was out of town just at the moment when my business must be attended to. He was gone, you know, to the yearly *Souls' Fair*, as your solitary purveyor in religious matters, hoping to get some celestial eye-water and heavenly ear-salve and angelic tonic to waken you up and cure your deafness and arouse your sleepy members altogether, for he is tired of repeating the siege of Sebastopol every Sabbath in his pulpit. I want him to disband the cavalry and artillery and give the infantry into my charge for a little time, and he will soon see what we will do. But he never acts rashly, you know, and believes less in revolution than amelioration; so he is reviewing the regiment, proclaiming freedom and equal rights to foot soldiers as well as officers, and goes on attacking the enemy with new

courage. I follow after with my little fife and drum, say-
ing, bravo! *sotto roce*, and carrying my own knapsack.
meantime, except when he *insists* upon relieving me."

"Good! you will conquer, I think. We are a rude and
lazy set of fellows to deal with, sure enough. But it is
a minister's work to attend to these matters; we have
enough else to do. But in what light are you going to
introduce our friend, Mr. Kuhn, to the world in your
Tale?"

"I have not made up my mind, whether to leave him to
the judgment of his own awakened conscience for prizing
it so lightly, or to steal that pretty little horse of his which
he drives too fast; for I have a compassionate consideration
for his future some thousands of years hence, when the
soul-spark in the poor animal, after passing through all
inferior metamorphoses, shall bloom into a beautiful young
lady in the heaven-sphere. Supposing that he should be
sailing along at the rate of a thousand leagues a minute,
upon a thunder-cloud edged with *tin*, which, you know,
shines pretty brightly and is so useful to you men that I
do not think you can *ever* do without it; and he should see
seated on the point of a rainbow, a bright and radiant sky-
nymph, clad in a robe made of the brilliant day-dawn, with
a zone around her waist cut from the bow of promise,
with diamonds in her hair and on her breast, and arms
crystallized from Sirius, such as Hilda loves; and he
should say, ' Come, take a sail with me.' Now if the fair
nymph were *à la she*, would not the witty answer be; ' I
thank you—no, I have learned better than to consort with
you, my one-time master, my equal, may-be, now. I know
not but in passing the *Yard and Ell* you would snap it in
two and use it for *Bits* to guide me, or snatch the comet's
tail to switch me with; or, if I paused a moment out of
breath, the twinkling of the stars as stirrups you would
force to do your bidding; or, at best, in passing by Saturn's
rings, whose refreshing waters I pant and ask for to quench

my thirst, 'Get up, gee-ho,' would all the answer be.' And
would she not serve him rightly by this tart speech, think
you? and would he not be sorry?   Or, if like Zoë were the
nymph, as tones of softest flute she would breathe her
reply, while like a mist the sun shines through, she floated
by his side. 'Hail, earth-companion on the dusty way; yea,
together we will quaff the ether of the New Jerusalem;
and while we glorify our good and loving Spirit-Father,
shining so gloriously, yet mildly from his Son, and be-
come one with them and this bright universe, and glitter in
star and reflect in moon and milky-way, and sing in the
music of the spheres, and paint with the never-setting sun,
now glowing with hues which earth but faintly dreamed of,
and poetize in measures which ever flow ' fast by the throne
of God,' whose inspiration lifts us to his own communion
not yet conceived of, we will, in trustful harmony, pursue
our way with backward, grateful, but pensive glance it may
be, at every trial of earth which but prepared us to chant
without a discord the song, in which shall mingle no harsh,
unloving symphony, *Glory to God, forevermore!*' "

" I hope you will not idealize any more horses, or I shall
lose my usual pleasure on Sunday afternoon."

" Only let me see your favorite one and at least you will
not drive it at the rate of ten miles the hour again."

" But really I think you had better leave that out about
the ' Wandering Jew.' "

"Impossible! It would be slighting the good gifts of
Providence not to make the most of him, for he is the only
character I have with a touch of the strange and awful
about him. All the rest of you I know like a book, and
you are as harmless and matter-of-fact as lambs; but he,
with eyes a mile deep, and mystery, and it may-be, mis-
chief back of that, is in some way to help me to a plot;
for our friend, Mr. Headrich, and even my sober, truthful
husband says a story is not worth much without one. How
I am to work it up is not at all clear to me, but it must

22

come through this stranger if at all, so you may as well ask me to stop writing altogether and close my brief life of authorship, as to banish him from the premises. Who knows but he was created on purpose to figure here? I should be no better than an infidel to reject him."

"You are very willful, I see."

"Yes, you must let me have my own way for once, and I shall live the longer for it, especially as I have been at the world's beck all my life in a certain fashion, more than I intend to be in future, I can tell you. So here I go at my own sweet will, and if any of you are sailing in a nice little skiff on some fine summer's day on waters which you have no right to, why look out for breakers when you see me ahead flying through the air on a broomstick."

"My gentle Lisbet!"

"O yes, gentle as old Boreas when let loose."

"My passive little sister can this be you?"

"Yes, passive as the sea in a storm, as the world in a general earthquake, as the sky when a hurricane sweeps over it; very, *very*, VERY passive, my penetrating brother! But really, there is no need for fear; I will commit no deed with pen and ink, which I am not willing you should repeat towards me. Indeed, if you please, in your first Tale you may have me for the only character, and show me in every possible light, provided you only do it in the loving spirit I do. So you see, I do not break the rule, '*to do as I would be done by.*'"

"Are you going to Mrs. Sarran's to-night, dear Lisbet?" said Mrs. Körner.

"Yes, I suppose so."

"Look as pretty as you can, for it will be a beautiful party in all its arrangements, I know; for hers always are."

"I will wear my best apparel, but my pretty looks depend very much upon other people. If you will tell the company to please let me look pretty and they will consent to, I shall be everlastingly obliged to you, for I have been longing to have them allow my beauty to shine out ever since I was born."

" What now, Mrs. Paradoxia?"

" Very plain and easy to understand. Such dull faces as Zoë's and mine, must be lighted up by interesting conversation to show well, and ten to one, there will not be any up to my mark."

" You must make it agreeable yourself. I shall watch you to see if you do your full part towards it."

" I shall try to as much as the prosaic times will allow me. I can talk with interest for a few minutes and be enthusiastic too upon the surface-subjects of the day — pickled nuts, the last new fashion, novel, news, or author, the prettiest belle, the different styles of matrons, magnificent, or discreet and plain—eloquent, artistic, *new* or *coming men*, war, pestilence or famine, but I tire of these transitional subjects and want to go on to the real and substantial, such as I indulge in in my day-dreams. Hey, Zoë!"

" Give us a specimen, by way of variety, to-night, to brighten up our circle a little."

" I have not the courage, when at the simple remark I made to you the other day, that when grapes grew almost spontaneously on the hillsides of more southern regions, it was a sign that the people might eat them and drink their juice, you laughed at me and called me fanciful."

" Never mind, talk as you like for all that. Drop the weather and expatiate."

" I want no better subject than the weather, if I can talk about it as I like."

"As how, for instance?"

" Well, supposing that Mr. Tubinger, who owns large wheat fields, comes to me with benevolent intent to play the agreeable, and after three repeated times informing me that the summer is delightfully cool and verdant but too rainy, adapting, as you see, his lordly mind to my capa-

city, I should answer: ' Yes, the seasons in their round are
in close correspondence with our inner and outer life.
Our sins and follies disturb the order of the physical, no
less than the moral and spiritual universe. Creation groans
till now with the foul and foolish deeds of those who should
perfect the work begun by its great Architect. Tempest,
storm, and inundation, which sweep with devastating fury,
are but expressions of the want of harmony between man
and man, and both with nature. Subdue the hurricane and
whirlwind in the interior soul, enlighten it upon the great
forces, which at God's bidding rule the world as second
causes; let each inhabitant of earth perform his part well
in conquering its arid plains and deadly swamps to use and
beauty, and the world would smile as an Elysium, and Uto-
pia would be no baseless fabric of a dream. Would he
not hem and ha, and think I was a lunatic? So, I say
quietly ' yes; but I think we shall have enough to eat and
drink.'

" Or, if I felt very cross, saucy and indignant, I should
add: ' Too rainy, is it? Is that an advertisement that your
crops are spoiled, and therefore, your prices will be heavy
for our staff of life? Shame, shame on you, when God,
with such abundance, pours from his garners food for the
millions of his children, that you should scramble to seize
an undue share by your monopolies, and make-believe a
dearth in the midst of groaning, bursting plenty! Ye shall
not have your selfish will. As there is justice and charity
above, ye shall be compelled to deal out your stores, in
meet obedience to true commercial laws. Gnash your
teeth—your avarice is impotent. Clench your hands—
your wickedness hath dealt its own death-blow, for in it,
as in a mirror, men will see how awful and unnatural it is
to pervert the free, unmerited gifts of Providence to their
own mean or selfish purposes, without thought or care for
the wants and miseries of others.' "

" Go on, I like it; hurra for Lisbet!" said Mr. Körner.

" O, you are too satirical!" said Lina.

" Not at all. Again, supposing you, my brother, should come to me, seeing me looking ennuyée, and should say brightly, ' What think of the times, little sister?' and exhilarated as I always am by you, I should answer, ' Bright visions beckon from over this dull waste of senseless folly, crudity, narrowness of thought and temporary swoon or captivity of all that is ennobling, beautiful and grand in European life. For out of this sad wreck of all free thought and frank and cordial brotherhood, from its atheism and mockery of truth, and low morality, from its closed artists' studios and authors' closets, double barred, and upturned printing-presses, and shut pulpit doors, and darkened courts of justice, shall come up a low indignant cry, which shall increase, and swell and burst at length, until it rends the welkin. It shall first rouse, like inarticulate thunder; it shall resound over the nations, its spirit, lightening as it goes, till these words, clear and commanding, shall, like the trump of God, make the dead live, and raise them to light and liberty. ' Citizen soldiers, standing armies, lay down your weapons, reeking with the blood of those *ye* have no quarrel with; disband your forces. *Ye* are the Gods of Europe. Without ye, the despot's hands fall in paralysis.' Let them see at last and tremble at the sight, that bayonets not only think, but speak and act. And this, their language is. ' Too long have ye wielded us for your own selfish purposes, too long have we been your slaves to do your hellish bidding. Wounded, bruised and maimed, made like the ravenous dogs in temper, like the wild brutes in soul, a spark still burns within us which shall flame up and scorch ye for the ruin ye have wrought upon us. Fight your own battles if ye will. If to the damned ye choose to go with the blood of millions on your skirts, ye drag not us beyond this very hour. We will not war against you in fearful revolution; blood has been spilled in floods, and still we are in chains. But we lay down our arms and

swear to fight no longer at your demoniac orders. Enough
to do in the short life allotted us, to live for God and our
own souls. Our children are born and live and die in
most unnatural severance from us, who gave them birth.
Wives, mothers, sisters weep till the eye loses its life and
stares sightless with the vain hope of greeting the son,
brother, husband of the sweet days long gone. For muti-
lated, worn and hopeless, with the springs of life all
broken before our time, with misery and sin high heaped
upon our souls, the cursed inheritance of cruel tyrants,
we totter home to die, a desolated troop. O spirit brave,
gentle and tender, whose name befits the music tuned by
Heaven within thee, who wert sent by God to soothe the
spirits of the *under-world* on earth, the battle-field and
camp, bind up the wounds of those poor, fainting ones,
steep them with cordials that strength may last for them to
travel homewards, and weep out their homesick souls upon
the bosom of their own and die, blessing you with their
last breath! O beautiful type of womanhood, made
strong by a faith, whose watchword is 'God and Humanity!'

    "'Kossuth! sublime, yet humble Christian Statesman,
braver in self-restraint than in the deeds ye wrought for
thy 'dear Hungary;' now is the time ye have long bided
for. Take what belongs to thee, thou leading man of
Europe, for thou wilt rule only to bless, till the time come,
of which thy prophetic heart failed but in this, that it
yearned to share too soon for its country's good, the rule
with lesser spirits. Lead for a while with firm, yet gener-
ous governance, the millions who look over to thee in thy
seclusion as their saviour. Marshal the forces, electrify
them with the spirit caught from him, who lived to bless,
and died to save mankind. Form Germany, Poland, Hun-
gary, many-sided, yet with one yearning heart, into a
Christian republic, each separate state an emporium for
art, or science, or learning, or morals, yet sending their
grateful tribute of life-blood to the centre, keeping it alive

with the true living ichor, fraternal love, then returning it
again in natural flow to every smallest member!

"'Louis, thou modern man-sphinx, with thy face of stone
and supple frame, now starting into this form and now that,
to riddle the gaping nations! thou wilt yet glorify the land
which the man of destiny, Napoleon, loved with such fond
but doomed affection. Thou wilt yet reveal thy genius in
a way more startling than any yet suspected. Thou wilt
take off the chains from Artists, Philosophers, and Poets
among thy countrymen, whose spiritual insight, whose in-
stincts, beauty-loving, spirituelle, shall flower in noble
action, prompting to greater labors, more enduring renown
than awaits those deemed stronger, more worldly-wise,
and mighty through rigid formalism. These sons of genius
thou wilt bid God-speed in fashioning and adorning *la belle
France*, till, charming, she stands forth in beauty bright,
the *graceful Lady of our continent*. Then it will be
proved to those who taunted her with capricious vacillation
and weak subservience, that though it was not in her chil-
dren to combine successfully for victory and power upon a
coarse idea, she has but waited for her soul to grow beauti-
ful, ay mighty, too, to announce her resurrection in heavenly,
poetic, artistic, eloquent utterance, and rise and shine with
glorious and growing lustre!'"

"What an oration!" said Mr. Körner. "Then that is
the way you would talk if you could, is it? Try it to-night.
I'll introduce you to the audience, and stand by you mean-
time."

"Of course I would not be so stupid as to be such a
nuisance in a party. Everything in its season, I say.
Conversation, light, graceful, tender, serious, airy, by turns
in the parlor, and orations and sermons in the lyceum and
church! When we women get the use of our tongues in
our legitimate sphere in the family circle, we will show
you how the thing ought to be done; but —"

" Indeed! everybody knows what chatterboxes you all are. What now?"

" Men are everybody, are they? Did you ever hear a woman say that her sex were the greatest talkers, making speeches four hours long in parliament, preaching sermons till they stretch to *twentiethly*, prosing hour after hour in private, standing in the door-way lengthening out their last words, *et cetera, et cetera!* I only ask you, or any of your brethren, to note the five next assemblings of—say three men and as many women in social converse, and see which division talks the most, and how many times any one of the ladies attempts to express herself and is not overborne by the louder voices of the other sex. That is all I want you to do. I am not anxious about the result. However, I am not entirely serious in *this* complaint at least. I believe that your sex ought to do the speaking in public. Let women write. They wield a pen of various power, and they can do it in the retirement they are fitted for. And even in private, I think that gentlemen may well form the *basis* of our conversation. Their substantial, granite natures are fitted for foundation-work of every kind. But if our thoughts, like vines and flowers, and rainbows and dew, or even a good pelting shower now and then, attended by thunder and lightning, which is very purifying you know, seek to gild and beautify and refresh, at intervals, do not say, ' pshaw, this is all flummery and nonsense. Let us brush the stuff away,' and then tramp on again with your heavy tread."

" Good. I'll agree to all this," said Mr. Körner.

" But to return to oratory," said she; " I simply meant that the spirit and subjects of our conversation should be more earnest and elevated than they are. I verily believe that many others as well as myself are revolving grave and stirring questions within, who simply give out the scum and froth of our best thoughts and feelings when we meet, and for that reason society has become tedious."

"I fully agree with you; let me stay at home and play with the children, I say. Yet if we would, through a broad culture, bring out what is in us all, each his separate gift, whatever it may be, society would be enlivening and elevating; but to stand up for four mortal hours and play and act the agreeable and interesting, with nothing inspiring in the tone or spirit of the gathering, is getting too much for my nerves, I confess," said Mr. Körner.

"I have not got to that pass yet," said Mrs. Körner. "I look forward with a child's delight to this evening."

"I am so glad," said Lisbet. "And why should you not, a sunbeam as you are, dance merrily here and there among those who love and court you for your warmth and brightness?"

"George Stephenson used to say, when his mother told him to dress himself for her evening company: 'Confound it, now we have got to stand and make faces at each other till mother orders in the provender, when we shall smudge round and eat apples in our prettiest way. Hilda, let's cut and run.'"

"Rather free-spoken was the said young American, but you seem to have a vivid recollection of him, my dear," said Mrs. Körner.

"I have. I wish I could see him now. I wonder if he is out in the western wilds of America, where he used to say he was going," and even Hilda looked dreamy and abstracted for a moment.

"But, sister mine, where did you learn so much, pray? What college gave you the prize for being *orator primus?* Tell me."

"Orator! did you say? I am no orator, only *men* are orators of course, who puzzle their brains and get angry if the children interrupt their awful lucubrations; who sit up till after midnight scratching their heads and drinking strong coffee, or brandy, gin, or what not; who smoke an extra number of cigars, or may-be take an opium pill or

23

two by way of inspiration. And when the mountain has brought forth a mouse, the procession forms, the best carriage draws up to the door, the *orator of the day* steps in, supported on either side by grave gentlemen in black relieved by dazzling vests, and through crowds he mounts the rostrum, rattles with cracked thunderbolts and lightens with mouldy electricity in long-drawn, faded streaks, while the initiated cry ' hear, hear!' When his eloquence has expired of inanition, he is borne away on shouts to the feast-table, where in deep potations he is drowned in the praises of his compeers, which soothe his vailed, wine-composed senses with the flattering unction of the *greatest Orator of these progressive times!* No, no, I am no orator, for I am only a woman and go about my daily work—now make a pudding, now smooth a pillow, sweep my parlor, prune my vines, and weed my flower-beds, or for recreation sew——and you know what; these thoughts and feelings meantime swelling and rising until they flow out for your and Lina's entertainment, and if for something better, my beloved ones, so much the happier for me. But I am no *orator;* that cannot be."

" What possesses you with the idea that Napoleon, the Little, is going to work such wonders, and how do you come by your spirit of prophecy? What is the secret of it, pray?"

" You must wait and see if my predictions come true, before you call me prophetic. How do I come by the spirit? Think of a practical Anglo-Saxon asking me, a dreamy Oriental, as I call myself, such a question! If you had not an aurora of poetry in you which shines out now and then, as when you tell the children their good-night stories, for instance, I would not deign to inform you. Why, man, I get it all through my *common sense.* Yes, simply my common sense, which you all boast of so much, but of which there is a disgraceful, diminishing, and dis-heartening dearth in these dreary, drudging, dreadful

times among *your* sex, to say the least.   Ours will have to
come to the rescue, I plainly see."

" But you have forgotten to answer my question."

" You should know yourself.   Our Journals have ex-
posed the result of Louis' great intentions.   Did you not
read yesterday's paper?"

" Yes, but I saw nothing of this kind."

" Strange, when it was so prominent!   You must not be
so busy with those law papers and then you would not fall
behind the times.   Why, in one of them was this announce-
ment: ' That the empress Eugenie's face was remarkable
for nothing so much as for its expression of a sense of
enjoyment,' which added to what I know of the emperor
through other sources, led me to this train of thought, and
I leave it to you if it is not very common-sensible.

" ' Now,'thought I,'if Napoleon were as mean and wicked
as the world says, Eugenie's face would wear a different
look from that.   There have been times since their mar-
riage when she seemed unhappy, and *they say*, that it
might be because her husband resolved in his mind
whether he had better not repeat the sacrifice of his uncle
in giving up Josephine.   But Louis and Eugenie's was a
real love marriage, and great good always comes from such.
At any rate, all seems right between them now.   Still, I do
not think it would be sufficient even for the happiness of
an empress, though I grant she is in a very false position and
one which is liable to make her very selfish, to throw over
her face the glow of a lively sense of enjoyment, simply to
have her husband love her if he were a very wicked man
at heart, or did not at least give strong symptoms of re-
forming.   No, Lisbet, you may depend upon it, she knows
a fact or two, and how to keep her husband's secrets too.
I have great faith also in *stone)faces*, and that trustworthy
newsman, *they say*, says that his is one of the purest water.
Depend upon it, that underneath this dull surface some-
thing great and good is revolving for her and the country

of her adoption. He has a strong will, a power of com-
mand, and executive abilities, all requisite in its present
condition. Yes, he is just the man suited to succeed at
this distance of time, that great genius and reformer, the
first Napoleon. He will, guided by his example where it
was wise, warned by his mistakes, with a sage insight into
the spirit of the times and the requirements of the age,
strike the first hour upon the horologe which is to usher in
a new era of civilization, in which Art, Science, Literature,
and Religion are to supersede Hatred, Tyranny, War, and
Diplomacy in preserving the balance of power in Europe,
and allow the peculiar genius of either nation to attain its
natural development and growth.' All this I read in Euge-
nic's face, revealed with a true woman's artlessness, and
you may be sure that she too will do her full part in bring-
ing about this new order of things.

"Now, do not say *absurd* to my mode of reasoning, but
wait five years and then pass your judgment upon it. I
see in Lina's face that she does not think I am an idiot."

"O Lisbet, day by day is it revealed to me, why, when
scarce beyond my infant years, as with fond care you led
me to our rustic day-school, I felt such pride in your pro-
tection, and why, when the stranger met us on our home-
ward way, I nestled close beside you, that he might know
I was *your* little sister. And now I greet you with glad and
grateful welcome in your new sphere of thought and duty,
sure that as with meek and patient spirit ye have gathered
treasures, too subtle for me, engrossed as I am, with my
maternal cares to grasp at, so will ye with true and graceful
feminine force express them in the great cause of raising
woman to her rights and duties. I only fear, that in your
zeal for truth, you may overstep the line beyond which the
world brooks not reproach and criticism. My loving heart
bids me to keep the chain of affection ever bright between
myself and others, and I do not compromise the truth, I
ween, in doing thus. And they must love you even as I am

loved, or half my happiness is missing. Keep in mind your mutual relations with the friends at least around you, and how painful will be a chasm between you wrought by too free a pen."

" Lina, I thank you for your kind greeting, and no less for the words of caution mingled with it. Think not that with unguarded spirit, I dash the crudities of my careless play-hours in the faces of my contemporaries. But with affectionate, reverent spirit, as befits a child of the All-Perfect, who, with wondrous skill made this our time-sphere, and pronounced it good; so do I gather the productions of my heart and brain, and weave them in simple fashion, but with serious purpose, with traits and incidents and expressions of my own and the little world about me, with careful hand pruning my work of every falsehood to Nature and God, hoping not to offend, but to give pleasure to the passing hour. But by the fiat announced by Him, who would have his children worthy of their high destiny, to immolate ourselves, rather than to offend one of the laws by which we are darkly held, I must reprove as well as praise. O, my sister, ye have called to mind our child-hood, with your infant pride in me, and I have ever deemed it as but a foolish fancy; though I loved you for it. But I will be worthy of your early instinctive admira-tion, nor mar with bitterness, the fair home of love, which is the necessity of your being, but strive to have it fairer, more worthy of you through my bold pen. For it is made of a precious metal, the gift of friendship and relationship, and dipped in the milk of human kindness, which cannot, if it would, draw else than lines which run parallel with truth and love, though in the process it may strive to sever in all good faith, the ruinous excrescences from our lives, and touch them with added healthful grace and loveli-ness."

" Then, dear, erase some of the most pointed remarks, please do," said Mrs. Körner.

" Lina. I mind the time, when sleeping on your baby-couch, our mother and I would gaze in rapture on your un-earthly beauty, as your cheek lightly rested on the tiny hand, the dark eyes closed in sweet repose, the lips divided by a smile, the forehead with delicate veins coursing across it, like rivulets repeating the upper sky-blue, and forehead expanded heaven-like, telling tales of the angels who joy-ously danced within. As with one breath, we would ex-claim, ' how lovely!' I would question sadly, why, when I closed my weary eyes to sleep, my brow would settle into a frown of distress, and strange and fearful and unchildlike dreams would lower from the darkness round me. Our fates to me are now interpreted. You have fulfilled your early promise. Affection, beauty, brightness and appro-bation attend your every act, for each is overflowing with sympathy and humanity. The suffering poor feed from your open hand, which meantime softly heals the soreness of their grieved natures. The sad and lonely cast but a glance at your ' kind loving eyes,' and straightway lay their burdens in your bosom. Birth, death, marriage, and burial among those whom colder hearts would deem no claimants are all familiar to you, who shed your sympathy like the sweet dew from heaven, on all who ask it by look or word or sign of grief, while, if it might be, you would gather to your Eden a multitudinous household, and ' keep them warm ' with your embrace."

" Do not flatter me, I but consult my happiness," said Mrs. Körner.

" It is no flattery, but the simple truth, my Lina," said her husband.

" I, on the other hand, like Memnon's statue, have stood in stony silence, my music sounding deep within me, wait-ing for the rising Sun's rays to strike my harp of thou-sand strings, and chant anew the song of Bethlehem's angels. Strange, that it should keep in tune so long amid life's chills and damps and heats, and the coarse world's

rude handling; for my childhood mates have lived, acted,
uttered their oracles, and died, or have been absorbed in
the spirit of the times, making bnt slight individual mark,
by which to date their memories. Children have risen
since around me, and soon outgrown my dull intelligence
in Fashion, Elegance, Esprit du corps, Science, Art, and
Literature, Mental Acumen, and Skill of Leadership, each
one measuring the other by prominent development in one
of these or all, as is the custom. But I have simply lived
a *Soul*, growing by every influence Our Father sheds
around me, but chiefly by stretching my stature heavenward
to grasp his beams of light shed downwards. They have
guided me through no mean gymnasium which has trained
and strengthened me till now. But such culture befits not
one who would stand forth distinguished enough to influence
largely, or give a prestige so as to be heard with gentle de-
ference, though truth and beauty may drop like honey
from the lips. Such manners and such regard are given
to strong colors, red, yellow, or black and white mingled
in striking contrast. But I, a neutral tint, though striving
to mingle in the shade the elements of all the rest in fitting
harmony, have been too insignificant to reflect the rays of
any inferior luminary, shining by borrowed light. I have
waited for the Sun of righteousness to revolve near my
orbit with his full day of splendor, dawning near, to waken
me to give forth such music as he approves.

"I am his instrument, and if the chords may sometimes
rudely jangle, it is, that through temporary discord, they
may be attuned to the sublimest harmonies and charm and
elevate the listeners. I give you what is in me. Take it
in the spirit of love with which I yield it. It is the concen-
trated essence of my life-song, ever sounding on through
all the weary years, but too much blended with the sounds
of Nature to be distinctly heard, except when some meek,
docile listener, with ear quickened by nightly chant of
spirits in his dreams, has placed his ear with loving trust

to my stone face and deemed the rising Sun's rays the sole awakening cause of what he called unwonted strains, but which I have ever striven to sing from every pore of my stony-tinted being."

" Dear Lisbet, Memnon's music has never been turned from with a deaf ear by me, though I knew not its varied power of utterance. But to drop the figure, I simply meant to express the idea that in a work designed for the widest good, much tact and judgment must be used in its construction, and in the handling of the different characters, so as not to place you in antagonism with any of your readers, or at least as few as possible. What you say about your husband's parish, for instance, may offend more than benefit."

" My dear, I write for people who are gifted with common capacities, of course. One must at least, presume upon thus much. I only ask for the judgment of patient and sensible readers.

" The parish! I have been thinking that, like Æsop, I must take a candle at noonday to hunt it up, so gracefully it was bowing itself away from our entreaties to build anew our sanctuary; though when the pastor's services are needed for its multiform requirements, it starts up obvious enough. But, supposing that I should, in playful fashion, place in opposite scales on one hand, the awful injuries inflicted upon it by my pretty golden goosequill, and on the other the wrongs of the sisterhood of ministers' wives. For they grow uneasy upon the Procrustean bed on which they are bound and cry out for freedom from their restraint. *I* have no great complaint to make, for a neutral-tinted object is seldom aimed at by the marksman, it is not sufficiently evident to the eye, you know. Or, if some very sharp-eyed hunter notes me and raises his bow, I pass on, saying, ' It cannot be for me, O no!' And even if the arrows hit me, I am guarded by such proof-panoply within, that they slide from me like rain from off a cabbage leaf. So it is not for *myself* so much as *them*, I use the scales of justice."

'Weigh on,'' said Mr. Körner; " we'll see which side kicks the beam."

" Well, *first item*.   To be made the subject of a long debate between wise men and sage elderly maidens, on our matrimonial eve, upon whether ' we'll *do* ' for the fearful responsibilities of our future position. *Item second*. After careful calculation upon how little salary will supply our husband's slenderest needs, *to be thrown in as a makeweight* in the scale which tips too lightly on his side to the eye of careful bargainers. *Item third*. To have the same wise men comment upon the undue attentions which the pastor pays the bride during the honeymoon, thereby neglecting them, their wives and children; and the said elderly maidens throw up their eyes at the extravagance of her wedding *trousseau,* and especially at that bright bow or feather which she presumptuously sports in their face and eyes. *Item fourth*. To be so unfortunate as to throw the whole parish into convulsions if she steps to music a half hour or two, though the wives and daughters may meantime dance to early dawn; or into an incurable fever, because, forsooth, she goes to see a drama enacted, though she may meet the parishioners in a body at the play-house, on the plea that she *sets a bad example! Item fifth*. To have her first-born, and all that come after him, looked at askance by the reckless youths of the community if he happen to frolic extravagantly, when misled, it may be, by them, with the sneering remark, ' pastors' sons are always dissipated.' *Item sixth*. To be chief surveyor, engineer, conductor, and engine-tender of the locomotive society, so far as it devolves on women to keep it running, in order that the *majority* of her sex who are more favored by fortune may sit apart in indolent, elegant, fastidious leisure and seclusion from the vulgar labors, social connections and interests of the rude world at large, so detrimental by its contact to the superficial gloss and tinsel of fashionable and dilettante living. *Item seventh.* While at the same time she denies herself a generous cultivation of her artistic tastes and literary aspirations for want of time, engrossed by her public and social duties and family cares, increased by the necessity of earning, by some means, her own wardrobe, denied by the meagreness of the living granted her by the *parish.* Now look at the scales please, and tell me which side tips."

" Stop," said Mrs. Körner; " put first into them the affection and its tokens which ever have attended you, brightening your face with smiles while saying, ' how good God is, shown in these symbols of their love, blossoming thus beautifully in kindly deeds!' "

" Ay, Lina, not one is forgotten, but the spirit with which they were proffered is cherished in my heart of hearts. The children walk delighted through my dwelling and say, ' How many pretty things our pastor's wife has!' and I answer gladly, ' Gifts all of dear affection, doubly valued for themselves and for their beautiful associations.' The custom of the ancient Cyrus is repeated, who, when the meat and bread upon his table was grateful to his taste, said: ' Take the other half to yonder friend, and say, Cyrus loves this, receive it from him.' And when I walk abroad, proud of my brave attire, I say of some ornament, ' this was the choice of friendship, it fits me well.' "

" Then what would you have? You surely are not sordid, though really your speech tends that way. Should the sisterhood have a separate salary in addition to their husband's, in consideration of their interest and aid in his labors?"

" O no, no, no! we are too conventional and commercial now in our modes of showing our interest in each other, and it divides those who should be members, one in spirit, as they are of one ' household of faith.' A cordial greeting, a look saying 'God speed you on your way!' a flower, a little mint, the slightest favor expressing our spiritual relationship, would go far to unite those who fear to make life a drudgery by too general a sympathy, and so look askance lest the least greeting should draw down upon them a host of social obligations such as the fashion of the times exact. What I mean is this: that no woman should be set apart, as too holy by her position to mingle in any sports or recreations suited to her associates. It degrades both her and them by a miserable superstition. Nor in the work of life are they, more than she, exempted from the responsibility, which each one owes as a Christian woman, to do her full part to bring the world up to the tone of God's requirements. Each one should be a priestess of the Most High, and not only see that she burn no strange fire upon the altar of her faith, but that the pure flame of holy life shine brighter and brighter to the perfect day. Then no unequal burden would heavily weigh on one, no better fitted nor gifted with greater strength than others to bear along the interests of humanity; but while she could claim her share of leisure for beautiful culture and refreshing recreation, many a one, now palsied in mind, heart, and body by indolence and ennui, and an aimless life, will waken as from the dead at the summons to the true life-work, which now is resting upon a few wearied, and anxious, and over-worked ones, starving their fancy and living taste for beauty for want of leisure and pecuniary means with which to indulge their cravings."

"You are very radical, Lisbet. The world will call you a disorganizer," said Mr. Körner.

"I am, and I care not what it calls me, provided some words of mine may express the indefinite wish which many have for a reform, and thus hasten on its progress. We are souls and should have a soul's true existence, for no one, however just, is unaffected by the atmosphere of society around him, and I, for one, yearn for the companionship which is shut out from me by overgrown conventionalism. Sects, coteries, societies but divide us from each other. Even those of the same household, who have lived through every experience of mortal life together, birth, death, marriage, heart-rending agony, sickness, sorrow, and success, are ignorant as unborn babes of what makes each other's life-pulse beat with highest hope or sink in sad disheartenment. I say farewell forever to paltry self-seeking, exacting friendships such as these; *Mene, Mene, Tekel, Upharsin* is written against them on my heart of hearts, dooming them to banishment and eternal condemnation. They rob us of half our life; for a soul shut up within itself, denied full expression of what it lives, and moves, and has its being for, is but half living. And how can Psyche spread her wings and soar to the empyrean with no elastic atmosphere to buoy her up and answer, breath for breath, to the timid fluttering of her gauzy wings? Psyche! strange work must be thine own in this enlightened age of *intellect*, but darkened and misled concerning thee and thy just claims! Fold thy delicate pinions and take the pickaxe, spade, and auger, and bore deep, deep down to the crystal fount of human nature; free the pure stream of truth which surely flows beneath all upper incrustation, however dense, discouraging and dubious it may seem to the weak in faith. Tire not, but work in love, in season and out of season, by night and by day, alone or with the cold, indifferent, or sneering world gathered around thee to witness thy defeat. God, through his Son who bade thee to the work, looks on and cheers thee. Patience a little longer, and the living waters, buried for ages, shall, freed from their dark imprisonment, mount up high and still higher to greet the upper sunlight, and then descend in purifying showers, cleansing the atmosphere of all impurities, and leaving it healthful and inspiring. Meantime, it plays in fountains, flows on in rivers, falls in cataracts, collects in reservoirs, and is spread

from thence through every household, clearing, purifying
and gladdening all by its life and lustrous virtues. Psyche!
then spread thy wings, refreshed by rest, strengthened by
labor of thy more corporeal members, and fly into the clear
transparent blue. Now shall men see thee as thou art, the
symbol, expressive of what their life should be, strong,
vigorous, manly for thy earth-labors, but with wings fitly
plumed for highest soarings — heaven and earth in closest
junction, as befits children of time, but heirs of heaven."

"Lisbet, destroy not unless you re-create a new and
better friendship than you condemn. How can we live, how
can society exist without connections, rude they may be,
yet necessary to existence and efficient action here below?
Tell me the remedy for our social ills; show me the sub-
stitute for what you banish."

"The Church! my Lina, formed of all living souls, each
one alive to the priceless worth of his own nature and its
development, burning with zeal to live like our great
Leader, our elder brother, God's most obedient Son,
nature's sole true interpreter, and to be one with him and
God! The Church! beginning with the household, going
out to our little company of fellow-worshipers, and spread-
ing and spreading till it becomes a Christian common-
wealth, embracing all people, tongues, and nations."

"A grand idea worthy of your husband! You have been
his docile pupil," said Mrs. Körner.

"I have; but do not think it caught by rote from him.
My soul is quickened, a-blaze with this great sentiment.
O Lina! join this great communion; come to his feast.
Spurn from your generous and child-like soul the coarse,
metallic spirit of the age, if but its shadow has crossed it,
which sees in these simple symbols nothing but elements
of material bread and wine. They come to us from that
dark hour when he, the brother of our purest heart of
hearts, was in life's dire extremity. They whisper to us
in tones sadder and softer than any voice can utter, to

remember him who died that we might live. They summon us to awaken from our lethargy and sins, and be renewed in spirit and glorified in life ; to commune through them with the great and good of all past, present, and coming time, with Jesus, as master of the feast, who blends in his great spirit the genius of all that is true and pure in the religions of the ages with the poetry of nature, to form the subtle essence of his own eternal Christianity."

" We come.

"Ay, ay, we come."

"O! let us join you also, in our youth," said Zoë and Hilda.

"And I too," said the child. "Do you love me, my aunty?"

" Yes, darlings, each and every one. The sweetest flowers shall be glad offerings to our Lord, no less than the ripened fruit. Come one, come all!"

" Now we will leave you better, I trust, and happier for our meeting. Adieu, my sister!" said Mr. Körner.

" Till we meet again this evening, adieu, dear Lisbet!" said Lina.

"O this evening! Yes, I think I'll go. I feel at home at Mr. Sarran's; his benevolent face, beaming a benison upon his guests, is even better than if his speech were freer without it, and the kind, gentle greeting of the hostess reminds me of our mother. But wear that full gray robe of yours, my Lina, please, that if I fail of courage in a large company—for my heart sinks in entering a crowd— I may hide my head between its folds, and, like the silly fowl, imagine myself not seen. Or, now I think of it, our hostess wears neutral tints, and I'll stand close by her, or, if she is called away, I can hide myself behind the busts and statuettes, or, if *they* are engrossed, I'll retire into the library and put my face close to the portrait of my early friend, and may-be they will think I am simply a shade of that, for when we were young, it was said we looked alike.

Or better still, I'll sit upon the sofa with Miss Farrel; her face is almost as stony as mine, ay, and covers as much too, which will shine out some day to the amazement of the superficial. We'll chat, and the guests will say: 'Are there two there? No, yes, no; on the whole, there is but one. How prettily she crochets!'"

"Lisbet, darling, let me say one word, and deem me not intrusive. Your serious words have sunk deep into my heart; your light ones jar upon my spirit, following in such quick succession."

"Why, Lina? Dive deep into your soul and note in your most natural hours, if various tones sweep not, one after another, over its harp-strings. If pure and loving in their spirit, they make no discord, but form a richer, more thrilling melody. Look abroad on nature. Now it rains gently, making sweet symphonies; now pours in torrents, lightening for stage lamps and thundering for the chorus of the orchestra. Momently, the sun breaks from behind a cloud, like the great Primus Don, to dazzle us with the splendor of his acting. Do these changes in the heaven-theatre seem rude, unfeeling, and untimely? O let me be free, at least with you, my sister! I am too grave and ser-monizing to suit *my* taste and fancy. My spirit is like a rainbow, many-tinted. Would that the atmosphere would reflect half its brightness! I live in the hope it some day will. But even now shadows are flitting across my vision, many-eyed and quick to *sense* the future. Heaven grant they may not darken around us! Adieu, adieu! Pray heaven for strength and guidance!"

CHAPTER XXI.

" The canker galls the infants of the spring
    Too often before their buttons be disclosed ;
    And in the warm and liquid dew of youth
    Contagious blastments are most imminent."—SHAKSPEARE.

ZOË'S eighteenth birthday had just passed, and she was beginning to look forward to rejoining her parents, from whom she had so long been exiled. A ship was soon to sail for Santa Cruz, and the question was debated by them whether she should return in it or wait for six months longer, when another opportunity would offer for her passage to the island. For a reason which will hereafter appear, they decided that, notwithstanding their yearning desire to see her again, which, on the part of her mother, had become almost a mania, it still was better that she should remain in Denmark for the present. In this Zoë more willingly acquiesced than she would have done before her intimacy with Mrs. Liebenhoff commenced. In her she found much relief from the devourings of her own nature, turned in upon itself for lack of proper sympathy and a nutriment congenial to it, and in that lady's high-toned and enthusiastic character and sentiments, accompanied, as they were, by a warm and growing attachment to herself, she found an approach to the ideal friendship of her day-dreams. On the one hand, the intimacy between them was beneficial to her. On the other, considering that her imagination was already unduly developed,

(290)

and her aspirations and religious sentiments in advance of
the character possible to an inexperienced young girl,
whose world had been as yet only within herself and her
school-room, and whose principles were not matured and
strengthened by practical life, the soarings of her friend
into the ideal and imaginative, as was her custom, acted
unfavorably upon her. These were but the flowering of
Mrs. Liebenhoff's nature on the summit of an experience,
which had strengthened her to the degree that there was
no exhaustion resulting from the act; the fruitage of a life
so matured by faithful labor, watchfulness, and a culture
suited to the soil of her mind, that it poured forth its abun-
dant harvest spontaneously, without danger of injury. If
the present influence upon Zoë were considered, she
might be said to have erred in her intercourse with her,
though in a way very natural. Never before had she found
one so much like herself in her original constitution, and
at the same time, with equal simplicity and unworldliness
of character. Wearied as she was with many of the con-
ventionalisms of society, baulked of a full expression of
her aspirations and feelings by the different way of look-
ing upon life and the future of most of her friends and
associates, when with Zoë, childlike yet mature, imagina-
tive and highly refined, and with a true eye for the beauti-
ful in literature and art, yet fashioned, as she was, very
much by the Hebrew Scriptures, and after the model of
the ideal presented by them, she felt such delight in her
companionship, that her whole nature gushed forth like
the crystal stream from the fountain, delighting and elevat-
ing, but, at the same time, dazzling and unduly exciting
her. To be sure, she gave her the wisest counsel, suited
to her years and her peculiarities; but these were to bear
fruit in her pupil-friend afterwards, while the intoxication
of her fellowship was working daily in this impassioned
child of the Tropics.

24

"O Hilda!" said she, as she walked homewards, "I feel as if Mrs. Liebenhoff were inspired whenever I am in her presence. Even when I am sitting in silence with her, when she is writing or sewing, or whatever she may be doing, I am raised above my common life. Do you not think there are some persons who shed virtue from them as our Saviour did, without their voluntary will, simply because they are so good and pure? I know I feel very differently when with her from what I ever do with Miss Ingemann."

"Miss Ingemann is good and pure, too," said Hilda.

"Yes, I know it; but compared with Mrs. Liebenhoff, she is worldly and common-place. They seem to me as unlike in character as this Madonna, on my breastpin, is from that portrait hanging up in the hall with a crape cushion on her head and stiff stays on."

"Mrs. Liebenhoff is *too little* conventional to suit my taste. I think she carries her ideas of fraternity and sisterhood too far. She would make people all alike, it seems to me. We should have no kings and queens, nor even noblemen and ladies, with common people and servants to work for and wait upon them; and I should not like that. I am for preserving my dignity and not suffering every menial and low-bred person to encroach upon me. I must say I like to use my power over those beneath me, and order them round a little. It makes me feel respectable;" and Hilda raised her head and made herself as tall as possible.

"I have never seen any one, not even Miss Ingemann, who had such control over other minds as she has, and I do not think it would be possible for one to treat her with disrespect," said Zoë. "Her power is within, and her rule, one which a proper self-respect, joined with love and sympathy for every human being, gives her. O Hilda, in the millennium, which I cannot but think is near, I believe that God will be the only King, and Jesus the great Leader of the world, with a more beautiful dominion than any there are now on the earth. *I* want no other."

" Then, if you were presented at Court, you would treat our King and Queen just like other people, would you?"

" No, indeed, that would be very absurd and wrong. God permits them at present to rule over us, and with a pretty mild sway, compared with that of other wretched countries in Europe. I should get instructions from some one who had been there before me of how I must behave with propriety, and I should not hesitate to say, ' your majesty,' as is the custom; and I think it a very pretty title for one who tries to deserve it as our good Queen does. But if I thought, that in her heart of hearts, she did not see, that by virtue of being a child of the Most High, and one who tries above all things, to serve him truly, I were as good as she, I should call her no lady."

" Indeed! Well these are new fashions of yours and Mrs. Liebenhoff's. I suppose you would like a republic, such as they have in America."

" I certainly should, only a better one, for Mrs. Liebenhoff says they retain still in that, a good many false, feudal notions in their government and social life. I want a real Christian Republic, such as Jesus would establish, were he to come on the earth, in which every one would be free to develop their natures according to their own and God's laws, government only serving to protect them in this great work, and placing as many facilities in the way of it as possible, and in which all the people would, in reality, feel that they were equal in the eye of God and adapt their manners and customs to the idea. You see that my year's intimacy with Mrs. Liebenhoff has not been lost upon me."

" No, I see," said Hilda, thinking at the same time, that although Zoë had been happier and less irritable in her feelings than before she knew her, yet, that she was even more given to abstraction and more positive than ever in clinging to what seemed to her extravagant fancies and opinions than formerly. At any rate, there was less and less sympathy if possible, between her and Miss Ingemann, and this and the evils resulting from it were the greatest trials of her own sunshiny life.

As has been said, Zoë's sentiments and imagination were in advance of her years; her physique reached its maturity at a later period than usual. While Hilda, at her age, had the development, character and bearing of a young lady, at least twenty-one, though mingled with great naïveté and vivacity; Zoë, on the contrary, at eighteen, wore still the appearance of a young girl just budding into womanhood. She was of medium height, of slender and symmetrical figure, graceful, but languid in her movements, with a face which seldom varied its expression from one of almost stolid repose, when with those uncongenial to her, or a pensive look of appeal and eager questioning, when with those she loved and trusted in. Her complexion was that of a clear brunette, her features regular, her eye being dark, soft and mournful, her nose delicate in its formation, though widening at the nostrils sufficient to give it character, and the lips just full enough to enrich and humanize a face, otherwise so ethereal in its beauty, as to mingle the pleasure with which she was regarded with the painful thought, that she would not be long for this world. Her hair was very dark and shining, and wearing it as she did, parted in front, confined by a band, with a rich mass of curls on the back part of her head, when she appeared abroad, she was always noticeable, no less for her beauty than for its foreign characteristics, which distinguished her from all her companions.

"How beautiful Zoë Carlan, your West-Indian pupil, has grown!" said a lady-visitor one day to Miss Ingemann. "I had no idea that she would develop so prettily."

"Yes," said Miss Ingemann, "but her face sadly lacks character, and for that it has ceased to interest me. It is but a transcript of her mind, which I have decided will always remain weak and childlike. I never shall be able to develop it beyond a certain point, and that a low one. She does not try me as much as formerly, because I see plainly her incapacity for high culture, and I resign myself now to her returning home with but a smattering of the branches taught her."

"Ah! I had the idea that she was very bright. Mr. Liebenhoff told me yesterday, that she had a rare nature."

" His wife has brought him over to her faith, I suppose. The two are very intimate," and she laughed. "A fitting companion enough for her she is too. I wish our Pastor had a partner who could support herself better in a position which calls for much strength and dignity of character. Were she really *superior* she might give such a high tone to our social circle. By way of complaisance, we have to place her in responsible stations when we meet for various purposes; but really, there are so many others better fitted for them, and who really do from necessity take the lead, that it seems a mere compliment."

" This, at least, can be said of her," rejoined her friend, that she claims no skill in leadership, and on the whole, we get along more peaceably than if she were always *queening* it over us. I sometimes think it is a principle with her to keep in the background, as she does, that others may take the parts they are well fitted for. You know she is pretty radical upon the subject of all government."

" I know but little of her opinions excepting that I con-sider her moon-struck generally, and for that reason, I have dreaded her influence over Zoë, who has no balance of mind and character. All that I can do under the circumstances, however, is to counteract it as far as possible through her school lessons. I endeavor to do my duty by her."

So there was no relaxation for her pupil in her daily studies, but her powers were unnaturally taxed for many hours each day in acquiring an insight into dry metaphysics, or still dryer mathematics, so that at the most critical period of a young girl's life, on which depends very much her future fitness or otherwise, for its duties and enjoyments, her brain and nervous system were taxed to the utmost, without their being supplied with that strength and nutriment necessary to their well-being by air, exercise, and proper attention to general physiological laws. Added to this, Zoë was homesick from morbidly dwelling upon her mother and the love with which she would cherish her, and which was denied in a boarding-school, where, if she had been ever so attractive to her teacher, she could share her favor only with forty others. She was heartsick from knowing that, do what she would in accordance with her natural genius, she never suited one, whose methods of culture were so rigid as Miss Ingemann's, and whose views of human nature were graduated by the standard of judgment, most favored in this practical and intellectual age, by the narrow, keen, coarse, one-sided Anglo-Saxon mind. Added to these unfavorable circumstances were her premature religious sensibilities. Had she been under the modern American *evangelical* influence, so called, where there is a regular system in vogue of blowing up the tender souls of the young into a flame of excitement before the character is fitted to sustain, or the religious knowledge sufficient to guide, or the wisdom ripe enough to protect and train it in its great life-work, she would either have become a maniac or a blasé religionist, or, perhaps, as many do, have gone to the other extreme in animalism or infidelity. But, fortunately, she was subjected to no such forcing process in this respect. Miss Ingemann was a conscientious, sensible woman, who believed that as soon as she had a religious conviction it was to be carried out in practice. She instructed her pupils in our Christian faith, as she understood it. She was a Lutheran; but dogmatics are not carried to the extreme, in Europe, that they are in

America, so that their minds were much less overlaid than they would have been there with articles of human creeds. They were taught Christian morals and piety—in a modified form, it is true—still with less admixture of error than would have been possible in such hotbeds of Calvinism. Then Mr. Liebenhoff was of a wise, enlightened, and deeply Christian spirit; and his pulpit instructions were adapted to the guidance of souls, who have a great and good life-work to accomplish, leaving but little time to sharpen the wits to unnatural shrewdness by polemics. At home and at school, the Bible was pointed to as the chart by which they were to guide their steps, and train their spirits, both through time and eternity.

Enough has been said to show Zoë's appreciation of this volume, and the part it had in her training. Her mother had given her one when she left her, saying, at the same time, " Read this, Zoë, every day, and not only God and Jesus will be with you when you do so, but your own loving mamma, too; for by the light of the holy Word I shall see that my darling is under their kind care, and that when they will it, I shall fold you to my arms again." For years she had a superstitious, it may be, but none the less strong feeling, that when she sat down to peruse its pages her mother was near her, though unseen, guiding her in the selection for the day, and impressing upon her childish mind a reverence and love for its truths. So that her filial affections were constantly operating to form and strengthen her religious ones, at the same time that her absence from her threw a vail of romance, not only over the image of her which was impressed indelibly upon her mind, but also over the Scriptures with which that image was indissolubly connected.

Human nature is the most delicate and precious creation of God, and to develop and mature it worthily of its great Author and its high destination, it must have no one-sided or eccentric culture, though even that may be of a purifying

and elevating character. Zoë's undue absorption in relig-
ion made her superstitious and fanatical. She suffered
from a want of confiding and affectionate intercourse with
a variety of minds, and a more practical knowledge of the
world and its concerns. Hence her feelings became un-
duly concentrated upon herself. Both her instinctive and
acquired sympathy with the character of Jesus was, through
a want of guidance, becoming a dangerous idiosyncrasy.
She felt that there was a similarity in their early fortunes
and characters, and it followed that, gradually, she imagined
that their destinies were to be similar. And here there
was what seemed an inconsistency in her, though, at the
same time, it was a very natural one. From having so high
an idea as she had of what she ought to be, and what it was
intended she should be, she suffered intense self-reproach
for her own imperfections, and every accusation thrown
upon her would deeply depress her, not so much from a
sense of its injustice as from its seeming simply the meed
of her deserts. And yet, whenever made thus miserable
by reproach and a sense of being misunderstood, she would
rush all the more eagerly to devotional musings, and in
simple converse with the Christ, forget that she, a few
moments before, had thought herself unworthy of being
the least of his disciples. "Yes, glorious elder brother,"
she would say, "first-born of a new creation, how little do
men know and love thee as thou art. But God has seen fit
to reveal thy brightness to me—me, a poor little, simple,
lonely, unloved girl. Jesus grew up a carpenter, and his
friends knew not how great and good he was to be. Only
his mother thought about the promise of the Father and
kept the secret in her heart. I wonder if my mother knows
that her child is to live over his life again in some way not
yet revealed to her, but none the less surely will it be
repeated. O come the time, Father in heaven, when I
shall see clearly how I am to fully perform thy great and
holy will."

These were thoughts which she never breathed, even to Mrs. Liebenhoff. Had she done so, she would have striven to correct them. But, on the contrary, that lady's glowing zeal for the improvement of society through the influence of Christianity, as embodied in his Church, served to fan her own sanguine hopes and aims to an intenser flame, and swell her heart with still wilder hopes, connected with her great mission. She would exclaim to herself, "Yes! the Church of Christ shall bring on, ere long, the millennial day, and I will be the leader to marshal in his second coming upon the earth."

These imaginations were more and more shaping her daily experience. They gave a point to all her reading, and through them she interpreted nature and the incidents of her life. Every change of the elements pointed to something in her destiny, and the most trivial words dropped by her associates were often big with meaning and suggestion to her. Her etherealized spirit sat lightly, in one sense, to the earth and its common interests and fashions. On the other, not a leaf could fall of the early autumn foliage, not an insect could flit across her sublimated vision, not an event occur either in her own private history, the social circle of which she was a member, or in the great busy, self-seeking world, without her reading in them the signs which were to usher in a new and glorious era of awakened Christendom.

The soul is a great realm. To the common eye it may seem shrouded in thickest film of sense and apathy, giving no sign even of ordinary action. And yet the outer revolutions of empires, the overthrow of thrones, and the construction of fairer kingdoms, principalities, and republics, upon their subverted bases, are simply the symbols and tokens of its workings. O reverence the human soul! thine own no less, nor yet more, than that intrusted to the keeping of thy fellows, for it is the vicegerent of the Almighty upon the earth, and woe, woe be unto it if it work
25

not with all good faith and with enlightened wisdom his lawful bidding.

Zoë was sitting one afternoon of a hot July day, in an undress, upon a cushion, on the floor of her own apartment, directly opposite the window, looking upwards at the fleecy clouds, which, piled in changeful masses, floated past, breathing in with luxurious delight the fast fleeting breath of the short Danish summer. She was startled from her reverie by a white dove flying in at the window. As it came towards her, she almost involuntarily opened the single loose robe which partially covered her person, and it rushed eagerly into her bosom, where it remained with its wings spread, fluttering with fear, looking up into her face with an almost human expression of appeal for protection.

It was probably pursued by some bird of prey, and such seemed the obvious reason to her of so unwonted a visit. But she was accustomed to look below the surface of the most trivial events to gather hints for her direction in life, and, in this surprising one, she read with clearer vision than had yet dawned upon her the nature of her life-mission.

Poor persecuted innocent, she cried, as she looked into its pleading eyes. God sent thee unto me, for my stricken heart, he knew, would yearn towards thee and protect thee from all that would work thy ruin. But what other message hath he sent by thee, thou carrier pigeon from His great white throne? Ha, now I see the missive folded in thy fluttering pinion, and this its language is:

> Zoë, life of my life, awaken, arise,
>   Clothe thee anew with zeal and devotion,
> Put on God's armor and strive for the prize,
>   The world wots not of 'mid its noise and commotion.
>
> O show it the way to the truth and the light,
>   As it shines in the face of thy Saviour divine,
> O save it from sin and the perilous flight,
>   Which awaits it while buried in vice and in crime.

She closed the window, as after the first fright was over

it seemed inclined to make its exit by the way it came in, but Zoë received it as a special messenger from heaven, and she had no idea of suffering it to depart without gathering from it its full meed of blessing. She gave it food and water, and called in Hilda and her other companions that they might admire its pure beauty, though, as usual, she was very careful not to speak to them of the deep significance which she attached to its visit. The next day the poor bird moped and seemed ill at ease, though carried into the open air of the garden, and wooed and petted with all the tender tones of endearment, which suggested themselves to her. Another morning came, and, cold and lifeless, it lay in the warm nest prepared for it by its gentle mistress. She looked aghast at first at the sacrifice made of it to improper diet and confined air, and, perhaps, to some injury received on its way to her. To Rinda's "I told you so," she made no answer, but stood and questioned with herself: 'What am I to learn by this?' and the answer came very readily to one so impassioned and absorbed in one idea as she was. "It bids me hasten to do my life-work, she said. The world is famishing, dying for the pure truth of God, revealed by Christ. Let me, even me, show it the way to the Father by the simple precepts and parables of our Lord; for has he not said that out of the mouths of the simple and tender he will perfect his praise?"

Filled more and more by this idea of being intrusted with a peculiar mission, nature, the incidents of her own life, the world and its events, became, as it were, but the running accompaniments, or, rather, the index pointing to this great object, each and all qualifying her for it, encouraging, guiding and sustaining her in its preparation, while, at the same time, God the omnipotent charioteer of the universe was reining it in to keep even pace with the hours, which were to usher in her ministry.

On her return from Mrs. Liebenhoff's she found on her

writing-desk this subject, upon which she was to write her theme for the coming week, which Miss Holberg, at the direction of Miss Ingemann, had just placed there: " The beauties and advantages of docility and obedience in the young." Zoë immediately took the hint conveyed by this sentence, and it provoked her, for she had ever striven to obey Miss Ingemann's instructions and rules, and when she had failed, it was only where her nature and sense of truth had drawn her irresistibly aside from them. She had strong impulses and a quick irritable temper, wrapped within a nature of true gentleness and refinement. These sometimes got the mastery over her to an extent quite ludicrous for one invested with credentials for so sublime a mission as she imagined, and her subsequent shame and remorse were, of course, proportioned to the height from which she imagined herself to have fallen. But in this instance when the blood mounted to her cheek and the flash of anger gleamed from her eye, she called them only the natural and just effects of a holy indignation, and she sat down with her pen and dashed off these burning lines:

" Docility and obedience are the two handmaidens to lead along our steps during our weak minority, in the path which our great Father has marked out for his children, beginning with their birth and leading on and on to the glories and sublimities of eternity after eternity. But does any weak, blind time-tyrant think to fetter the immortal child of the ages, the *soul* of the souls of lesser spirits, dwelling in darkness on this earth-sphere, within its own narrow intellectual dimensions ? No, no, for like the mist which the rising sun looses from the mountain's brow, like musical sounds freed from the heavy-toned organ at its swell and fall in the lonely midnight, like the poet's measures sung to the winds in moments of rapt inspiration on the solitary sea beach, so is the soul, enfranchised by obedience to its own great laws and the word of its Maker, and shame, contempt, and woe shall be the doom of him who seeks to chain it any more than them. O ! come the time when freedom's breath and religion's inspiring, directing wand shall be its only mistresses, clarified and sublimed, as it will be by the millennial light. So yearns and agonizes for this great spiritual truth the liberty-loving spirit of

"ZOË CARLAN."

She folded the paper upon which she had hurriedly written these sentences, and placed them in the usual repository for the pupils' themes, from which they were taken by the teachers for correction.

It will be seen by this style of her composition, that she had been strongly influenced by her interview with Mrs. Liebenhoff, for, though her habitual thoughts were in harmony with hers so far as their different ages would allow, with the exception of her own personal idiosyncrasy, yet her usual method of expression was more subdued, excepting when very much excited, and then she expressed herself in poetical strains, but limited more or less by the bounds of metrical verse. To the narrow and superficial this quality of imitation, which showed itself also in her religious development, may seem a servile and inferior one. Taking, as she did, the Saviour for her model not only in the spirit of his teachings, but too much, as it would seem, according to the letter also, since it led her into the extravagant notion of her own future Messiahship, she would be judged by the so-called philosophers of the present speculative and inventive age as wanting in the higher characteristics of genius and intellectual endowments. But when it is considered that the universe is a great school of all the sublimest arts, sciences, literatures, and philosophies, with God for the great central inspiring Spirit, who opens one arcana after another of its mysteries as his children, by their obedience to his generous and wholesome rules, are prepared for them, and that Jesus is the pure, true, sublime, and loving revelator of the just and right principles by which these mysteries are to be interpreted, appropriated, and made practical to our daily life, it follows that the most docile pupil and obedient follower of these laws and of their great Archetype is in the true path which leads to the inner temple, where shines evermore the celestial light, revealing the cherubim which keep their perpetual guard over the Holy of Holies. Like the student artist who wanders from one hillside to another, sketching, as it would seem, with *slavish* exactness each rock, tree, mountain top, and rivulet within the scope of his vision, spurning all aid from his own imagination or the suggestions of another, so tender and reverential is his love for each time-worn feature and furrow of the dear old mother Nature, and deems that his likeness is befitting and true, until he holds it up to her mirror with affectionate longing for her smile of approval, and her wave of "God speed you," when lo! disappointment. For the, but now, haggard and ancient dame Nature, so hoary and wrinkled, has doffed her garments of gray and her visage of eld, and shines out lovely and fresh as a bride on the eve when new life has been breathed through her being from the perennial Eden of love. He dashes his picture, the pride of his heart and the hope of his future, in rage and tears at her feet. "O mother, capricious and cruel!" he cries, " why have ye deceived me?"   But hark! hear her gentle and musical voice, which now elates him with joy and enhances his love to the pitch of devotion to Him, her great Author; for before his couched vision, *His* glory now shines in each line of her youthful and radiant face. And these are her words, " O Son of my love, who, still groping and blind, didst see too minutely each fissure and stain, each decay and excrescence, yet loved me no less, ay, even more for these weather-marked lines, indented by caring and laboring for thee, receive now the reward of your trust and affection."

She touches his eyelids and there thrills through his being, a divine inspiration, and now is revealed the great truth that he, who in reverent faith follows, step by step, the leadings of nature and God through his Christ, in his feeble minority, shall be one with them and the angels in blissful communion; and his soul shall be trained, and his hand shall be guided by a holy idealism, to paint for immortals the *spirit* of earth and the *essence* of the heavens, not on canvass alone, but on the ever during tablets within.

Another influence besides Mrs. Liebenhoff's had been, of late, assisting to mould Zoë by its effect upon her imagination and feelings. This was the acquaintance and instruction of her German teacher. His method of tuition was unlike any which she had been subjected to, and more in accordance with the nature and character of her mind. Discarding all tedious, elementary rules, he, at once, through the aid of an interlined copy of the Gospel of John placed that most beloved portion of Scriptures within her grasp, through a form of expression novel and suggestive to her. She made rapid progress, both in the pronunciation and translation, so that when Miss Ingemann asked him of his success with this, her most discouraging pupil, she was surprised by his cordial encomiums upon her mental capacity and docility of disposition. The thought crossed her mind that she might have made a mistake in her attempt to inclose Zoë within her own cast-iron methods, but like the oak tree, which, for a moment, may sway to a powerful passing wind, only to return again to its usual imperturbable sturdiness, so she soon regained her usual self-complacency on this point.

But in other ways was the Hungarian shaping her thoughts and sentiments more powerfully than through the German language. He was a man of a strong, acute intellect, trained both in the Jewish rabbinical schools and in the cloister-like universities of Germany, filled with curious and profound learning, both of the ancient and modern schools of theology, philosophy and literature, at the same time that his imagination was lofty and well controlled. But what impressed her more than any other quality of his character was his moral force. This was the commanding element, which gave aim, energy, and perpetual vitality and inspiration to his own life-work, and carried on his pupils from day to day to unprecedented success in every branch which he taught them. Like the waves of the sea at spring-tide, which bear on their resistless current all lighter substances, which, floating near, they draw within their influence, so did his strong will, and high and never-flagging sense of the great possibilities of the human mind, when awakened to its duties, propel them with glad but resistless impetus to high attainments. When a woman feels this influence buoying her up and impelling her on-wards, she joyfully acknowledges the leadership of man. Her clear, spiritual glance *sights* from afar, the true, the beautiful, and right, and she plumes her butterfly wings and flutters gladly towards it, but with feeble and unsteady motion, unless his strong, eagle-eye and pinion, which never blinks or tires, cleave the air and make a swell, so that she be strengthened and sent onwards in her flight. If he do this, his heaven-ordered part, she sparkles brightly and more brightly as she nears the upper sunlight, playing about his head, resting her grace and beauty upon his heart, flying ever and anon in advance, sustained by his strong breath, then nestling with joyful acknowledgment of weak ness upon his kingly form, even making herself tinier than need be that he may be glorified the more in the view of the great skylight. O man! beware how ye come within the sphere of any base, destroying elements, for, though ye may escape utter ruin to your coarser immortal fabric, her more ethereal and tender one may be irremediably bemired. Keep her beside you in your highest soarings, and she will preserve the curtain of your eye cleansed to the point of clearest vision, and give you such glad impulse by her cheering that the rarer ether will never weary, but change more and more your earthly being to the celestial temper of her own, only relieved by what she most looks up to and admires, your strength and manhood. Zoë *felt* this force more than she *reasoned* upon it, and her progress was in accordance with the conviction. So delightful was it to be cordially praised for any acquisition, that, through her study of German, her whole nature took a start, and the school-girls, quick to perceive each other's inner or outer changes, laughed at her for actually growing taller under the new administration.

"Zoë," said Adelgunda Heiliger, one day as she was assisting her to dress, "you must get a new frock and charge it to Ben Ezra. He is the cause of this sudden outgrowth from the old one, and it is but right that he should replace it, for really this is too scanty for you in the present fashion."

"Let her piece it out to the proper length with her German exercises," said Rinda. "They will answer for phylacteries which, you know, she will have to don by-and-by, as is the custom of certain people. Hey, Zoë!"

"Of all things in this world, don't call our teacher a Pharisee," said Zoë, "for he is at the moral antipodes from that sect."

"At any rate he intends, from present appearances, to be no Essene," said Freya. "Zoë, love, invite me to the wedding, will you not, and introduce me to Ruth? I have always wanted to know her better. I will help her glean, next time she goes to the field of Boaz, and I will be as little fascinating as possible too, so as not to damage her prospects with her kinsman."

"Here are some nice smooth stones," said Adelgunda, "which I picked up on the sea beach, which I shall drop into David's pouch as I sit at the feast-table with him. I am going to strike for the throne and cut out Michal altogether. *I* never shall reprove him for dancing, but will waltz till the ark drops to pieces from old age. I shall have an opportunity to learn some new figures, shall I not? and I will astonish Mr. Ernestine next time he comes to give us our lesson."

"And I," said Hilda, "shall accept nobody's attentions but the magnificent Solomon's, and won't I scatter the inmates of his harem, and reign supreme over Israel, no less than himself? The Queen of Sheba need not think to come again and delude him by her flattering compliments. I will give her the go-by in a way she never experienced before. But we forget the principal personages of the occasion. Zoë, darling, what *rôles* will suit you and Ben Ezra best, besides that of bride, Madonna-like and saintly, and—what shall I call him of all his metamorphoses?"

"Call him the Prophet-Priest and King Melchisedec of the coming dispensation, who, without beginning of days or end of years, remains forever the emblem of peace and justice, on whom devolves the ministry divine of ushering in the representative of the second coming of the Son of God," said Zoë.

"Ah! King of Salem! I salute thee and hail with joy the day when thou, man of the ages, mysterious and mighty, born without father or mother into our time-globe, takest to thy arms of eld my Zoë to give thee youthful life again, and carry her on to her high destiny!" said Hilda, bowing to her German class-book.

"When is this wonderful union to take place, Zoë?" said Rinda. "I like to know of great events in season so as to be in proper readiness."

"Ask the great High Priest of heaven and earth, even our heavenly Father," said she with great seriousness. "There are secrets which even Jesus was not let into when on earth, much less am I. But cease your mirth and raillery, my friends, for I never expect to marry," and she walked out of the room absorbed in her own thoughts.

This was a part of her idiosyncrasy, which strengthened as she grew older, that, like Jesus, she should fulfill her mission unbound by the strongest ties of life. To-be-sure, she was shaken for a moment, now and then, when in the presence of her teacher, whose increasing interest in her became suspected by her companions. When his voice sank to a tender tone as he addressed her in her recitation, or she caught his eye resting upon her face when she raised it in inquiry to his own, while following his reading, she forgot for a moment her peculiar fate and felt a thrill of youthful love's first dream, but it was soon forgotten in her life-long musings.

CHAPTER XXII.

"If she be a traitor,
Why so am I; we have still slept together,
Rose at an instant, learned, played, eat together,
And wheresoe'er we went, like Juno's swans,
Still we were coupled and inseparable."—SHAKSPEARE.

WHEN Miss Ingemann read Zoë's outburst of feeling in her theme, she was shocked and almost discouraged; but being both strong and decided in character, and, at the same time, conscientious and faithful, so far as she saw her duty, she determined to make a strenuous effort to cure her pupil of her extravagant fancies and willful opposition to reasonable restraint. She sent for her to her room. Zoë knew what was coming, but she had got to the point, at last, where a determined purpose and strong conviction of being in the path marked out for her by God and her nature will bring even the most plastic and gentle. Therefore, with head unusually erect and eye expressing courage and enthusiasm, she stood before her teacher.

"Miss Zoë," said Miss Ingemann, "here is your theme. Its expression does not come within the limits of propriety and good sense, and therefore we cannot accept it from you. We require you to re-write it in a mode consonant to what you know is our reasonable expectation."

"Excuse me, Miss Ingemann, I cannot do it."

"What do you mean, Miss Zoë? That you intend a willful disobedience to the rules of this establishment?"

(300)

" I have no such willful intention. I have simply written
my true feelings and thoughts, and I cannot falsify them
by a different expression."

" You amaze me by your presumption. I demand of
you a more subdued and rational composition. The
thoughts are extravagant and fanatical, and the expression
wild and highly improper, and we cannot permit such
within these walls. This is my unalterable determination,"
and Miss Ingemann arose and stood at her full height.

Zoë was completely roused, and she burst forth like a
torrent to the astonishment of her teacher, who had never
seen her under such excitement.

" Madam, I have uttered what is in me, and woe be unto
my soul if I turn aside the inspiration of God into another
channel at the bidding of human lips! I read yesterday
in a journal from that far-off land which God opened, that
his children might have one abiding-place for freedom to
worship God according to His and nature's laws, that her
ministers, instead of being guides to lead and light along
the people to the millennial day, enchain their minds
each five years by a promise to utter nothing but what its
creeds of ages gone by have ordered. So they squeeze,
and trammel, and wind their thoughts like serpents, ever
striving to be free, around a time-worn, bloody, lying parch-
ment. Only now and then one frees himself, so as to inter-
pret the Word of God as He demands of the growing
powers he gave him. But hark! a hiss and sting, and the
poor timid spirit coils himself again in meek submission
to the dismal parchment, whispering, ' I said it not,' or, if
I did, ' I meant the same as you!' And what is the conse-
quence? Why, sins of every shape and hue start rampant
round them, emboldened by the falsehood and treachery of
the priests and prophets, scattering misery and darkness, and
hurling to perdition millions whom God has given into their
keeping. No, madam, even in my simple school-girl

theme, I will take warning of this fearful doom. I change it not."

" What heroics are these?" said Miss Ingemann, indignant and astonished; then paused to look critically into Zoë's face to see if she were not insane. Her pupil knew well that gaze, and it always turned her into stone. She simply bowed and left the room.

Once out of her sight, she ran like lightning into her apartment, where she found Hilda.

" What is the matter?" said she, alarmed at seeing Zoë's excited face.

" The matter is, that I am going to sail to-morrow for Santa Cruz."

" Why, what has happened? tell me."

" Hilda, I have lived entrammeled long enough. My chains gall me to the point of desperation. God and my conscience command me hence, and I obey them. The ship departs to-morrow, and I shall take passage in her."

" But, Zoë, you cannot go alone. You never have been away from this retreat, and think how you would feel upon the deep or among uncongenial strangers!"

" Hilda, you know me not. I can do anything. I have powers within me that can shake the nations, ay, and shall do it too; how much more guide my own way across the waters. In God I trust. He will watch over me."

" O Zoë! I know you better than you think. I have noted your genius and rapt, poetic soarings, so different from the working of my mind, and I have striven to reveal them to our teacher, but your own failure of response to my encomiums by ever wearing before her your stony face, has made them seem to her only like my childish preference for you without a base of truth. I know too, that your broad vision takes in the practical, as required within our little circle, for we, your schoolmates, ever come to you for a decision upon our little tastes and decorations. But, darling, you are not strong as we are, and one day

your spirits rise to the mountain top in exultation, and the
next fall into the abyss below. Does she not aid and
soothe thee then, thy own strong Hilda, of this common,
naughty earth-sphere? Zoë, how canst thou live without
me, or I without thee, if thou art far away?" and she
began to weep.

"Hilda! my own, my good and true, who hast borne
with such meek yet cheerful patience with my wayward
temper, and hast had ever a word and smile of gladness
for my strange woe, the cause of which I hardly know of,
though it pervades my being, checking each gladsome
thought ere it is fully formed, casting a shadow over each
smile ere it shines forth to brighten my dull face, thinkest
thou I love thee not? O my friend! though a strange gulf,
riven not by me but by our Maker, for I have vainly striven
all these years to cross it, to cover it up, or make believe
that it existed not, divides our deepest souls, yet are you
dear to me as my own life. When you are not by, I am
restless and forlorn, I gaze into the distance to catch the
first glimpse of your beloved form, and strain my ear for
quick intelligence of her who is my sunshine, my tower
of strength to lean upon, the interpreter of my thoughts to
the stern world, which chills them ere they are expressed
by its cold glitter and its icy breath. I know not how life
can be life without thee, but God points with direct, com-
manding index towards the great ocean, and I go; for in him
I live, and move, and have my being in a way which seems
to me most peculiar, and if I disobey his counsel, not I
alone but the whole universe is jostled from its orbit. Of
this I must say no more; but, O Hilda! pray that I may
have strength and guidance for my strange destiny."

"Zoë, my life, my inspiration, guide, restraint, and ten-
derest friend! I go with thee. Whatever betide thee shall
be shared by me, so far as God permits. Thou shalt not
leave me to the desolation which would come over my lot
unshared by thee, my childhood's mate, the sharer of my

room by night and day, and to whom I have grown each
year by finer yet stronger ties, even to my opening woman-
hood, when judgment, taste, fancy, and deeper religious
yearnings all point to thee as my best earthly satisfaction.
Can I relinquish thee for all the world beside? No, never!
we go together."

The two girls embraced each other with all the enthu-
siasm suited to their different natures, united as they were
by a strong and disinterested affection, high principle, and
the purest sentiment. To Hilda there remained a painful
and difficult task, which was to inform Miss Ingemann of
her determination. They loved each other. With the one,
the affection was mingled with pride and a just satisfaction
at the successful result of most conscientious training;
with the other, gratitude and admiration for this oldest and
most faithful teacher and guide. But she hesitated not a
moment in view of this trial. "Zoë needs me more than
any other one in the world, and how can I live without
her?" she said to herself, as with the quick decision and
courage which characterized her, she threaded her way to
Miss Ingemann's apartment. She found that she and Miss
Holberg had gone on a visit to a friend in the country, and
would not return until late in the evening. What was to
be done now? Zoë was the directress in this emergency.

"I must go and bid Mrs. Liebenhoff farewell," said she.
"She has been so confined for the last week, nursing our
pastor in his severe sickness, that I have not met her for
several days; but I must see them both."

"Yes," said Hilda, "and Mrs. Körner and other friends
too, and above all, Mr. Andersen. Then the captain—we
must make arrangements with him immediately. O, how
much we have to do!"

"Here is your hat, Hilda," said Zoë, as she put on her
own. "Come, we can tie them on the way."

And the twain, with gloves in hand, arranging their
mantles as they walked along the street in a way which

would have shocked their teacher's nice sense of pro-
priety, walked with rapid strides towards Captain Keiser's
dwelling.

As they came within view of the sea, they saw a ship
just sailing from port. They looked at each other and
said nothing, but quickened their pace almost to a run to
reach the captain's house. The servant at the door told
them that he had just sailed for the West Indies, and that
they had been misinformed in supposing that the next day
was the time of his leaving.

Zoë looked bewildered for a moment, for guided, as she
felt herself to be, by a special inspiration, this obstacle
she could not account for. They were slowly retracing
their steps when an acquaintance of Miss Ingemann, an
elderly gentleman by the name of Sarran, whom Hilda, in
her fondness for playful titles, had dubbed "the Viking,"
from his frequent voyages, met them.

"Good evening, my Volkyria!" said he to her. "Why
droop your wings in that fashion? Come, give me a shake
of the hand, ay, and something better too, as a parting
blessing, for I suppose you know that I am off to-
morrow?"

"No, sir; for where?" said Zoë and Hilda in one breath,
catching at the faintest hope of release.

"To Santa Cruz. Do you think I am going to winter
my old rheumatic frame among the ice and snows of old
Denmark? Not I. I hope I know what is best for myself.
Any commands? I am at the service of any fair damsels
of Valhalla, who may wish to send anything, mayhap in
the shape of a love-message to the other world, and keep
it a secret, too, from the powers at head-quarters," said
he, winking at them. "Neither Odin nor Freya get any
revelations from me. Hey, ladies!" and the good-natured
old gentleman laughed at his own bright wit, as it seemed
to him.

"May we go with you?" said Zoë. "O, pray, let us!"
26

"*How* are you going?" said Hilda, "the ship has sailed."

"By England. The monthly steamers to the West-Indies are a better conveyance than any other, in these days. Besides, I have business in London. You go with me? Bless my stars! ain't I in luck? To-be-sure you may, and you need not fear but that I will take good care of you too. There is no gallantry in these days like what I was bred to. But be sure and not be tardy, for I like to be in season. At five o'clock, to-morrow evening, we must be on board, bag and baggage. Remember the hour, please," and the old gentleman bustled away more self-important than ever.

"It is just what I want," said Hilda. "Mamma has always said that I might visit her relations in London, before I left Europe, and now is my opportunity. But here is the parsonage. I hope that Mr. Liebenhoff is not very ill."

They ran up the steps and asked for their friend. Mrs. Liebenhoff at first sent down her excuse, saying, that she could not leave her husband; but on telling the servant that their urgency was extreme, she appeared, but sad and worn by night-watching and anxiety. They told her in hurried terms, of their sudden determination, but forbore to enter into particulars in her present state of feeling, and she, though sad and tearful at the thought of losing them, was not so much surprised as they expected. The fact was, she knew that they were to go home in the course of the year, and preoccupied as her mind was by her husband's illness, it did not seem strange to her that they should be summoned to return a few months earlier than they anticipated, so she did not question them about it.

"Can we not see Mr. Liebenhoff, one moment?" said Hilda.

"I think so. I will see," she said.

In a few moments they stood before him. He was

propped up by pillows, pale and emaciated, and they were
shocked to see the change which a few days of suffering
had produced in him.

"You are going to leave us then, and next Sabbath you
were to join us in our renewed communion? We shall
sadly miss our dear young friends. It may be, however,
that I shall be absent too; what think, dear Lisbet? Well,"
seeing her turn aside in agitation, "it must be as God
wills. Farewell, little ones! be good children and remem-
ber us, as we shall you, with love and prayer, that God
may bless you and grant us to meet again!"

They kissed his pale forehead, then were folded for a
moment in the arms of Mrs. Liebenhoff, and weeping left
the house.

A few more calls, and tender adieux, and many tears,
and then they returned to gather their goods together
for their voyage. They sat up late packing their boxes,
writing farewell notes to friends whom they should not
see again, and arranging everything with a discretion
and sense of fitness remarkable in two young girls,
who had ever been watched over by careful guardianship.
But it seemed as if a great purpose had matured them in
a day and carried them to its fulfillment, as with the force
of inspiration. They talked over their plans till late at
night, then fell into fitful, dreamy sleep to awaken by the
broad sunlight shining into their window.

After breakfast, hand in hand they appeared before Miss
Ingemann. She looked up from her book and started, as
if she read a strong resolve in every feature of their faces.
Hilda, who thought she had nerved herself for the crisis,
began to cry.

"What means this?" said their teacher.

"We come," said Zoë, "to inform you, madam, of our
determination to return to Santa Cruz. We are in readi-
ness and shall leave this evening. We ask your blessing
on our way."

Miss Ingemann looked from one to the other, doubting the evidence of her senses, then with dignity and a slight curl of the lip, said to Zoë:

"And who has given you permission to leave your guardians so abruptly?"

"God and my conscience," answered Zoë.

Miss Ingemann had high respect for principle and a strong resolve, and though she saw lamentable fanaticism in her pupil, yet she could not but respect the determined bearing of the young girl, though she meant that it should yield to her own strength of will.

"Zoë," she said, "I do not wish to be harsh with you; but you are entirely in the wrong in this matter. People are not inspired in these latter days. We have other aids to guide us. It is very wrong for you to think of leaving your school before your father sends expressly for you."

"My father had in view only my greater ease and pleasure in bidding me stay a few more months. But I know he is in trouble from the unsettled condition of our island at this time, and I wish on that account, if on no other, to return. I am not selfish, as I wish to prove to him. Already he has spent beyond his lessened means in my education; and my mother and I are pining to meet each other. I wish to go. Mr. Sarran will protect us on the voyage."

Miss Ingemann's methodical mind was not convinced by these reasons. There was always much formality in the manner of the dismissal of her pupils, and this extemporaneous leave did not consort at all with her strict notions. She waved her hand and said, "It is of no use to exchange words upon this subject. I dismiss you, young ladies, to your studies."

Zoë was roused and burst out again. "No, madam, it is of no use, as you say, to lengthen words upon my leaving you. A greater than my teacher bids me go hence, where my every respiration is drawn at the expense of truth, of nature, and the high behest of God.

"Last night in dreams I saw myself upon the broad and fearful waste of waters. Strangely did they sustain my weight, as with most natural self-possession, with drooping head and hands suspended by my side I walked upon them. There was darkness behind, and gloom and a fearful wall of briny waves before me, but a bright gleam from heaven, shining through a silvery cloud, lighted my footsteps close before me, and the mists blew westward, and the waves flowed fast towards the same goal; and the wind, the sun, and every voice of nature sounded in my awakening ear—' Onward, still onward,' and I *must* go."

Seeing the girl's determination, and knowing that, in a few months, at farthest, she was to give her up, the thought came to Miss Ingemann's mind, like a flash, that she had better not contend longer with a nature with which she had so little sympathy and success; and as she knew Mr. Sarran well, and that she could confide her to him with safety, she changed her tone and said: "Well, Zoë, if you choose to take the responsibility of disobeying your father, I will no longer fetter you, as you, in your high-flown language, accuse me. I will write to your parents, explaining to them the reasons for permitting you to leave. I am sorry if my care and labor for your good have only given you the sense of bondage. I have striven to do right by you," and her voice trembled.

Zoë was completely subdued by this expression of feeling. One of her accustomed revulsions came over her after a time of excitement. She threw herself on her knees before her teacher, wailing out, "Think me not ungrateful for all the good I have derived from you. My heart is burdened with a sense of unworthiness; for I well know I have not met your plans and exertions in my education as you have desired. Forgive me, and yet pity me, for I know not what I am, nor what God would have of me. I could not be what you wish, and yet I am weighed down by remorse that I am not."

This unwonted revelation of her struggling feelings, which was forced from her by the softening influences of the occasion of parting from her home and teacher of years, brought out strongly the opposite characteristics of these two beings.

Zoë, gentle, affectionate, and humble from ever looking upwards to an exalted ideal; poetic, sensitive, and delicate in her feelings and of quick insight into character, felt no resentment at the obstinate efforts of Miss Ingemann to warp her nature aside from its rectitude and beauty by a culture unsuited to it. On the contrary, she looked at the conscientious motives which had governed her in the main, forgetting now what she had previously felt very forcibly, that wounded pride was also a cause of her being no better liked by her teacher. She simply wished to be free as God and her own soul irresistibly impelled her, and, therefore, the step she was taking, accompanied as it was by so much heart-rending feeling.

In Miss Ingemann's character, on the contrary, pride, self-reliance and self-esteem were combined with a strong, clear, but narrow intellect, and a reason which took in but little besides the obvious, striking, and practical in life and character. To this was superadded a religion, which though abstract, speculative, and mystical in its creed, and favoring a certain cast-iron form of sentiment and con- tracted mode of religious experience for all souls alike, frowned upon all indications of an awakening religious life in accordance with the advancing mind of the age, and the natural influence of a more rational understanding of the spirit of our faith in its gradual emancipation from a slavish obedience to the bare letter of Scripture. The consequence was that there was in her a hardness, direct- ness, sternness, and even scorn and intolerance towards what was the deepest life and inspiration to Zoë, her poeti- cal sentiment and rapt musings with the ethereal spirit of nature and the universe, quite crushing to all her confidence and trust.

These qualities were revealed in her answer to Zoë's simple expression of gratitude and confession of self-reproach.

" I am very glad, Miss Zoë, that you show symptoms of a proper consciousness of your faults, and that you are not *entirely* unmindful of all that has been done for you. However, I am very direct, as you know, (this she often said with much emphasis,) and I must say to you that there are reasons why I, of late years, have not expected the same of you as my other pupils, so it may serve as some alleviation to your sense of imperfection as well as to my own disappointment. But let me advise you, as a friend, to give up your foolish and sinful fancies and be governed by common sense and evangelical faith in God. I wish to part from you in friendship," and she erected her head with self-satisfaction at her magnanimity.

Zoë keenly felt all that was conveyed in this truly coarse speech, though Miss Ingemann did not intend it as such. It was simply the natural expression of a woman highly bred by aristocratic, conventional, dogmatic life, just in the proportion that she was vulgarized by losing sight of the eternal principle of the equality of every immortal soul before God, blinding herself to the truth, that if one seems inferior to another, it is because circumstances have made it so, or what is equally probable, because her own standard of judgment is too low for her to see the truth as it really is. The conviction flashed upon her pupil with lightning force, that while she, in her simplicity, had opened her heart to her teacher as in the presence of God, she had been met by a severe, selfish, worldly spirit, revealing itself quite as much through her religious wishes in her behalf, as in her implied inferiority of caste and mental endowment. She too erected her head and left the room, her sorrow and self-reproach turned into a sense of injustice and indignation.

In this mood of mind she ran into one of the recitation rooms for a book, where she found her German teacher. He had just heard from Mrs. Liebenhoff of her intention of leaving Copenhagen, and came immediately to see her. They gazed into each other's faces for a moment, and a quick intelligence revealed their mutual feelings before Zoë had time to train her eye to its usual look of passionless repose. At this moment the youngest "child of the regiment" of school-girls, a favorite of Zoë, and who was often hanging about her during her recitation, came into the room. She was artless, and affectionate, and a great chatterer.

"O dear!" said she, "you shan't go away, Zoë, shall she, Mr. Seüll? Why don't you make her stay?" said she. "If I were a great, strong man, I would. Do try, won't you?" and she took a hand of each, and endeavored to draw them together.

"You believe in intimations from above," said he. "O! accept this, through one, about whom heaven lieth in her infancy. Will you not stay? or may I not go to you?"

Zoë said nothing, but her face expressed the opposite feelings, striving within her.

"I know she will stay if you want her to; because she told Hilda she was very sorry to give up studying German; that she liked to speak it better than Danish."

"Let me interpret that," said he, "for my own soul holds the true key to it, or I mistake me. 'Because you can think aloud in it better than in the more northern tongue.' Tell me that it is so."

She smiled and blushed, and emboldened, he approached her. She waved him back, for the thought of her great mission came between her and the rapture of a first affection. Still, partly swayed by passing suggestions, various thoughts flashed through her mind. "It may be that God

intends him for a helper in my great work.   But shall I
return to my dear parents with my life's partner chosen
without their knowledge?   I will not be so unfilial."   She
partly turned from him, saying, "Wait but a year."

"What say you?" he said, not wishing to believe that he
heard aright.

"Be my friend for a little year," she said decidedly,
"and, in the meantime, I go to the arms of my beloved
mother."

"Have pity on me first," said he, "and give me surer
hope than this.   I have dreamed that at last heaven was
propitious to my prayer, and was granting that in you I
might see the completion of one arc of my weird destiny,
and that in your loving care and tenderness, comfort would
flow into my stricken heart."

This had the opposite effect upon Zoë to what was
intended, for her own life had been one of such suffering
and privation, that when she thought for a moment of the
possibility of marriage, it was as a refuge and consolation
to herself in some degree, and the oft-repeated words of
Mrs. Liebenhoff, implicating his sex for its low view of
woman, now came forcibly to her, chilling her feelings
very perceptibly.

He saw this, and interpreting it wrongly, said: "It may
be that far away, you will forget, in the smiles of others,
even to wait one little year."

Zoë flashed up at the possibility of any want of truth
and rectitude in herself.

"Do you believe that I would trifle with your most sacred
feelings?" said she.

"I know well that the youthful of your sex are not with-
out caprice, and lack, sometimes, a faithful memory of those
they leave behind.   How can I trust my fate to the few
words you have spoken, and those so enigmatical?   I am
in chains, and you would sail away unshackled into the
dim distance, leaving me —"

27

"Free as the air that blows over the Carpathians from even the bonds of friendship," said she, turning abruptly from him and walking out of the room. If Ben Ezra, after months' acquaintance, in which she had revealed herself to him more than to any other one, believed her so worldly and common-place, she wished to be bound to him by no tie whatever; and indignant and disappointed she ran to complete her arrangements.

Hilda remained with Miss Ingemann after Zoè left the room. Her teacher did not dream of her going, too; for loving her as she had always done, she felt sure of her being obedient in every respect to her wishes. Seeing her in tears, she said, "I am sorry for this misguided girl. She gives us all much trouble, but dry your eyes, my dear. I am going into the country to pass the next Sabbath with my friend, Mrs. Petersen, and you shall accompany me, love. In the meantime make yourself as happy as possible, and—perhaps you would like to assist Zoë in her preparations the next hour or two. If so, I will excuse you from recitation this morning."

"I must go with Zoë," said Hilda.

Miss Ingemann started and paused before she would trust her voice to speak.

"You, my dear Hilda, my pride and joy! You will not disappoint me by any disregard of my hopes and wishes? Why should you go now? Another opportunity will offer six months hence. Zoë will leave this establishment in disgrace for her willfulness and ingratitude. I wish my *darling* to carry with her all the honors it can give her."

Here, too, Miss Ingemann failed in her appeal, though to a nature very much like her own in its original characteristics. But Hilda had been moulded by Zoë, quite as much, though more indirectly, than by her, and now that her gentler friend was in trial, she clung to her. She had gradually been awakening to the wide difference between the two, and her mature preference was for the more poetic and spiritual one, though she was not blind to the extravagances in her development.

She wiped her eyes, and with as much decision and coolness as Miss Ingemann could manifest when occasion offered, she answered to what she considered a low motive for her to place before her for staying. "I must go with Zoë, Miss Ingemann;" and then left her.

At five o'clock, all was in readiness for them to leave; the last box corded, the last little gift exchanged with their favorite companions, and the last kiss given to Miss Hol berg, who was in and out all day assisting them by kindly suggestions, and exchanging many a word of affectionate interest. The final duty was to go and bid Miss Ingemann farewell. The latter was cold and dignified to Hilda, in proportion as her affections and pride were more severely wounded by the step she was taking, and Hilda acted the same *rôle* in a little less lofty and dignified style, while Zoë was overwhelmed with sorrow. Miss Ingemann, partly touched by this, and partly to rebuke Hilda, with whom she was really offended, condescended to say, "Miss Zoë, perhaps at some future time you will again visit Denmark?" Her pupil, softened by the thought of leaving the only home of which she had any distinct knowledge, and her sole guardian since infancy, longed to throw herself into her arms and respond warmly to this chilly, non-committal invitation; but she thought what a gulf there was between them. She never yet had uttered an untruth, and in mournful accents and with drooping head, leaning with sinking form on Hilda's arm, she slowly answered, "*No.*" So she went forth to meet her destiny; a reed, shaken by every passing breeze; a wind-harp, now tuned to melody by each gentle breath, now its cords snapped asunder by a rude touch or gale; a vase, inclosing in its depths a store of sweet perfume, essence, and spirit of lore and science, by no means meagre for one so young; a failure, it is true, in the discipline of mind deemed essential by the calculat

ing, critical spirit of the age; yet a trophy of success in
the great school of Christ, for she had learned of him to
be meek and lowly, at the same time that she was brave
and true to Nature and her most enlightened conscience,
and had caught a glimpse of the power and grandeur of a
life like his, and by what struggle it was to be attained, so
that, come death, come woe, or·serenest happiness, it mat-
tered not; the goal was before her, and for that, her aim
was set, and never-ending labor.

As they drove away, Miss Ingemann said to Miss Hol-
berg, " I am more than ever convinced that there is no use
in trying to educate the masses, excepting to suit their low
position.   In this instance, I have been unsuccessful, while
Zoë has been a great detriment to the really superior mind
of Hilda."

" I feel," said Miss Holberg, weeping, " that we have
not been able to interpret her nature successfully, and
hence our disappointment.   Depend upon it, she has trea-
sures within her, which only need the right key to unlock
them, to astonish and delight us."

" Do you think so?" said Miss Ingemann, and stood
thoughtful for a moment. She was truly religious, and
seeing her assistant in such grief, she said, " Well, my
dear, we have striven to do our duty by her. May God
forgive us if we have been guilty of an unintentional mis-
take. We can only commend her to Him now, and may
He supply what may have been lacking in our instruc-
tions."

The Pastor's wife watched with sinking heart, the sands
of her husband's hour-glass running silently, but none the
less surely towards eternity. In one sense, she was pre-
pared for this premature ultimate of a life, taxed in mind
and heart beyond the possibilities of a healthy longevity.
But more than actual exorbitant work, in its injurious
effects upon the physical system, was the heavy weight of
responsibility thrown upon him, by the want of co-operation

of the surrounding community in his labors, for what he
felt to be its absolute and imperative need.   Quickened as
his soul was to a high point of spiritual insight and eleva-
tion, the prevailing materialism, and the lack of a full and
living appreciation of the high duties devolving upon every
human being towards itself and the world, weighed upon
an already fractured constitution with destructive force.
Lacking her keen imaginative glance and ever-living hope-
fulness, he was sustained in his unflagging self-devotion
by firm principle and love for truth, more than by any pros-
pective vision of eventual success.   He was invested with
every quality of mind, character and culture incident to
humanity, save the single one of *passion*, which would
have given to the others the magnetic dart, necessary to
pierce through the heavy crust with which mammon and
sense had covered up the hearts of his people.   But all
was over, and she, like Marius upon the ruins of Car
thage, sat upon the grave of her desolated hopes, and thus
her soul sighed out its dirge, broken in its strains by the
anguish of many loving friends of his flock, no less than
by the sense of her own life-loss.

And is thy pale, worn corse all that
Is left to me of thee, my beautiful, my true,
And good!   This the end of earth to one,
Of whom, in his boyhood's purity, it was said
By the wise and saintly, " there is no stain upon
His life I would efface, no virtue suited to
His years, if it were given me, that I could add !"
This the end of time to one, so bravely knit
In his corporeal frame, by nature, frugal fare,
The fresh breeze of Heaven's country, and willing obedience
To all its varied laws, unfolded to his eager
Yet reverent seeking?   O!   what befell thee, my beloved,
That thou, ere thy full prime, shouldst droop
Thy noble head, so busy in its varied workings,
Now coping with philosophy, now gathering wisdom,
From science, history, life, and the economy of God's dealings?
What came to thee, dear heart, so full, yet gentle, in its beating,
That it drew towards thee, equally, the sage, the learned,

The little child, and humblest pensioner upon thy bounty?
What blight could fall upon thee, dearest, that thy hand should
    early fall
So cunning in its artifice, that it could pen
Thy clear-eyed, eloquent truths, which shall be
Memorials of thy Christ-like power, no less
Than stars of light and leaves of healing
To the ages ; then turn to fashion with artistic skill
Many a thing of use and beauty, to be a joy forevermore
To those who love thee?   O! my eyes of blue!
Twins of my own, waken to answer
Smile to smile, to give intelligence by their sweet approval
Subdued to the point of mystic,
Secret sympathy, invisible to others, of my every feeling,
Deed, and aspiration!   Drowned are they in deeper night
Than erst we've shared together!   Mute are they
As ne'er before to my still questionings !
O meekly, yet with the might of faith,
Thou didst enfold thy hands upon thy breast,
Saying, " Thy will be done, be it as thou wouldst have it,
Though scarce intelligible thy decree,
So much have I to do for thee, O Father !
So many have I yet to bring within thy circling fold,
So wide to spread thy worship, and renew
The angel song, Peace on the earth, good-will to men,
And glory to God forevermore ;
To lead the youthful and the world-beset,
To living waters, ceaseless in their flow,
And quenchless in their potency of thirst-cure ;
To walk with freer bound in fields of light and loveliness,
Strewn with the flowers of Art and Poesy,
With her whom Thou hast given for my completeness.
Can I relinquish this thy costliest gift?   Can heaven
Be heaven without her?   Can I withdraw from her
My arm, strong to support, provide and guard ?
O help my unbelief: I would believe and meekly bow,
To thy behests, vailed as their wisdom is from my weak vision !"

Cease ye my sinless, pure and sanctified,
With no faltering wing shalt thou ascend to the heaven of heavens,
Thy birth-place, home, and ceaseless aspiration.
No broken pillar art thou, fractured 'mid high, untimely.
No torch, inverted, telling of no relighting,
But a glorious, full-orbed sun, whose strongest burning rays,
Can pierce sublime through murkiest, earthliest ether.
Thou hast baptized me " thy Completeness,"

So will I be in this, thy soul's extremity,
And sing the song thy lowly spirit deems not meet for thee ;
Rise to thy rest, reward, rejoicing,
Even to the inner temple, where God's purest light is shining,
See and adore and love with sense all purified,
What the dim eye of earth may not conceive of,
And when thy soul hath slaked its first deep longing,
Take the credentials tendered thee for the mission,
Thou, in thy charity, greater than required
By the letter of the Word, didst pant for,
'To be the ministering spirit to the lost underworld.'
Ah! well I know the cause of thy untimely exit,
And as Achilles by Patroclus' death-bed
Vowed to avenge him, so do I thee, my own,
Twice slain, once by excess of care and labor
For the selfish world : then by the foul city's breath,
Made poisonous by sins, too mighty for thy cure,
Too monstrous for thy slackened power of life's continuance.

Man of the ages, mysterious and mighty,
Whose strong but tender ministering helped me
To soothe the weary frame, support the aching head,
With words of holy cheer to waft the passing spirit
To its upward haven, where no tossing, booming waves
Can make stern shipwreck of the richly-freighted soul-ship.
Was it for this, weird man, the ages, car-like,
Have borne thee to my dying one,
To be the sage and gentle fate by God appointed,
To cut the thread of life, worn to attenuation,
And close the eyes, couched for the skies' clear light,
More than for the cold, dim, smoky earth-air?
I would fain have pleaded with the sisters dread—
"Spare him! O spare him yet a little longer!
Pity me! O pity me! gentlest of the three!
Ye say, 'ye have learned to love the life, whose beauteous web
Charmed even thee, conversant with Infinity.'"
But soft and low, with tender aspect, Parca whispers :
"I cannot, God commands, and while I snap the thread,
Cast your eye upwards and say, 'God speed you, brother!'
And half the pain will spend with thy submission."
        Man of the ages, dear to the departed,
For thy truth of spirit and thy life, forever uprising,
For these, I too will garner thee in my treasury of jewels,
And if the key should ever rust, which would admit thee
To the sanctum of my friendship, only retouch it with the wand,
Left in thy hand by my ascending, saintly one,

And it will be the "Open Sesame"
To my most holy confidence.

O my *deepest* soul! how fares it with thee
In the rude shock, Time with his scythe hath dealt thee!
Hark! hear its answer low, but strong as life, and firm as destiny.

> Gathering in, gathering in
> Grain for the winnowing,
> Gold for the purifying,
> Gems for recrystallizing,
> Trees for rejuvenating,
> Flowers for retinting,
> Humanity for renewing,
> Heaven and earth for re-uniting.

After due care and observance, Ben Ezra left the re-
mains of the dead to bid a more satisfactory farewell to
Zoë, than she, in her impatient excitement, had allowed
him.   As he passed the quay, he saw a ship with its sails
fully set, just sailing away into the thick mist, which at the
hour of evening was enveloping the harbor.   He inquired
of a bystander its name and commander, and found it was
the one in which she and Hilda had embarked.   A double
sense of desolation settled on his spirit.   His dearest friend
in the present scene of his lengthened experience had just
departed, and now the hope, which had gilded his latest
life, was fast fading away into the grave which the ages
had been lowering and ever lowering.   Thus he wailed
out his lament:

"Gone! gone! another ray of sunshine over my pathway stealing.
   How long, O Lord, how long dost thou deny my heart's sore
      pleading!
   Am I the sport of a blind destiny, the caprice of a stern fate!
   Who ever answereth to my anguished cry for love — too late, too
      late!
   Enlighten me, O Father, upon the purpose of my wandering!
   Unvail to me thy great designs on which I tire of pondering.
   Give me, O give me life in love! that I, renewed for aye,
   May ever worship God, through Christ, and toil for his humanity!

For lo! from age to age, phenomenal, I gather,
With the assemblies of the people — one with them — yet, alas!
    another.
Give me, O give me life in love! that I, renewed for aye,
May ever worship God, through Christ, and toil for his humanity!

Zoë fades from my sight, like the mist of the night.

Call to me, Ocean, from thy deepest soundings,
Blow to me, breezes, from thy remotest boundings,
Stars, from your blue profoundest shine articulate,
Sun, with your melting beams, her love perpetuate!

No answer comes from them to my deep heart's appealing.

Speak to me, my deepest nature,
Reveal the presage of the future.
Hush all discordant whisperings.
Listen to its revealings.

No answer comes to me from its abysses.

Woe! woe! is me! the oracle of all Time is dumb,
Lonely and sad I wander. God! do thou yet sustain!
Still be my light, my life's exceeding gain,
Ever I trust in Thee, though crash of worlds should come!

CHAPTER XXIII.

"The youth, who daily farther from the east
Must travel, still is nature's priest,
And by the vision splendid
Is on his way attended."—WORDSWORTH.

" Lord! 'tis not ours to make the sea,
And earth and sky a home for thee:
But in thy sight our offering stands,
A humbler temple 'made with hands.' "

WILLIS.

(*Mrs. Liebenhoff dedicates her book, " THE WAY,"
to the children of Mr. Liebenhoff's Sunday-School.*)

"I have been thinking, if there were any so simple and unlearned that I could dedicate my book to them, and it has come into my mind that you, my little ones, may have preserved your child-like temper, so as to receive it in the spirit in which it was

(322)

written. There are plenty of shrewd and knowing people, who will tell me if it is formed according to the rules laid down for authors, if the sentences are too long, if the facts agree with the time stated, if the characters speak and act as they ought to, and make many other remarks upon it which you would not, and I hope, never will understand. But I wish to give it in charge to those who will love it for its *spirit*, its *deepest meaning;* so I come to you, and if a part of it is too old for you now to take a lively interest in it, you will, I hope, grow to like it better by-and-by.

" My children, you know all too well that we are left without his guidance, who was ever faithful and loving in his instructions to us, so we must be all the more true and earnest in laboring for ourselves. He loved each and all of you, little ones. It cheered him, each Sabbath morning, to come to you, and look into your sunny eyes, and mark your obedient attention when he spoke to you of God and Jesus. And when weighed down in spirit by the lack of interest of his older hearers in the truth he gave them, which was dearer than his own life to him, he would say: ' The children will drink into their young hearts its beauty and purity, and their souls will bud and bloom into sweet flowers for the garden of our God; and they will build a temple for his worship, and each of them shall be a living stone in it, polished to fittest grace and loveliness.'

" And now that he is gone, they say, ' we cannot rebuild our church, so we will leave it as it is, a wreck for passers-by to gaze at, and, may-be, scoff for our lukewarmness.'

" My children, *we* will build the church, new and complete in every part, a fit offering to the great, good Father and our Redeemer. Come one, come all, Mary, and Freya, and Edgar, and Carl, and Gunhilda, and Louise, and Eva, and Fritz, and many more that I cannot name. *We* will dig stones from the quarry and fashion them into a glorious church, worthy of our Maker, and the souls he gave us; and the few faithful ones, who loved to teach and talk to

you of the way to be good and happy here, and afterwards
in heaven, will lend a helping hand, when most it may be
needed. And little Petrea shall sing for us, meanwhile,
the simple song she learns at school, and Meta shall come
and dance for us, and if she trips with graceful step to
help, by her playful, winning ways, to build a temple where
she can learn of Him, who loved more than all else, little
children, then she will grow up and never be proud and
vain because of her 'flouncy gown.'

"Do you ask, how we shall have strength and money
enough to build our church? Never fear, my children.
'God will provide.' Only begin with loving hearts and an
earnest purpose, and the sweet heavens and every gracious
influence of earth will aid us. Never fear, but commence
the work in fullest trust and love, and more than the half
is done.

"What shall its form be, do you say? It shall grow
into grace and beauty under our hands, even as a forest-
tree. Strong and massive shall it be, to live for ages, so
that our children's children shall see where their parents
worshiped, and say, 'we will praise God even more worthily
than they, because of their blest instructions and the ever-
living, growing action of our own souls combined.'

"Its pointed doors and windows shall uplift us as
we gaze towards the heavens. Its two towers, one sur-
mounted by an anchor, the other by a cross, shall speak to
us of consecration of ourselves to duty, however trying,
and of high hope combined. Its shell, with open ear, shall
teach us to be awake and listening to every hint borne to
us from God without and God within us. Its pillars,
many-branched, shall, like the trees, tell us of God, walk-
ing amid the cool wood's shade, of which our temple shall
be a symbol. The angel blowing the trumpet over the
preacher's desk, shall ever prompt him to utter the whole
sacred, needed truth, as it flows in upon him.

"It shall be light, airy, and home-like, with the seats all

rounding towards one centre, as if we loved, one the other, and liked to look into each other's faces, and wished no one to hide himself in a dark corner, where he might steal the Word, but lack the sympathetic charm of loving hearts, which gives it half its potency. The minister will give us in simple, earnest fashion, the pure truth of Christ. He will read, too, of God's dealings to his people before his coming; and then of his full, consummated truth, exemplified by his great life. And we will chant the psalms and hymns together—turning our faces towards the choir and organ—each one as he best may, with melody of utterance, or by the sincere and voiceless spirit.

"It shall be adorned with pictures, which speak to us, at times, even with plainer voice than words. The infant Jesus, in his sweet mother's arms; she, smiling upon us, saying, 'Lo! this beloved, holy child is a new era in the world's life. Love and grow like him, and the spirit within you shall be pure, tender, beautiful, strong and mighty to prevail over the inner and the outer world as his was.'

"Christ, walking upon the water, an emblem of the electric spirit's potency, shall be a hint to us of the power of the coming future. The Prodigal Son, welcomed by his Father, will show us the forgiving love of God for sinners. And we will not forget our *suffering* Saviour, for his crucifixion tells us trumpet-tongued, of the high cost of every man's redemption; for, not alone by Jesus dying to ease, to glory, and to earthly love; nor by his resignation to what God appointed, but by our own likewise, do we gain the crown, and reign as conquerors over sin and ruin forevermore.

"We will build high our church, with steps ascending to it, so that the 'Children's Chapel' underneath shall have full air and sunshine. It shall be broad and spacious, even as the Church above, for many will come to our Sunday-school, I ween.

"Pictures shall be here too; Christ blessing little chil-

dren; holy ones praising God with prayer and song, and
many others, with medallions and statuettes, such as you
will love to look on. I have many ready for our Chapel
now, my own.

"It shall be open each Sunday evening too. Sometimes
we will gather to hear one, who can tell us well of the
wonders of the stars. Again another shall teach us of the
beauty and high uses of the trees and flowers; another, of
the marvels of the tinted shell, linking each with thoughts
of God, and his many-sided goodness, loveliness and
power. And thus the Pastor will be relieved and cheered
by the aid of many minds, intent like him, upon spreading
God's truth and love, and making our lives harmonious
therewith. Sometimes, too, we will meet in our Chapel-
home for social converse, brightened by intelligence and
thought, and warmed by sympathetic interest in high
themes.

"And now, I am going to speak to you, my children, of
what many pious people will think a very sinful plan, but
it is not nevertheless, to my simple faith. So be attentive
to me. You know that the Sabbath was given us to rest
from labor, to grow good, to do good, and be happy in.
God has not told us exactly how, though all the ages have
pointed to the Church and its simple and holy ordinances, as
one great means of becoming thus; so every Sunday morn-
ing, if possible, we will come to church; and in the after-
noon, there are so many good books to read, it seems a
very pleasant way to spend the hours in, to learn some-
thing from *their* teachings. But sometimes, on Sunday
evenings, we will have dramatic representations in our
Chapel. Is it so very dreadful? You have felt, I dare
say, after being serious all day long, as if you would like
to sport and play. God put this love of change into your
feelings. You only must learn to guide it rightly. It is
no more wicked to laugh than weep, indeed much less so,
I think, in a world which God has made purposely for us

to be happy in.   So we will be merry a part of Sunday, will we not?

" And do you not think, if a little boy or girl were striving very hard to grow up good, and wished to learn how, in every way he could, that, if he saw, represented by living persons, the struggles, trials, and at last the victory of some great and good man or woman, who had toiled from childhood for this high aim, that he would learn as much, as if he went to a darkened church three times each Sunday, to hear a gloomy-looking man say in the morning, over and over again, ' that sin is exceeding sinful;' and in the afternoon, tell of the ' terrors of the law,' and in the evening, ' that God was going to burn up a multitude of his children for ever and ever ?'

" I think we should learn a great deal more.   So the young people, with little trouble and preparation, will use the talent which has been given them, for some good purpose, to make our Sabbath evenings happy and beneficial to us.

" And now, I go into the sweet country and the bright tinted woods to gather comfort and hope again from their refreshing influences.   Farewell, my children, and when I return, come to me, for a little while, and a few at a time; for I have much to do, and your noisy prattle when too long listened to, disturbs the current of my many thoughts. And you shall see my pictures, and select one, each of you, as you best like; for I have many which have been suggestions to me while I wrote my book for you, and which I will with pleasure give to my little friends.   Farewell."

END OF VOL I.

CPSIA information can be obtained at www.ICGtesting.com
Printed in the USA
BVOW05s1011041215

R6580900001B/R65809PG429133BVX5B/3/P